Sicily: An Archaeological Guide

Archaeological Guides
General Editor: GLYN DANIEL

Sicily:
An Archaeological Guide

*the prehistoric and Roman remains
and the Greek Cities*

MARGARET GUIDO

FABER AND FABER LIMITED
24 Russell Square London

First published in mcmlxvii
by Faber and Faber Limited
24 Russell Square, London, W.C.1
Reprinted mcmlxviii
Printed in Great Britain
by Ebenezer Baylis and Son, Limited
The Trinity Press, Worcester, and London

FOR LUIGI

Quacunque enim ingredimur, in aliqua historia uestigium ponimus.
(For walk where we will, we tread upon some story.)
CICERO, *de finibus*, V, 5

Contents

Foreword   *page* 21

A Brief Outline of the Prehistory and Early History of Sicily   23

Museums in Sicily   29

Glossary   29

Some Early Greek pottery styles and their dating   32

1. MESSINA, the AEOLIAN ISLANDS,★ LONGANE, the ROMAN VILLA at CASTROREALE SAN BIAGIO, and TINDARI★   33

2. HALAESA, CEFALÙ, HIMERA and SOLUNTO   47

3. PALERMO,★ ADDAURA and SEGESTA★   56

4. ERICE, TRAPANI, LÉVANZO and FAVIGNANA, MOTYA and LILYBAEUM   73

5. SELINUNTE,★ SCIACCA and HERACLEA MINOA   85

6. AGRIGENTO★ and SANT'ANGELO MUXARO   107

7. CALTANISSETTA, ENNA, REALMESE, AIDONE (for Morgantina), PIAZZA ARMERINA★ and CALTAGIRONE   131

8. GELA★ and RAGUSA   143

9. CASTELLUCCIO, NOTO, HELORUS, SYRACUSE,★ PALAZZOLO ACREIDE, PANTALICA★ and THAPSOS   155

10. MEGARA HYBLAEA, LENTINI, CATANIA, ADRANO, RANDAZZO, NAXOS and TAORMINA★   199

Bibliography   212

Index   215

★ The more important sites are marked with an asterisk

I wish to thank the following for kind permission to reproduce their photographs: the *Soprintendenza alle Antichità* for Syracuse (nos. 1, 9, 11 above, 12 and 15); the *Soprintendenza alle Antichità* for Palermo (nos. 3 below, and 4); the British Museum (no. 8); the Ashmolean Museum, Oxford (no. 10); Oliver Benn (nos. 5 above, 6, 7 below, and 14); and Ditta Galifi Crupi, Taormina (no. 16).

Illustrations

PLATES

1. The start of the excavations at Capo Graziano in Filicudi (Aeolian Islands) and excavations on the Lipari acropolis
page 35
2. Tindari. The Propylaeum of the Agora   45
3. The Temple at Himera, and one of the lion-head water-spouts from the Temple   53
4. The Addaura cave near Palermo. Upper Palaeolithic incised figures   63
5. Segesta. The Temple and Theatre   71
6. Selinunte. Metope from Temple E (now in the *Museo Nazionale* at Palermo). Actaeon attacked by Artemis' dogs and Temple E from the west   93
7. Agrigento. The Temple of Concord and one of the giant *telamones* re-assembled from fragments, in the Temple of Zeus   119
8. Sant'Angelo Muxaro. One of the gold bowls. (Now in the British Museum)   130
9. Piazza Armerina. Detail of one of the mosaics in the Roman Villa   135
10. Gela. Terracotta relief of Aphrodite holding a goat. (Ashmolean Museum, Oxford)   151
11. One of the rock-cut tombs at Castelluccio, and one of the sculptured figures of Cybele at Palazzolo Acreide (Akrai)   157
12. Detail of a painted *krater* from the Giardino Spagna cemetery at Syracuse   173
13. Syracuse. Inside the Cathedral. The Temple of Athena   177
14. Syracuse. The Greek Theatre, and the Euryalus Fort, showing some of the towers and part of the inner defensive ditch with entrances to underground passages   185
15. Pantalica. Some of the tombs in the South cemetery   193
16. Taormina. View of the Theatre with Etna in the background   209

Line Illustrations

1. Sicily. The main archaeological sites   *pages* 16–17
2. Sicily, showing the route followed in this book, the division into chapters, the Sicilian railways and the route of the Europabus tours   18–19
3. Isometric plan of a Greek temple showing some of the architectural elements   30
4. Tetradrachm of Messana   34
5. Tindari   43
6. The *Museo Nazionale* at Palermo. Plan of the three floors   58
7. Segesta   64
8. Segesta. Suggested reconstruction of the scene structure of the theatre (after Bulle)   72
9. Lévanzo. Engraved figures of a bull following a cow   78
10. Plan of Motya (based on Whitaker)   79
11. Selinunte   86
12. Selinunte. The Temples. (after Dinsmoor)   90
13. Selinunte. The Sanctuary of Malophoros and secondary deities (after Gabrici)   97
14. Two-headed stone stela from the Sanctuary of Malophoros 98
15. Heraclea Minoa   101
16. Coin of Akragas with eagles devouring a hare   107
17. Agrigento   110–111
18. Agrigento. The Sanctuary of Demeter, San Biagio. Suggested reconstruction (after Carta)   116
19. The Temple of Zeus. Plan and reconstruction of the façade, showing the probable position of the giant *telamones* (after Prado)   123
20. Agrigento. The area to the west of the Temple of Zeus   126
21. Terracotta model of a shrine. Native work of the VI c. B.C. from Sabucina. 1/6   131
22. Piazza Armerina. Plan of the Roman Villa   136
23. Coin from Gela, showing *quadriga* with Nike above   143
24. Gela   143
25. Gela. The Capo Soprano fortifications   148

26. Castelluccio. Carved grave slab   *page* 156
27. Syracuse and district   159
28. Syracuse   160
29. Syracuse. The *Museo Nazionale*. First floor   170
30. Syracuse. The *Museo Nazionale*. Ground floor   174
31. Syracuse. The Temple of Athena incorporated in the present Cathedral   178
32. Syracuse. The Temple of Apollo and Temple of Olympian Zeus (after Dinsmoor)   181
33. Syracuse. The Greek Theatre   183
34. The Euryalus Fort, outside Syracuse   189
35. Pantalica. Sketch map   192
36. Thapsos. Native pots and imported Mycenaean pots, dagger and beads   197

Fig. 27 is reproduced, by kind permission of A. G. Woodhead and Messrs. Thames & Hudson, from *The Greeks in the West*.
Figs. 3, 29, 30, 31, 32, 33 and 34 are reproduced from *Syracuse: A Handbook to its History and Principal Monuments*, by M. Guido, by kind permission of Messrs. Max Parrish.

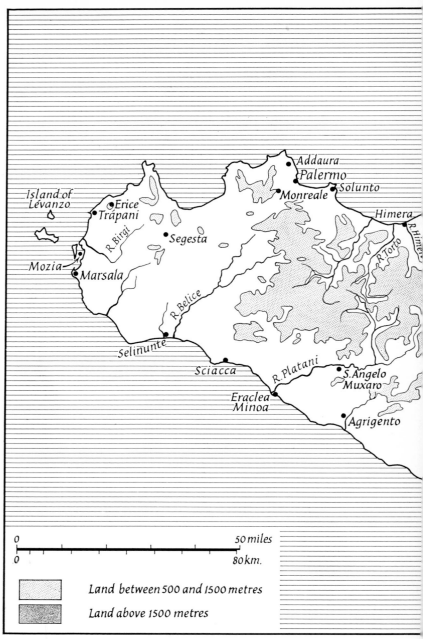

Fig. 1. Sicily. The main archaeological sites

Panarea
Milazzese
Filicudi
Alicudi
Capo
Graziano
Salina
Lipari
Lipari Islands
Vulcano
Milazzo
Tindari
Longane
Messina
alù
Halaesa
Taormina
Naxos
Mt.Etna
Enna
R.Dittaino
R.Simeto
Catania
ltanissetta
Morgantina
Piazza Armerina
Lentini
Caltagirone
Pantalica
Megara Hyblaea
Thapsos
R.Anapo
Gela
R.Gela
Palazzolo Acreide
Siracusa
Ragusa
Castelluccio
Noto
Helorus

H.A.Shelley

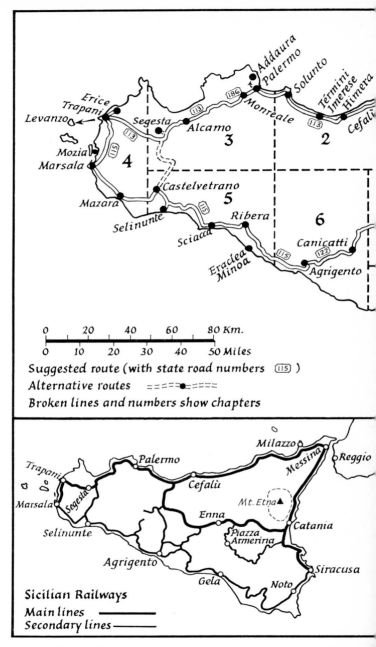

Fig. 2. Sicily, showing the route followed in this book, the divis.

Foreword

I have tried in this book to describe the principal archaeological sites in Sicily from the Palaeolithic to Imperial Roman times.

The book is arranged in ten chapters, beginning with Messina (where most visitors with their own cars are most likely to land), and working round the island in an anti-clockwise direction in conformity with much of the route followed by the main bus tours (Nastro d'Oro, Europabus): the places described in the various chapters can quickly be seen in Figure 2. This system enables anyone beginning his visit at, say, Palermo or Syracuse, instead of Messina, to orientate himself equally well whether he travels in a clockwise or anti-clockwise direction by bus, train or car.

Bus Tours. Details about the Nastro d'Oro, Europabus tours (which by careful planning can be so used that a day or two may be spent in a number of places), can be obtained from the *C.I.T.* Travel Service offices in London (10, Charles II Street, S.W.1), in New York (11 West 42nd Street, N.Y.10036), or in the larger towns in Sicily. Archaeological tours of Sicily are arranged by: *Discovering Sicily*, 156 Shaftesbury Avenue, London, W.C.2.

Hotels and Pensioni. A list can be obtained from the *Italian State Tourist Office* in Regent Street, in London, and at 626 Fifth Avenue, in New York.

Maps. Anyone travelling by car would be well advised to acquire maps before arriving in Sicily, where good maps are not easy to find. The following can be recommended, both issued by the *Touring Club Italiano* in Milan, and can be bought at the Map House in St. James's Street, London, S.W.1., and at Rizzoli International Bookstore, 712 Fifth Avenue, New York City; sheet 4 of the map of Italy at 1: 500,000 (an excellent general map), and sheets 25, 26, and 27 of the 1: 200,000 map which are for more detailed use.

Museums (see list on p. 29). The opening hours are frequently changed, and students wishing to see small collections or reserve collections should apply directly, well before their visit if possible, to the *Soprintendente alle Antichità* for the area concerned. There are three of these areas, with their centres in Palermo, Agrigento and Syracuse, respectively. (Students and teachers should enquire about free passes from the Italian Institute, 39 Belgrave Square, London, S.W.1, or 686 Park Avenue, New York City.)

The choice of places to be visited is, of course, a purely personal one. I feel, however, justified in giving more emphasis to the description of the Greek towns, not only because they represent the moment of Sicily's highest achievement, but because they hold greater interest than do the prehistoric sites, for the majority of cultivated visitors. The prehistoric sites have not, however, been neglected, and I have included many of outstanding importance.

During the period following the VIII century B.C. we can complement our archaeological knowledge of the Greek towns with the innumerable details given by early writers (many of whose works are available in the Loeb or other translations), concerning the history, and the eminent personalities, political men, tyrants or leaders, poets, philosophers, historians or soldiers, who lived there, and it is this combination of archaeological and historical documentation which enables us to reconstruct a far more detailed picture than would ever be possible were we dependent on only one of those disciplines. So, in this book I have tried to insert the various monuments into their historical setting, and to quote from classical writers whenever these may help the visitor to take a more lively interest and pleasure in what he sees.

For the unspecialized visitor I have included a fairly full list of dates and events (see below), as well as a short bibliography. Perhaps the two most useful books for 'background' reading would be L. Bernabò Brea's *Sicily before the Greeks*, for the prehistoric period, and A. G. Woodhead's *The Greeks in the West* for the Greek period: both are published by Thames and Hudson, in London, and Frederick A. Praeger, Publishers, in New York.

In case this book should have a second edition, I would be very grateful for any criticisms or corrections.

                                                      Margaret Guido

A Brief Outline of the Prehistory
and Early History of Sicily

Sicily was first inhabited by Man in the *Upper Palaeolithic* period, at the end of the Würm glaciation. Vestiges of this age have been found in many caves all over the island, particularly around the coast, and the two most interesting caves, those containing incised or painted figures of humans and animals, can be visited near Palermo (Addaura) and in the island of Lévanzo which, at that time, was still joined to the mainland of Sicily.

IV millennium
The Neolithic
Age

For several thousand years this cultural tradition lingered on, and was only brought to an end in about the early IV millennium when new people arrived on the shores of Sicily – people who belonged to a culture ultimately stemming from the East Mediterranean and which was gradually diffused over the whole of its shores. The pottery they made, decorated with impressions of shells, bird-bones, etc. is the earliest known from Sicily, and it is characteristic of the pre-historic villages of the so-called Stentinello culture near Syracuse. These Neolithic peoples were already exploiting the obsidian from the Aeolian Islands. They were soon followed by other peoples, some using plain (Diana style) pottery, and others painted pottery, and the cultural fusion of some of these groups led to a number of regional variations.

III millennium
The Copper Age

Once again new and more evolved peoples of Eastern Mediterranean origin – this time bringing the first knowledge of metal-working – arrived in Sicily. These were the people who introduced the custom of burying their dead in tombs cut in the rock – a custom which was to linger for many centuries. As navigation improved, and boats became more seaworthy, the trade connections grew wider, and Beakers were imported from Spain and France, perhaps via Sardinia. The various regional cultures in Sicily at this time are recognized by such names as San-Cono-Piano-Notaro, Conzo, Serraferlicchio, Malpasso, Sant'-Ippolito, etc.; these, as well as the culture of the Conca d'Oro near Palermo, and the contemporary cultures in the Aeolian Islands, are richly represented in the Sicilian museums.

About 2000 B.C.
The
Early Bronze
Age

The Early Bronze Age began in Sicily at about this date. The most characteristic culture is named after a rich group of tombs at Castelluccio in eastern Sicily. The people from the nearby village and from other sites in Sicily were importing curious bone plaques, decorated with bosses and finely incised lines, which can be fairly accurately dated in other parts of the Mediterranean, where they belong to the transition between the Middle and Late Helladic periods. Again there were many regional variations among the various groups living in Sicily at this time. One of the best known is the Capo-Graziano culture of the Aeolian Islands, and another culture, known from the north-east coast around Tindari, was perhaps ancestral to the Middle Bronze culture of Thapsos.

About 1400 B.C.
The
Middle Bronze
Age

The Thapsos culture is called after a group of tombs near Syracuse, and can be fairly closely dated from the imported Mycenaean ware and bronze objects, etc., found in them. This is the period of the so-called Milazzese culture in the Aeolian Islands, again dated from Mycenaean imports. In one site in the island of Salina a necklace of faience beads included some segmented ones of a type which, originating in Egypt, was widely popular in the Mycenaean world, and has been found even as far afield as the Wessex culture in England. These beads are invaluable for the chronological links they provide.

About 1250 B.C.
The
Later Bronze
Age

Once again Sicily and the Aeolian Islands were invaded, by peoples this time claimed by the early writers to be Ausonians, Morgeti and Sikels from the mainland of Italy. The inhabitants of the coastal villages fled into the interior where they seem to have absorbed, rather than have been dominated by the culture of the newcomers. So far the Ausonian culture has been recognized in the Aeolian Islands and northern Sicily, but that of the Sikels is harder to identify, and the most possible claimant seems to be the so-called Pantalica culture, named after the vast and impressive settlement, and the thousands of rock-cut tombs near Sortino – a site which evidently took the place of the more vulnerable coastal villages at about this time, and which continued to be occupied until the VII century B.C. Italic cultural influences were strongest in the second of the four phases into which this culture is divided, and Phoeni-

About 1000 B.C.

cian navigators were beginning to trade objects from all parts of the Mediterranean. These commercial activities gradually replaced the earlier, Mycenaean ones.

About 850–650
B.C.

The third and fourth Pantalica phases coincided with the first settlements of the Phoenicians in the west, and the Greeks in the east of the island. By the end of this time Sicily was ethnically composed of Greeks, Phoenicians, Elymians (around Segesta and Erice), and the mixed, native peoples generally known as Sikels in the east, and Sikans in the west, though the real difference between the two latter groups, if it ever existed, is still not well understood.

The Greek
Colonies

From the mid-VIII century onwards a number of Greek colonies were founded from parent cities in Greece and subsequently from expanding colonies in Sicily itself, and the next few hundred years witnessed a period of vigorous growth and of great cultural achievement among these colonies – a cultural achievement whose progress was continually interrupted by warfare, either between the Greeks and Carthaginians, or between one Greek city and another. The men who rose to power in these cities were known as 'tyrants', a word which, in Greek, does not carry so pejorative a sense as in English, and in fact some of these men such as Timoleon, Dion, or Hieron II of Syracuse were motivated far more by idealistic and democratic ambitions than by the desire for personal advancement which inspired many others for whom the English word tyrant would by no means be too strong.

The colonists came from many parts of the Greek world. *Corinthians* settled at Syracuse, Camarina and Akrai, *Chalcidians* at Himera, Mylai, Zancle, Catane, and Leontinoi, *Megarians* at Megara Hyblaea and Selinus, and *Rhodians*, *Cretans* and *Cnidians* at Gela, Akragas and Lipara.

Trade contacts between Greeks and natives led to the gradual Hellenization of the indigenous areas, so that, in time, the Greek tongue became widespread, and continued to be used for common parlance throughout the Roman period as well.

The following dates of events and personalities are of particular importance:

Foundation of the earliest colonies — The first of the Greek colonies, including Naxos, Megara Hyblaea and Syracuse, were founded around the middle of the VIII century. Others, nearly all sited near the coast, followed at intervals.

491–478 B.C. — *Gelon* in power in Syracuse.

480 B.C. — *The Battle of Himera.* The Carthaginian forces defeated by the combined armies of Theron of Akragas, and Gelon.

478–466 B.C. — *Hieron I* of Syracuse.

456 B.C. — Aeschylus dies at Gela.

415–413 B.C. — Defeat of the Athenian expedition at Syracuse.

409 B.C.　Carthaginians land expeditionary force and sack Selinus, and then Himera, Akragas and Gela.

405–367 B.C.　*Dionysius I* of Syracuse. Syracuse becomes the most powerful city in Europe. Wars against the Carthaginians.

397 B.C.　Motya sacked.
Plato visits Syracuse.

345–336 B.C.　Timoleon takes power in Syracuse and initiates plan for rebuilding many of the destroyed or damaged cities in Sicily.

Hellenistic Period　(about 325–30 B.C.)

315–289 B.C.　*Agathocles* of Syracuse. Wars against the Carthaginians.

278–276 B.C.　*Pyrrhus* in Sicily.

265–215 B.C.　*Hieron II* of Syracuse. During his long and prosperous reign the first Roman-Punic war was fought. Until his death Syracuse remained an ally of Rome, and during his life Sicily became a Roman Province.

213–211 B.C.　Syracuse, having broken her alliance with Rome after Hieron's death, was besieged and taken by Marcellus. Archimedes accidentally killed.

The Roman Period　During the Roman period Sicily was exploited for everything she had to offer, particularly for grain for the Roman armies. The land was divided into huge corn-growing estates and conditions were so harsh that two major revolts broke out, the so-called *Slave Wars* of 135–132 and 104–101 B.C.

1 century B.C. Cicero visited Sicily to investigate the crimes of the Praetor Verres. Civil wars between Pompey and Caesar, and then between Pompey and Octavian (later Augustus) and Mark Antony. Diodorus Siculus writing his *History*. Many towns which had been great in the past had now dwindled to such an extent that in several instances Augustus re-colonized them.

Imperial Roman times Christianity came early to Sicily. St. Paul visited Syracuse.
The latest building described in this book is the great Roman villa at Piazza Armerina, erected at the end of the 3rd century A.D.

The Byzantine Period *From the end of the Roman Empire to the Arab conquest.*
In the 5th century the Goths and Vandals raided Sicily, which was then freed and annexed to the Byzantine Empire in the mid-6th century A.D.

The Arab Domination The 9th century saw the Arab raids and the establishment of Arab domination.

The Normans controlled Sicily in the 12th century, but following the Wars of the Sicilian Vespers at the end of the 13th century, Sicily passed into the dominion of the Spaniards.
All these various invaders or settlers, Greeks, Phoenicians, Romans, Arabs, Normans and Spaniards have brought their contribution to the rich cultural and architectural heritage of present-day Sicily.

Principal Museums in Sicily

(Minor collections are indexed under Museums and collections)

(The numbers in brackets refer to the pages.)
Note that opening hours are subject to change, and vary between summer (May 1st–October 1st) and winter.

*Adrano (205)
Aeolian Islands (Lipari) (36)
**Agrigento (128)
Caltagirone (142)
* Caltanissetta (131)
* Catania (205)
Cefalù (49)
**Gela (150)
Heraclea Minoa (106)
*Lentini (203)
Megara Hyblaea (200)

*Messina (33)
*Motya (83)
*Noto (158)
Palazzolo Acreide (192)
**Palermo (56)
*Ragusa (153)
Solunto (55)
**Syracuse (169)
Taormina (211)
Tindari (46)
*Trapani (76)

**National Collections

*Other important collections

Glossary

Abacus. The flat slab on the top of a capital.
Acroterion. Sculptured figure or ornament placed on the apex of the pediment (and sometimes on its outer angles as well).
Agora. Market-place.
Anaktoron. Princely palace.
Anta. See 'in antis'.
Antefixes. Ornamental blocks on the edge of a roof, to conceal the ends of the tiles.
Archaic period. About 700 to early V century B.C.
Atrium. Colonnaded open court inside a Roman house.
Biga. Two-horse chariot.
Bothros. Pit for votive offerings.

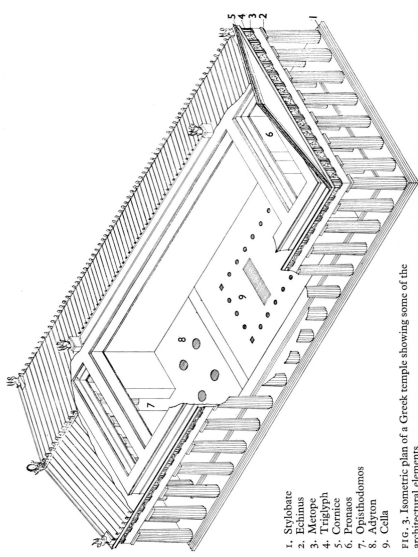

1. Stylobate
2. Echinus
3. Metope
4. Triglyph
5. Cornice
6. Pronaos
7. Opisthodomos
8. Adyton
9. Cella

FIG. 3. Isometric plan of a Greek temple showing some of the architectural elements

Bouleuterion. Council chamber.

Cavea. The auditorium of a theatre.

Cella. See Figure 3. This was the hall where the cult-statue of the deity was kept.

Diazoma. The semicircular corridor running round the middle of the *cavea.*

Echinus. See Figure 3.

Entablature. The upper part of an order, consisting of architrave, frieze and cornice.

Ephebe. Young man between 18 and 20 years of age.

Favissae. Underground storing-places for offerings.

Fibula. Brooch.

Frigidarium, tepidarium and *calidarium.* Cold, warm and hot rooms in Roman bath buildings.

Geometric period. About 900–700 B.C.

Hellenistic Period. Conventionally from Alexander the Great to Augustus. About 325–31 B.C.

Hypogeum. Underground vault.

'*In antis*'. With the long side walls of the building extended to form the walls of a porch, and with two columns between the *antae* (wall-endings) to support the roof.

Kouros. Standing male figure of the Archaic period.

Megaron. Large oblong hall, especially in Cretan and Mycenaean palaces.

Metope. See Figure 3.

Mutule. Projecting square block above the triglyph.

Nymphaeum. Temple of the nymphs, often a Roman pleasure-house containing statues and fountains.

Odeion. Small theatre-shaped building for concerts and recitals.

Opisthodomos. See Figure 3.

Orientalizing period. About 700–575 B.C.

Peristasis. Part of a temple, around the outside of the *cella.*

Pithoi. Very large pottery vessels.

Pronaos. See Figure 3.

Propylaeum. Columned entrance gateway to a sacred enclosure, market-place, etc.

Proskenion. The front of the low building supporting the stage on which the action took place.

Punic. Carthaginian.

Quadriga. Four-horsed chariot.

Sima. Ogee moulding on the entablature.

Situlae. Tall pottery jars.

Stelae. Stone slabs to mark graves, or bearing an inscription recording a victory, treaty, etc.

Stereobate. Stepped foundation platform of a temple.

Stoa. Roofed colonnade, or portico.

Stylobate. The upper surface of the stereobate.

Telamon. Support in the form of a sculptured male figure.

Temenos. Enclosed area around a temple.

Ticlinium. Dining-room in a Roman house.

Ti glyph. See Figure 3.

Some Early Greek Pottery Styles and their Dating

c. 1000 B.C.	Proto-Geometric period begins.
900–700 B.C.	Geometric period.
700–575 B.C.	Orientalizing period.

ATTIC		CORINTHIAN	
c. 710 B.C.	Proto-Attic.	Before 630 B.C.	Proto-Corinthian.
c. 680 B.C.	Proto-Attic with orientalizing.	630 B.C.	Archaic.
		600 B.C.	Middle.
600–490 B.C.	Black-figure period.	570 B.C.	Late.
525–400 B.C.	Red-figure period.		

1 · Messina, the Aeolian Islands, Longane, the Roman Villa at Castroreale San Biagio, and Tindari

MESSINA

Many visitors who drive to Sicily with their own cars will land in Messina from the train and car ferry which leaves from Villa San Giovanni or Reggio Calabria on the mainland; alternatively they will find Messina well provided with car-hire services, information about which can be obtained at the tourist information office at the Central station.

Although Messina was the site of the ancient Greek colony of Zancle, the town was so largely destroyed by the earthquake of 1908 that there is little to detain those with archaeological interests. There is, however, an important Museum to visit, and before leaving Messina, those who intend to visit the Aeolian Islands should enquire about the boat services from Milazzo, and in summer also about the hydrofoil service from Messina itself. Information can be obtained either at the Central Station or at the offices of the *Ente Provinciale per il Turismo* in Via Santa Maria Alemanna 3.

The Museo Nazionale is in Viale della Libertà, just outside the town to the north. Opening hours: 9.30–4.30; holidays and Sundays 9.30–1.30. Closed on Fridays.

The following very short outline of the town's early history may perhaps be found helpful in the Museum where the finds from Zancle-Messana are displayed.

The Greek colony of Zancle was founded in about 730 by settlers from Chalcis and from Cumae, and although the precise site of the early settlement has not been identified, it was almost surely on the south side of the big sickle-shaped harbour which no doubt attracted the colonists. On the extreme point of the natural mole which encloses this harbour they built one of the first of their sanctuaries, dated from its late VIII-century Corinthian pottery to the early years of the settlement. Although Zancle stood in a favourable position for commanding the straits, it lacked agricultural resources, and to overcome this difficulty a dependent settlement was founded at Mylai (the modern Milazzo). In about 493 the town was captured by refugees from Samos and Miletus, and not long afterwards it was seized by the tyrant of

Reggio who changed its name to Messana. Destroyed by the Carthaginians in 396 B.C. it was rebuilt and repopulated by Dionysius of Syracuse, but again fell to the Carthaginians and was liberated by Timoleon. In the III century B.C. the Campanian mercenary troops in Messana, who had fought for Agathocles and who called themselves Mamertines (or sons of Mars), became so powerful that they took complete possession of the town and extended their control not only in Sicily but in southern Italy as well. Hieron II of Syracuse marched against them and defeated them in 265 B.C., and later, in response to their plea for help, the Romans landed in Sicily to wage the first of their Punic Wars. During the last two centuries B.C. Messana reached a state of some prosperity, and was a large town at the time of Cicero. Caesar used it as a naval base against Pompey in 48 B.C. and a few years later it was sacked by Octavian.

(The Museum also contains a lovely 15th-century triptych by Antonello da Messina, and some other important paintings.)

FIG. 4.
Tetradrachm of
Messana

THE AEOLIAN ISLANDS

These small islands of volcanic origin lie off the north-east coast of Sicily, from which Lipari, the largest of them, is 38 kms. away. The other main islands are Vulcano, Salina, Filicudi, Alicudi, Panarea and Stromboli. There is a regular steamer service to Lipari which leaves Milazzo early each morning (the most convenient hotel for the previous night is the Diana, but there are also others), and in the summer months a hydrofoil service from Messina. The other islands can all be reached from Lipari, where there are several hotels, amongst which the Rocce Azzurre and the Augustus can be recommended.

Those wanting to visit the islands' archaeological sites will need to spend a day in Lipari and to make excursions at least to Filicudi and Panarea.

Plate 1 (*above*) The start of the excavations at Capo Graziano in Filicudi (Aeolian Islands) (*below*) Excavations on the Lipari acropolis

Owing to excavations which have been carried out during the last twenty years, the islands have suddenly gained in importance and interest for the rich sequence of prehistoric cultures represented there, vestiges of which have been found in stratigraphical relation, so that their development from the Neolithic period onwards is clearer than in any other place in the Western Mediterranean. The most complete sequence was obtained on the 'acropolis' of Lipari, where, as in a 'tell', the superimposed remains of the various periods had accumulated to a depth of over 30 feet (Plate 1).

To get a clear idea of these prehistoric cultures, a visit should first be made to the Museum, which is housed in two separate buildings, one on each side of the Cathedral. The earliest remains are in the building to the right, once the bishop's palace. Opening hours: winter 9.30–4; summer 9–1 and 3–6. Sundays 9–1.

The earliest period of occupation is represented by the Neolithic cultures of the IV–III millennia B.C. – four consecutive phases characterized by different pottery; the first three of these seem to show a continuous evolution:

(a) *The Stentinello Culture*, named after one of the ditch-enclosed villages near Syracuse. The pottery is decorated with impressions made with fingernails, shells and sharp implements, and there is a little pottery painted with red bands. These people were using flint knives but their chief industry (one which brought prosperity to the islands for about 2,000 years) was the working of obsidian, the volcanic glass which can be chipped into extremely sharp implements, and which was in demand over a wide area of the Mediterranean world before metals were available.

The distribution of this 'impressed' pottery is so widespread that it undoubtedly stemmed from one origin, probably in the Middle East, and from there it was carried by various seaways to Greece and other lands bordering the Mediterranean, bringing to them a more advanced culture, based on farming. It only reached Sicily and the Aeolian Islands at a rather late stage, when its bearers were already acquainted with painted pottery, unknown in its earliest phases.

In the Near East this culture was brought to an end by the arrival of the much more evolved cultures of Samarra and Tell Halaf; the approximate date of its western diffusion can therefore be placed a little before 4000 B.C.

(b) *The Second Neolithic Phase* (Capri period) has pottery painted with red bands bordered in black, and a light-coloured slip. In some cases this is associated with another ware, decorated with scratched lines filled with red or white, or occasionally with a third ware bearing meander-spiral motifs in relief. Stentinello pottery is no longer present. Both these two early Neolithic cultural phases have their counterparts on the Italian mainland, in the trenched villages of the Matera district, etc.

(c) *The Third Neolithic Phase* is represented by pottery painted with meander-spiral motifs in dark brown on a light ground – the so-called 'Serra d'Alto style'. Its quite different pottery resembles some from Southern Italy and Apulia as well as from the Middle Neolithic of Arene Candide in Liguria; but it seems rarely to have reached Sicily.

(d) *The Fourth Phase of the Neolithic* (Diana style) has no painted pottery but plain red ware with cylinder or so-called 'trumpet' lugs. This culture is well known in Italy as well as in Sicily, and very similar pottery has also been found in Malta. Some metal slag from this archaeological horizon shows that the people were just beginning to start metal-working. An oval stone cist-grave was found in a late stage of this culture.

(e) *The Copper Age* (Piano Conte). The coming of the Copper Age is marked by an abrupt change. The pottery, with its decoration of wide, shallow grooves, is like many of the wares in the 'Western' Neolithic Lagozza-Chassey-Cortaillod complex of N. Italy, S. France and Switzerland, and the culture has some links with those on the Italian mainland (the early Copper Age cultures of Gaudo, Rinaldone, etc.) Some sherds of Sicilian Serraferlicchio style and from the Conca d'Oro cultures around Palermo provide a useful chronological connection.

Another and slightly later Copper Age phase is known from Piano Quartara in Panarea. In Lipari it was stratified above the Piano Conte levels and below those of Capo Graziano. It has a variety of pottery forms, and many very tiny pots with perforations just below the rim; tall conical feet and pointed handles are common. This culture is probably contemporary with the Sant'Ippolito culture in Sicily. This was a depressed period for the Aeolian Islands, for the demand for obsidian was dying down; but in the Bronze Age prosperity began again with the improved navigation which opened the seaways to more intensive trade activity.

(f) *The Bronze Age*. The Capo Graziano culture is named after a hut village in Filicudi (Plate 1). It had a few oval huts and a number of burials made in cavities of the rock, as this could not be cut into tombs like those in the limestone of Sicily. In Lipari another group of ten huts were found clustered round a bigger one within a roughly squared enclosure, some huts overlying others. The village must have had a long life, lasting into the beginning of the next phase.

The coarse pottery, decorated with wavy lines and dots, is sometimes associated with imported Aegean wares, the latest of which (Mycenaean III A) suggest that the village lasted until about 1400 B.C. These are the first direct connections with the Aegean, and there is no equivalent phase in Sicily, where the contemporary cultures were those of Castelluccio and Vallelunga. Some pots of Capo Graziano style were found with bell-beakers at Villafrati in Sicily. Evidently Lipari had few contacts with Sicily at this time, but it had closer links with the Tarxien cemetery phase in Malta.

(g) *The Milazzese Culture* is named after a site in Panarea, where 23 huts were found on a rocky promontory. All the huts were oval except one which was square. Another village of this type was found in Salina. This culture is contemporary with the Thapsos culture in Sicily, and the pottery is almost identical, though the Aeolian Islands were also receiving 'Apennine' pottery imported from Italy.

Here again Mycenaean pottery was being imported, and its scarcity by Mycenaean III B shows that the culture probably ended before about 1250. The stone industry had already finished, and metal was being worked, for there are moulds for swords and ribbon bracelets. One of the Salina huts produced a necklace of faience beads, some of which were the segmented type found in the British Wessex culture and elsewhere.

A cemetery of this period was excavated at Milazzo on the Sicilian mainland. There were about fifty burials with skeletons crouched in big pithoi, and some of these, like some of the Aeolian pottery, had been stamped with potters' marks perhaps related to the Cretan Linear Script. Both this custom, and the funeral rite of burial in big pithoi, are of Eastern Mediterranean origin.

The Late Bronze Age and the Iron Age

Ausonian I. The coming of this culture was marked by another abrupt change: the islands were again invaded and contacts were broken with Sicily, though they continued to be strong with Southern Italy. Since, according to Diodorus Siculus, the islands were colonized by Liparos, son of the king of the Ausonians of central-southern Italy (a claim which is substantiated by archaeological evidence), the name Ausonian has been given to this culture, which represented one of the *facies* of the Apennine culture. It was these people (thought to include Sikels and Morgeti as well) who drove the villagers of Thapsos and the other coastal villages around Syracuse to take refuge in the interior, and who sacked the villages of the Milazzese culture in Panarea, Filicudi and Salina. The pottery brought by these invaders has a great variety of handles, often high and knobbed, axe-shaped or horned.

Ausonian II developed from the first phase. A large village on the Lipari acropolis (Plate 1) had huts with low stone walls inset with holes which held the vertical posts: the same kind of huts, more or less rectangular in shape, as have been found on the Palatine hill in Rome and on the Metapiccola hill at Lentini. Some of them had situlae buried under the floor containing cremations and occasionally vitreous paste beads. The pottery, developed from that of the previous phase, also includes some so-called Villanovan bowls and some pottery strainers like some from Pantalica I. There were also two kinds of painted pottery: one, rare at Pantalica, was found in the Lentini huts and in Apulia; the other, wide-spread in Sicily, was the ware decorated with feathery designs, present at Pantalica and common at Cassibile. This phase, to judge from the many bronze objects, must have lasted from about 1150–850 B.C., when the village was violently destroyed.

Two important cemeteries of this period have been excavated: one in Lipari and the other on the mainland at Milazzo. In Lipari the tombs were of two types, the earlier ones contained skeletons (sometimes buried with necklaces or bracelets) in big pithoi; the later tombs contained ashes in situlae, for the rite had changed to cremation; both phases belong to Ausonian II (about 1150–1050). In the Milazzo cemetery the burials had been placed in urns covered with 'Villanovan' type bowls; this was a true 'urnfield' of proto-villanovan type dating from about 1050–800. But here the early Greek period is represented in burials dating from the VIII to the early VI century: a period during which the islands seem to have been largely abandoned, for when the Lipari village was destroyed, in about 850, the population dwindled to a few hundred people living in constant fear of Etruscan pirates.

Lipari was given a new lease of life in 580 B.C. when it was colonized by Cnidians, and it remained a Greek settlement until 252 B.C. when the Romans, during the Punic Wars, captured the islands, at that time in Carthaginian hands, and built a naval base there. Trial trenches have revealed parts of the Greek levels, in which East Greek, Attic, Corinthian and Laconian wares were all present, and a stretch of the archaic city wall made with huge polygonal lava blocks has also been uncovered. The street layout in Hellenistic times, and possibly much earlier too, was on the grid plan.

Many Greek and Roman finds in the museum came from the cemetery near the Santa Lucia valley, dating from the VI century B.C. to the 2nd century A.D. Over 100 inscribed stelae were recovered. Note also in Room XVI an important collection of IV century terracottas, tragic masks, and statuettes of comic actors. Rooms XIV–XV contain locally made polychrome wares and a fine IV century B.C. *krater*.

Sites to Visit

A large excavated area has been conserved near the church of the Immacolata and diagrams fixed to the sides of the trenches enable visitors to understand the various superimposed levels, from the Early Bronze Age to the Iron Age and later.

Salina. There is a village of the Milazzese period between Santa Maria and the lighthouse.

Vulcano and Stromboli are still volcanically active but have little of archaeological interest.

Filicudi. There is a big village of oval huts on the Capo Graziano promontory, the type-site of this Bronze Age culture (Plate 1). Ask for the custodian at Filicudi Porto.

Panarea. On the Milazzese promontory, on the south-east coast, is the type-site of this Bronze Age culture, with over 20 huts.

In the Calcara area some smoking holes ('fumarole') were evidently venerated from the Neolithic to the Early Bronze Age, when a series of round pits were made with big boulders lined with volcanic clay: perhaps these were intended for offerings of grain.

THE SIKEL TOWN OF LONGANE (RODÌ)
AND THE ROMAN VILLA AT CASTROREALE
SAN BIAGIO

A short distance from Milazzo, on the road to Tindari, and close together, two places of archaeological interest should be mentioned. Just outside Barcellona a small road turns inland to Rodì and Militi, and here, on a plateau overlooking the two villages, is the site of the ancient *Longane*, an interesting place to explore even though very little excavation has been carried out, and there is not a lot to see. This was an important Sikel centre in the archaic period, but seems to have completely disappeared by the late V century B.C. It is only in the last few years that this site has been identified as Longane, the existence of which was once known only from a V century coin and an inscription on a bronze *caduceus* (the official emblem of Hermes and of heralds) in the British Museum; the provenance of neither of these is known. Undoubtedly, however, the river Rodì (or Termini) must be the river *Longanos*, mentioned by early writers as the place where Hieron II of Syracuse defeated the Mamertines in 269 B.C., and it follows that the settlement nearby must be Longane. The town developed between two hills or acropoleis, a small one to the south, on which are the remains of a block-house, and a much larger one to the north, once surrounded by walls, set with square towers; to the west two gate-houses project from the wall, which are thought to belong to the V century B.C. The inhabited area which grew up between these two hills on the site of a much earlier Bronze Age settlement, was not fortified, and nothing remains of its houses which may well have been made of wood or mud-brick. Only one building survives in this area: it was built with large stone blocks, and may have been a sacred structure.

The other site, a very short distance away, on the main road, is a large Roman villa at Castroreale San Biagio. This was built in the second half of the 2nd century A.D. and it has a number of rooms with mosaic pavements grouped round a central colonnaded hall. There is nothing of special merit here, but the *frigidarium*, which has marble-lined baths, has a delightful black and white mosaic pavement showing men fishing from a boat, surrounded with very big fish. All the other mosaics are simple geometric designs without interest.

TINDARI (Tyndaris) (Fig. 5)

To reach Tindari from the main road (113), continue westwards through Falcone to Locanda where a side road turns off towards the coast and winds up a short distance to the hamlet of Tindari and the ruins of the Greek and Roman town. The Tyndaris Hotel is a very pleasant place to stay; it has a terrace looking over the sea and to the Aeolian Islands on the horizon.

Tyndaris was founded (very much later than the other Greek colonies) by Dionysius of Syracuse in 396 B.C. His intention was to establish a military outpost to guard the north coast and to block any Carthaginian attempt to approach Syracusan territory from the narrow but easily traversable coastal strip. He peopled the new colony with refugees who had left Greece at the end of the Peloponnesian War and had been temporarily living in Messana, and he called the town Tyndaris after these people's gods, the Tyndaridae, or Dioscuri, whose cult is attested there both by coins and mosaics. These original colonists were soon joined by others, and Diodorus says that the population quickly rose to 5,000.

On its high and rocky promontory with steep drops to the sea or to lower land around it, the town had a naturally strong position which was relatively easy to approach only from the west, and here the defences had to be particularly strong. The first defensive walls were intermittent, and were built only in those places left vulnerable by nature. The acropolis, the sacred area, is now occupied by a Sanctuary dedicated to a black virgin, and to its north-west stood the *agora* linked by one of the three main streets (*decumani*) to the theatre. This layout is thought to date from the colony's foundation.

The next mention of Tyndaris refers to the year 344 B.C., when Timoleon had landed in Sicily and the town was one of the first to give him allegiance. As far as is known, the next sixty years were years of peaceful development, when the theatre, and no doubt other public buildings, were built, but when the Mamertines (the gang of rebel mercenaries from Messana) seized power in their town in the early III century B.C. Tyndaris was suddenly menaced, and Hieron II opened a campaign against them which ended in their defeat at Longane in 269. It was probably in response to this threatened danger that the city walls of Tyndaris were reconstructed and strengthened: the original walls were replaced with much more massive ones, faced on both sides with

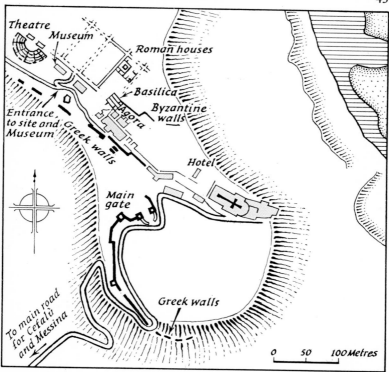

FIG. 5. Tindari

squared blocks which often bear mason's marks. Posterns and towers
were set at intervals along their line (which did not always coincide with
that of the earlier fortifications) and remains of a strong semi-circular
'pincer'–type gateway, flanked by two massive towers and side posterns
belonging to this period, can still be seen on the left of the road leading
up to the site.

At the beginning of the First Punic War Syracuse (and consequently
Tyndaris) was allied to the Carthaginians who used Tyndaris as a
defensive position, against, apparently, the will of its inhabitants who
tried on one occasion to switch their allegiance in favour of the Romans,
and were only prevented from doing so when the Carthaginians removed
some of their leading citizens. By 254 B.C., however, the whole of the
north coast of Sicily had fallen into Roman hands and the people of

Tyndaris were at last able to satisfy their desire to join the Romans, to whom they remained faithful throughout the later Punic and Slave Wars. In recognition for their loyalty they were honoured by the special privilege of being one of the Sicilian towns allowed to make offerings at the Temple of Venus in Eryx, and its prosperity was such that Cicero, visiting it in the I century B.C., referred to it as a *nobilissima civitas*. Speaking on behalf of its citizens, he claimed: 'We are counted among the seventeen favoured states of Sicily; in the Punic and Sicilian Wars we always remained faithful allies of Rome; and Rome has received every aid from us in war, and every respect in peace.' Needless to say Cicero was investigating the accusations made against the praetor Verres, whose behaviour at Tyndaris had been more than usually offensive. He had carried off, among other treasures, the much prized statue of Mercury, said to have been presented to the people of Tyndaris by Scipio Africanus in gratitude for their loyalty and for having supplied him with ships, and this theft so infuriated the people that when Verres finally left the island his statue was publicly torn down and demolished.

In 36 B.C. Caesar Augustus gained possession of Tyndaris and subsequently re-settled it; it was probably at this time that the basilica was built on to the porticoed agora, and the recent discovery of a colossal 2nd century head of Augustus inside the basilica suggests that it was still in use at that time. In Imperial Roman and later times the history of Tyndaris is little known. Pliny mentions a dreadful calamity which must have taken place before the end of the Ist century A.D., when half the town fell into the sea as a result of a landslide, but his account was probably exaggerated, and the site of the landslide has not yet been identified. During this time the theatre was completely modified to adapt it as an amphitheatre, and some spacious colonnaded houses were built over remains of Greek houses of the IV century B.C. and prehistoric remains of the Bronze Age (XVIII–XIV century B.C.). By late Imperial times the city wall had fallen into such a ruinous state that it was repaired and completed by building a new stretch along the seaward side, constructed with much re-used material from the theatre and other abandoned buildings. A few centuries later, in the Byzantine period, when the town had become much smaller, new walls were set up to enclose the acropolis area; these extended only as far as the basilica on the north-west.

The Theatre is thought to have first been built at the end of the IV century B.C. but it was entirely rehandled in Imperial Roman times when the four lower tiers of seats were removed, the orchestra lowered

PLATE 2. Tindari. The Propylaeum of the Agora

to form an arena for gladiatorial combats, and the stone scene-structure (in certain respects rather like that at Segesta, Fig. 8) was demolished. The building was evidently no longer in use by late Imperial times when some of its stones were used in the new city walls.

The Basilica is thought to have been built at the end of the I century B.C. It is really a monumental propylaeum belonging to the porticoed *agora* from which it leads into the main street of the town (Plate 2). Its façade on the side of the *agora* (which is now covered by modern houses) must have had five arches, the central one leading into the long vaulted gallery or basilica, flanked by a street at each side; the external pair of arches opened into stairways leading to an upper floor. The gallery was ingeniously contrived so that it could be shut off at each end to make a large hall for public meetings, and when these were taking place the traffic was switched into the two lateral streets, spanned by arches designed to help take the thrust from the barrel vaulting of the gallery. Niches in the walls of the gallery may once have held some of the Roman sculpture now in the Palermo Museum. This building is particularly interesting because it bridges two different traditions; structurally it is still linked with the Greek building techniques, but at the same time the incipient Roman technique of covering a space with a vaulted roof is just beginning to be apparent.

Roman Houses. Two large houses with colonnaded courtyards have been uncovered; one at least of these had two storeys. They are of Imperial Roman date.

The Antiquarium contains a model reconstruction of the original scene-building of the theatre, IV–III century Greek ware found below the Roman levels, Rhodian wine amphorae, lamps and other small objects of the I century B.C., Roman pre-sigillata and Arretine wares, and Roman objects of the 4th and 5th centuries A.D., sculptural fragments, inscriptions, etc.

2 · Halaesa, Cefalù, Himera and Solunto

HALAESA

Another Sikel town, again, like Longane, only a short distance inland, is *Halaesa*, near the coast at Castel di Tusa. To find the site, you continue westwards from Tindari towards Cefalù through S. Stefano di Camastra, 8 kms. after which a turning to the left leads to Tusa. Follow this road for 4 kms. up the left bank of the river, and the site of Halaesa lies to the right near the chapel of Santa Maria di Palate.

According to Diodorus Siculus Halaesa was founded in about 403 B.C. by Archonides of Herbita (one of the unidentified Sikel towns of the interior) who had left his native town with some of his subjects after having been forced to make a treaty with Dionysius of Syracuse.

The new town quickly prospered, and sixty years later was able to benefit from the peaceful conditions which Timoleon brought about in almost the whole of Sicily, when many of the towns which Dionysius had destroyed were built up again and newly fortified, and other colonies were founded; in the case of Halaesa the fortifications on the upper part of the hill were built at this time (late IV century). These fortifications, which closely resemble those at Tindari, have square towers at intervals, and the wall which bounds the terracing of the acropolis is reinforced with strong and closely spaced buttresses.

During the III century, perhaps partly owing to its maritime trade, Halaesa grew both in size and wealth, and its condition was further improved when, having submitted to the Romans at the outset of the First Punic War, it was granted special privileges for remaining loyal to the Roman cause. By the I century B.C. it was so wealthy that the praetor Verres imposed excessively heavy levies of corn and money, and from that time Halaesa seems to have declined, for it was only an ordinary municipal town at the time of Augustus.

Excavations have so far been very limited, but the *agora* with its surrounding porticoes has been discovered, and the street layout is now known to have been very like that at Solunto, where parallel streets with wide steps lead steeply up the hillside. The walls in the southern part of the site are now being excavated, and remains of a Hellenistic temple, probably dedicated to Apollo, and of another contemporary one to its east, have been found on a small plateau on the highest point of the hill. The city walls are now thought to be of two different periods.

CEFALÙ

(There are several hotels in Cefalù, including a Jolly Hotel, and a few miles inland, at the Sanctuary of Gibilmanna, the Bel Soggiorno is in a lovely position in the hills; open in certain seasons only.)

The story of Cefalù (the ancient Sikel city of *Cephaloedium*) is very far from clear, and only excavations can one day throw light on the problem. Perhaps at the time of Thucydides, who never mentioned it, it may have been only a fortress on the great headland above the town, from which it takes its name (Greek *kephale* = head). This hill was evidently occupied as early as the IX–VIII centuries B.C., and at some subsequent date (perhaps in the VI or V century) a wall was built to link this 'acropolis' with the small harbour at its foot. Just when these defences were put up it is not yet possible to say, but part of the wall, very massive and built with huge polygonal blocks, can still be seen in the town.

The first mention of *Cephaloedium* was in 396 B.C. when a treaty was concluded with the Carthaginian leader Himilco. It was then captured by Dionysius of Syracuse, and at the end of the century, owing to its friendly relations with the Carthaginians, it was attacked and taken by the Greek Agathocles of Syracuse in 307. By 254 the town was occupied by the Romans, and it was described as prosperous in the I century B.C. But like so many towns in Sicily it suffered very heavily from the exactions and oppressions of the Roman praetor Verres whose monstrous misdeeds were investigated so carefully and indignantly by Cicero, who gathered information in one place after another and left us detailed reports of the conditions in many Sicilian towns in the I century B.C.

Never very large, the town probably dwindled at that time, but continued to exist into the Norman period when some of the stones from its ancient walls were incorporated in the Cathedral. One of the finest medieval buildings in Sicily, the Cathedral at Cefalù is renowned for its magnificent 12th century mosaics.

The archaeological sites to visit are not many: a small museum, the polygonal walling of part of the early defences, and a curious and interesting building known as the 'Temple of Diana' on the hill.

The Museo Mandralisca (No. 13, Via Mandralisca) is open on week-days from 10.30–11.30 and 4.30–6.30. It contains Greek vases, some pottery from the Lipari excavations, early Sicilian coins, etc. Among the pottery there is a bell *krater* of local Siciliot make (red-figure ware of the IV century) painted to show a man selling tunny fish to another who is disputing its value or price. (There is also a very fine portrait of a man by Antonello da Messina.)

The Ancient Walls are, at one point, right on the sea. To find them follow Corso Ruggero northwards until it is joined on the left by Via Roma. At this point turn right and then second left and you can see the walls by going down to the shore. Another stretch can be seen in Piazza Garibaldi at the foot of the campanile of the little church of Santa Maria della Catena.

The so-called Temple of Diana. A steep footpath leads up to this from a small street, the Vicolo dei Saraceni, to the east of the southern end of Corso Ruggero. This building is certainly a very strange one, and it is improbable that it was ever a temple. Consisting of a huge rock-cut cistern surrounded by a wall of big rough blocks of stone, it has a rather 'dolmen'-like roof supported on a column of big blocks; this cistern was fed by a trickling spring, and it may well have been built by the VI century B.C., perhaps even earlier, for some IX–VIII century pottery was found when some excavations were made there some years ago. Another structure, whose lower courses at least were made with poly-gonal masonry, was built up against the cistern building; thought to be a fountain-house, this may have been put up in the V century but it has been rehandled and doors added at a later date, for the door mouldings are now thought to belong to the II century B.C. At all events the building, which is far from being clearly understood, must have been considerably modified in Roman times.

HIMERA

Himera (Imera in Italian) is now almost exclusively visited for the ruins of its famous Doric temple, which stands right beside the road (113) following the coast westwards from Cefalù (20 kms.). It stands to the north of the road just after it crosses the river Imera (or Fiume Grande) at Buonfornello.

The town of Himera also extended over the hill to the south, where

4

excavations have begun to uncover remains of walling, and two cemeteries have been found nearby. But so far the circuit of the ancient town
walls has not been accurately traced. Probably the high land to the
south-west of Rocca del Drago was enclosed by walls which stretched
north-eastwards towards the coastal plain to defend the harbour at the
river mouth. The temple in its sacred *temenos* must presumably have
stood within these walls. We know that the territory belonging to
Himera was extensive, its eastern frontier being near Cefalù, and its
western one at Termini Imerese (originally *Therma Himeraia* from its
hot baths).

The colony was founded in 648 B.C. by Chalcidians from Zancle
(later Messina) who were joined by some exiles from Syracuse. So far
some, but not very much, pottery belonging to the early years of the
colony has been recovered, but its scarcity can be explained by the fact
that so far excavations have largely been concentrated on the later
temple. By the VI century B.C. traffic with Spain was intensifying, and
perhaps the availability of Spanish silver accounts for the early coinage
at Himera, which was one of the first colonies to mint its own coins.

One of these original colonists from Zancle was the father of the great
lyric poet Stesichorus who was born and wrote in Himera, though later
in his life he moved to Catania. (His name was really Tisias, but he was
known as Stesichorus (chorus master) probably because he instructed
the chorus at Himera.)

The great moment in Himeran history was, however, in 480 B.C. when
the combined armies of the Greeks from Syracuse and Akragas routed
a powerful invasion force sent by the Carthaginians. To celebrate their
outstanding victory the triumphant Greeks built the temple of Himera.
The events preceding this battle were as follows. A petty despot,
Terillus, who had set himself up at Himera, was promptly driven out by
Theron of Akragas, who probably wanted to obtain a good port on the
north coast of Sicily from which to trade with Etruria and Spain.
Terillus begged for assistance from the Carthaginians, who landed a
mighty expeditionary force under the command of Hamilcar. So powerful was this force, which is said to have comprised 300,000 men, 200
galleys, and other ships, that it is quite obvious that the squabble over
Himera can only have served as a pretext for a large-scale invasion, to
meet the danger resulting from the unpalatable fact that the Greeks now
dominated an area stretching right across Sicily, barring Carthaginian
expansion to the east. In the first encounter Theron was defeated, but he
had sent urgently to Gelon of Syracuse, who immediately marched to

his assistance, and together they routed the Carthaginian army in an historic battle which is said to have been fought on the very same day as the battle of Salamis in Greece. According to one version of the day's events, Hamilcar was killed by Greek spies while he was offering sacrifices to Poseidon before the battle, but another version claims that, knowing the day was lost, he threw himself into the pyre. We are told that a fantastic quantity of spoils was taken from the Carthaginian army. Some of them were nailed up in the temples at Himera and others were sent to the sanctuaries at Olympia and Delphi, where Gelon dedicated 'golden Victories and tripods'. So great were the Carthaginian losses that Diodorus says 'only a few survivors in one small boat reached home to give the brief news that all who had crossed over to Sicily had perished'. The triumph was widely acclaimed and lavishly celebrated, for the victors claimed to have 'conquered the barbarians and extended the friendly hand of freedom to all Greeks'. Special issues of coins were struck in Syracuse, where some of the most renowned coin designers were employed, and the indemnity taken from the Carthaginians doubtless went towards payment for the many temples built in celebration, not only the one at Himera, but the Temple of Athena at Syracuse, and others at Akragas as well. Perhaps the most important effect of this victory was that it ushered in a period of peace which allowed art and literature to flourish as never before.

Returning to Akragas, Theron left Himera to be governed by his son, but the townspeople rose in rebellion against him, only to be severely punished by Theron who had many of them put to death or exiled. He then drafted in new settlers, mostly Dorians, to take their place, and like the victorious cities of Syracuse and Akragas, Himera enjoyed many years of peaceful development.

But the Carthaginians had never forgotten the defeat they had suffered at Himera, and were only awaiting the right moment for revenge. This presented itself at the end of the century when the Athenians, defeated at Syracuse, could no longer offer support to their allies in western Sicily. The Carthaginians now launched their second great invasion. This time Hamilcar's grandson Hannibal was in command, a man who eagerly sought the opportunity to avenge his grandfather's defeat. Having first sacked Selinus, he marched against Himera, where he found the town poorly defended. He massacred thousands of the inhabitants and razed its buildings to the ground in an attempt to wipe it right out of memory. Diodorus says that it was never built up again, but in fact, though most of the survivors were sent to the newly founded Carthaginian town of *Therma Himeraia* (Termini Imerese) which took the place of Himera, others were allowed to return, provided that they paid tribute to Carthage. But the blow dealt to Himera had been mortal: the hill top was now largely deserted, and the buildings in the plain, including the great temple, were no more than charred and battered relics of a once proud city.

The Temple (Plate 3), which may have been dedicated to Zeus Eleutherios, is thought to mark the actual site of the battle of 480 B.C., and in spite of the devastation it has suffered, sufficient still remains to show that it was an exceptionally interesting building with architectural features in common with temples both at Akragas and Syracuse.

It was a Doric building with 6 front and 14 lateral columns, a *pronaos* and *opisthodomos in antis*.

Rectangular stair-wells can be seen on either side of the cellar doorway, with steps which once led up into the roof-space. This is an unusual feature also present in several temples at Akragas, which suggests that at least some of the designers and craftsmen may have been sent from that town. (In Temple A at Selinus there was also a stair-well, but it was round, not square.)

The original design was for the columns to have double contraction on the fronts and single contraction on the sides, but Dinsmoor has drawn attention to the fact that before the stylobate blocks had actually been cut to fit the column spacing, the design was modified to allow for double contraction on the sides as well. This led to complications for, as he writes, 'in order to effect this with the whole length of the stylobate already fixed by the lower steps, it was necessary to widen all intervening axial spacings on the sides by $\frac{7}{8}$″'. He also noticed another curious fact: the lion-head spouts of the side *sima* were spaced without any relation to the spacing of the triglyphs. Many of these lion-head spouts (more than 50 were recovered, probably carved by various sculptors) can be seen in the *Museo Nazionale* in Palermo. (See p. 57.)

Leaving Himera, the road to Palermo passes through Termini Imerese where there are slight remains of a Roman amphitheatre.

SOLUNTO (Solus or Soloeis)

The ruins of this town stand on the slopes of a rocky headland from the highest point of which you can see up the coast eastwards as far as

PLATE 3.
(*above*) The Temple
at Himera
(*below*) One of the
lion-head water-
spouts from the
Temple

Cefalù and westwards to Monte Pellegrino above Palermo. This is a
lovely place which is worth visiting both for its position and its ruins,
and to reach it you fork off the coast road (113) at Santa Flavia, 17 kms.
east of Palermo.

For many years this was thought to have been the site of the Solus which, together with Panormus and Motya, were mentioned by Thucydides as the three main Phoenician sites in Sicily, and whose origins must have gone back to the VIII–VII centuries B.C. Excavations have now shown that this was a mistaken assumption, and the town whose remains can be seen at Solunto was built by Timoleon to replace the earlier town nearby, destroyed by Dionysius of Syracuse in 397 B.C.

The original site of Solus is now known to have been some 7 kms. to the south-west of Solunto, at a place called Cozzo Cannita where there is now nothing to see except a few traces of walling and a scattering of potsherds dating from the VI–III centuries. But sporadic finds of greater importance have been found there in the past, including the two large V century anthropoid sarcophagi now in the Palermo Museum, and, in all probability, the statue of a big seated figure of Isis (VI century?), as well as the statue of a headless goddess on a throne with winged sphinxes, which is partly Punic and partly Greek in style. This town must have been built as an outpost of Panormus (Palermo) at a time when the Carthaginians, anxiously watching the foundation of new Greek colonies in the VII century, wanted to block any possibility of Himera spreading its territory westwards.

After its destruction in 397, the site was abandoned, and a new town was built by Timoleon about fifty years later on the present site of Solunto. Laid out after the most up-to-date plan, the town grew rapidly, and Diodorus records the fact that after Agathocles of Syracuse had been defeated in his war against the Carthaginians in Africa, the remnants of his great army where given permission either to join the Carthaginian forces as mercenaries, or to settle at Solus.

This town was laid out on the grid plan, with streets at right angles to each other, a plan which was not infrequently adopted in the IV century B.C. and which derived certain characteristics from Hellenistic sites in Asia Minor, such as Pergamon or Miletus.

Of the later history of the place we know very little. During the First Punic War, after the fall of Panormus, Solus was annexed by the Romans as a *civitas decumana*. This accounts for the predominantly Roman character of many of its later features, when the population must have been a mixed one, with people of Punic, native, Greek and Roman descent. An Antonine inscription implies that the town was still in existence in the 2nd century A.D., but there is nothing to suggest that it continued to be occupied much later than that. It can never have been a place of great importance, but it may not have been finally destroyed until the Arab period (about the 9th century).

The approach from the car park and Antiquarium leads into the wide main street, or *decumanus*, partly paved with large terracotta bricks, and leading along the side of the hill towards the rather fragmentary remains of the public buildings, the *agora*, the theatre, and a small *odeion* used probably for council meetings. Cutting across this street are others leading up and down the slope: these were lined with houses and shops, some of them (like the one with Doric columns on the left of the main street) belonging to the Roman period. All these streets have a central gutter for carrying off the rain water.

At present only less than a quarter of the town has been excavated, and the buildings have been found to date from the IV century B.C. onwards, for a great many of them were rebuilt in Roman times. A group of rich Roman houses with colonnaded courtyards and fine mosaic pavements were found at the north end of the main street, beyond the insignificant remains of the theatre and *odeion*, both of which, though begun in the IV century, were rehandled in Roman times. Just below these two buildings stood the *agora*, a long rectangular piazza with nine small rooms with coloured plaster walls on its upper side. A big cistern can be seen nearby, and no doubt many others will be discovered, for the town was entirely dependent on these for its water supply.

The Antiquarium is dedicated to finds from this site. Among the earliest finds are some fragments of Greek red-figure ware and some Italiot sherds, both dating from the mid-IV century when the town was founded. (See Case 1.) The Punic contribution includes an open-air altar and three stelae, as well as some small terra-cotta heads which are very eastern in type; it is clear, in fact, that the Punic taste lingered on for a long while. A Greek inscription and many Roman finds, including Arretine pottery, reflect the very mixed character of the population.

If you are driving on to Palermo, it is well worth making the short deviation round the promontory before rejoining the main road. Visitors particularly interested in baroque architecture may like to be reminded that only a short distance from Solunto is Bagheria where the Villa Palagonia is ornamented with some of the most exuberant and freakish stone carvings to be found anywhere in Sicily, or even Europe. (Open to the public on application to the caretaker).

3 · Palermo, Addaura and Segesta

PALERMO

Accommodation. There is a wide selection of hotels and *pensioni* of all categories. The Hotel Sole is good and very centrally placed. Less expensive but also to be well recommended is the smaller Hotel Sausele near the Central Station at Via V. Errante 12. Mondello is on the coast, a few miles to the north; it has a number of hotels and a camping site in the Parco della Favorita.

Palermo (or *Panormus* as it was anciently called) was one of the chief Punic colonies in Sicily, and together with *Motya* and *Solus* (Solunto) acted as a Carthaginian base of the first importance. It was fortified with a strong enclosing wall in the VII century B.C. and remained in Carthaginian hands until the mid-III century B.C., when it fell to the Romans. Hamilcar Barca camped on Monte Pellegrino and tried for several years to regain it, but without success, and it remained a Roman centre of some importance for many years.

Its period of outstanding prosperity was during the early Middle Ages, under Arab rule between 948 and 1061, and during the Norman period, particularly under Roger II and his successors in the 12th century. These few centuries witnessed such a magnificent flowering of artistic achievement that visitors will rightly be more interested in Palermo's medieval rather than its ancient past, and will want to see such buildings as the churches of the Eremiti and of San Cataldo, in the Arab style, the many Norman churches including the Martorana and the small but exquisite Cappella Palatina, with its mosaics which are rivalled only by those at Monreale and Cefalù. Apart from these there are many fine buildings in the Spanish gothic or baroque styles.

For the archaeologist the *Museo Nazionale Archeologico* is a collection of extreme importance; it not only houses the finds from the Conca d'Oro (the fertile plain around Palermo) and most sites in Western Sicily (the counterpart of the Museum of Syracuse for the East), but the famous temple metopes from Selinus (Selinunte) in it form one of the richest collections of Greek sculpture in existence.

Museo Nazionale Archeologico. (Fig. 6) (Piazza Olivella). Most easily reached by Via Bora, either from the Teatro Massimo, or Via Roma.

Opening Hours. 9–4 (150 lire). Sundays 9.30–1 (free). Closed on Mondays.

GROUND FLOOR

Entrance Court (1) with two small rooms (2 and 3) opening off it. Among other sculptures these contain a fine orientalizing-style lion attacking a bull, from Halaesa (p. 47) and two huge V century anthropoid sarcophagi from Cannita (the first site of the town of Solus). Punic inscriptions, and a VI century B.C. male torso, perhaps from Motya.

Large Main Court (4). Architectural and sculptured fragments, and Roman period inscriptions, sarcophagi, etc.

(5) Reproduction of enormous capital from Temple G at Selinunte, and IV century and Hellenistic sculpture.

(6) Collection of twin-headed stelae (VI–IV century B.C.) from the sanctuary of Malophoros at Selinunte, a dedicatory inscription to Apollo from Temple G, and V century lion-head water-spouts from Agrigento.

(7) V century lion-head water-spouts from the temple at Himera (p. 49).

(8) Part of the entablature of Temple C at Selinunte, and other architectural fragments.

(9) *The most impressive room in the Museum, with the famous metopes from the Selinunte temples.* (See p. 92). Some of the archaic metopes come from a small, elaborately decorated temple (*Temple Y*), whose exact site on the acropolis is not known. One shows a sphinx, another three deities (Apollo and Artemis on each side of Leto), and a third shows Europa being carried off by Zeus in the form of a bull, with dolphins symbolizing the sea. In another Herakles is struggling with the Cretan Bull. This temple was probably demolished in antiquity, and some fragments of triglyphs, etc. which may have belonged to it were found re-used in fortifications added to Selinus at a later date. Originally the metopes were all painted, and they are thought to date from about 550 or soon afterwards. Their archaic character may be partly due to provinciality, and in fact they also show Ionic influences which are unlikely to be before 550 B.C. In certain respects they are strongly Peloponnesian in style.

Temple F. These metopes date from about 500–490 B.C., some years after the temple was begun. There are many scenes depicting a duel between gods and giants. In one a goddess (?Athena) has mortally wounded a giant; the acute suffering on the face, and the Corinthian helmet thrown back in the agony of death, are magnificently portrayed.

Temple C. As in Temple F the metopes were applied to the façade. One shows Apollo in a 4-horse chariot with Leto on one side and his sister, Artemis, on the other. Another shows Herakles and the Cercopes, the Libyan thieves who tried to rob him. In the third Athena is helping Perseus to kill the Gorgon, from whose blood Pegasus is born. Others are very fragmentary.

Although, as in Temple Y, these metopes are still somewhat archaic in treatment, and also reveal Ionic influence, they are in much higher relief, and probably date from about 550–530 B.C.

Temple E. A late and very classical temple, dedicated to Hera, and probably begun after the battle of Himera in 480 B.C. Of the original 12 metopes, 4 remain. They are later than those so far noted, (they may be as late as 460 B.C.) and represent the highest achievement of Selinuntine art, even if there are still signs of lingering archaism in comparison with Greece itself. The faces and arms etc. are sometimes of Parian marble, separately carved and then inserted into the figures made of local limestone. In one metope Athena can be seen killing the giant Enkelados; the others show the marriage of Zeus and Hera, Herakles killing an Amazon, and Actaeon being attacked by Artemis' dogs (see Plate 6). Unlike the earlier temples C and F, the metopes here were set above the porches.

See also an *arula* (small altar) from the Sanctuary of Demeter Malophoros at Selinunte. It shows Eos and Kephalos. Probably early V century.

(Rooms 10–13 contain finds from Etruscan sites.)

FIRST FLOOR

(1) Long gallery. Topographical collection of Greek and Roman Sicily. *Antiquarium* (3 rooms overlooking the main court). Small works of Greek, Punic and Roman origin in precious metals, etc. Coin collection.
(2) Terra-cottas, archaic altars, statuettes from Centuripe and Solunto (p. 52). Large masks from Selinunte.
(3) Small bronzes. Greek, Etruscan and Roman statuettes.

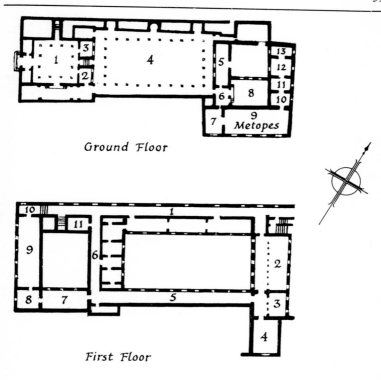

Ground Floor

First Floor

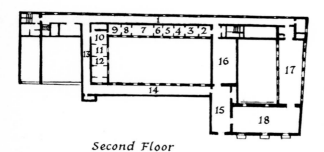

Second Floor

FIG. 6. The *Museo Nazionale* at Palermo. Plan of the three floors

(4) Large bronzes, including a III century B.C. ram, once one of a pair.
(5) Long south gallery, with some of the 12,000 votive terra-cotta figurines found in the Malophoros sanctuary at Selinunte (p. 96), showing typological development from VII–V century B.C.
(6) Recent finds from near Palermo, including some from a Punic cemetery.
(7) In course of arrangement.
(8) Greek sculpture and Roman copies. Fragment of Parthenon frieze.
(9) Roman sculpture. 1st–2nd century A.D. statues, imperial portraits, etc.

SECOND FLOOR (in course of arrangement).

North Gallery (1). Western Sicily Palaeolithic. Flint implements, etc. from Lévanzo, Addaura, etc. Copies of incised drawings from these two caves, and palaeontological material.
(2–9). Small rooms containing Neolithic and Copper Age finds, including beakers from Torrebigini (Partanna), and Villafrati, together with other pottery from those tombs; Capo Graziano style pottery from the Grotta di Moarda (Alcofonte). Finds from other tombs in the Conca d'Oro (district round Palermo), including the Sant'Isidoro tombs at Boccadifalco, etc.

Then follow the finds from Serraferlicchio, Malpasso, Castelluccio and various Copper and Early Bronze Age sites. Huge painted pot from Petralia.

Next come the Castelluccio and Thapsos cultures. Painted wares from Naro and Partanna, etc.

The Castelluccio culture which was centred in East Sicily spread to the west where its character changed. The pottery is often black or yellow or red with geometric patterns, and sometimes shows influence from Serraferlicchio. The Thapsos culture is not well represented in West Sicily (the type-site is near Syracuse, see p. 195), but the material from the Boccadifalco village is important.

After these rooms there is one containing pottery, etc. from Sant'-Angelo Muxaro (see p. 129), and Late Bronze and Early Iron Age finds.

Rooms 10–15 will house a magnificent collection of Greek vases, and finds from the Greek colonies including local imitations of Greek wares.
(16) will have mosaic pavements from Palermo and Marsala, and some frescoes from Solunto.

The Third Floor will house the reserve collections which will only be opened to students by special permission of the Director.

The *Museo della Fondazione 'I.Mormino'*, endowed by the Banco di Sicilia, is housed in their premises in Via Vaglica, a turning off Via Ruggero Settimo. It has been open to the public since 1963, and can generally be visited on request, up till about 6.30. It is a small but well displayed collection including two very fine black-figure *kraters* of the VI century, an archaic statuette (VII century), Greek and Roman coins from Sicily, etc.

ADDAURA

The Grotta di Addaura, with its famous Upper Palaeolithic incised drawings of human beings and animals, is only a few miles from Palermo, on the northern slopes of Monte Pellegrino, overlooking Mondello. It can only be visited by special permission of the *Soprintendente alle Antichità* (whose office is near the Museo Nazionale Archeologico), and it is therefore only advisable for those really interested. The same applies for the Upper Palaeolithic caves at Lévanzo and Favignana.

In recent years a number of caves with incised drawings have been found in Sicily. Besides the three caves at Addaura itself, there are others in the Niscemi neighbourhood, and near Trapani and Termini Imerese, as well as the well-known ones on the island of Lévanzo in the Egadi Islands (p. 77).

In only one of the Addaura caves is the human figure portrayed, in the central cave of the three, but human figures are also known from Lévanzo, and from the Grotta Geraci near Termini Imerese, where they are painted with a black outline.

The most westerly cave at Addaura has produced palaeolithic material, and remains of dwarf elephants from the earlier levels. (Speleologists can sometimes make arrangements to visit the cave by applying for a guide from the Club Alpino Italiano, Via Ruggero Settimo 73, Palermo).

The drawings in the central cave, or rock-shelter, came to light by a curious accident. Some bombs, dumped there by the Americans in the war, exploded accidentally, and the blast flaked off the layers of incrustation which had formed over them. This layer still covers most of the walls of the shelter, and the greatest skill will be needed to remove it. No archaeological strata have been discovered there, but the occupation level must originally have been much higher than the present floor, for traces of it were observed on the walls at a height of about 3 metres. The drawings, too, are high up on the walls and have to be seen from a ladder.

The incised drawings (see Plate 4), which represent single figures or groups of people and animals, have been divided into three groups. Those regarded as the earliest are rather lightly drawn human and animal figures, sometimes overlaid by stronger, more deeply incised human figures and animals (mostly bovids). The third group is also strongly incised, and is composed of two or three animals whose treatment is stylistically different from the other groups: they are more rigid, and were perhaps drawn by people of a rather decadent and backward culture. One of these overlies a figure of the first group.

The most sociologically interesting figures are perhaps those of the second group, for they allow us to catch a glimpse of human activities which are very rarely seen in Palaeolithic art. A group of hunters and warriors are arranged in a scene which is difficult to interpret, though it appears to represent a ritual dance centring upon two ithyphallic men, lying one above the other and facing in opposite directions. At least eight other people wearing what seem to be bird-head masks, are standing round or dancing. This fascinating scene may represent an initiation dance or propitiatory rite of some sort. Below these figures a hunter is pursuing a galloping deer.

The drawing of all the figures is assured and sensitive, full of vitality and movement. Strangely enough no hands or feet are shown. An attempt has been made to relate them to other series of Palaeolithic drawings. The first two groups are very like the Lévanzo figures, and the presence of human figures with uplifted arms has also suggested connections with some painted drawings which may be rather later in date, from North Africa. This suggested comparison has recently been supported by an interesting discovery of comparable figures from the Gebel-el-Akhdar in Cyrenaica, one of a chain of sites running from Tunisia into Tripolitania. Very provisionally these seem to fall within the VI or VII millennium B.C., and if the Addaura drawings really prove to be comparable in style and date, the latest, rather debased, drawings from there may even fall into the very early Neolithic. Such a late date is also possible for some of the Lévanzo drawings though at present the hypothesis has little support.

It is interesting to note, that although they are not present at Addaura, groups of simple incised lines are sometimes found in Sicilian

PLATE 4. The Addaura cave near Palermo. Upper Palaeolithic incised figures

caves, and these may be related to the so-called 'traits Capsiens' which have recently been carbon-dated in Tunisia to the VII millennium. For instance the Grotta Racchio all'Isolidda (Trapani) has both animal figures and simple incised lines, though they need not, of course, be contemporary.

For the time being the close dating of the Addaura drawings must remain a challenge.

SEGESTA (Fig. 7)

Segesta can be visited by train from Palermo (there is then 20 minutes' walk from Segesta Tempio station) or by the Nastro d'Oro bus, whose route is shown in Figure 2. If you go by road from Palermo you should leave the city by the state road (186) which continues westwards from Via Vittorio Emanuele, or it can be joined by following Corso Tuköry from the Central Station. This road passes through Monreale, with its splendid 12th-13th century mosaics in the Cathedral, and the richly ornamented cloisters which once formed part of a Benedictine Monastery, (in summer closed to visitors between 1–3).

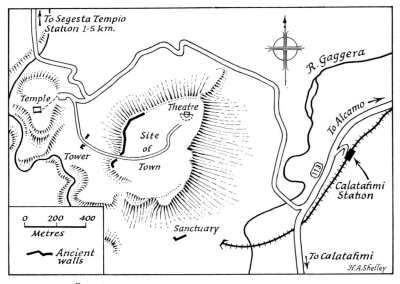

FIG. 7. Segesta

After Partinico (a focal point of Mafia activity) you take the road 113 to Alcamo, and near Calatafimi a turning to the right winds up through lovely hilly country to Segesta.

Accommodation. The nearest good accommodation is at Castellammare del Golfo, 17 kms. to the north, on the coast.

Perhaps more than any other place in Sicily, Segesta arouses sentiments and emotions in the travellers who, for many centuries, have been visiting its ruined temple with admiration and wonder. Certainly the earlier visitors had the inestimable advantage of arriving there after the slow ascent on mule-back from Calatafimi, their mules picking their way across country by the few bad roads and the stony *trazzere* which, winding between the hills, afforded them a glimpse every now and then of the distant temple. Tired and triumphant, and imbued with the 'romantick' approach to antiquities, one such traveller was inspired, as he contemplated the temple, to write, 'The clear colour and majestic disposition of so many columns on which light and shade are cast in various directions, and the insulated situation of so grand a building on a bold eminence in the midst of a desert, have something singularly awful and sublime in their effect.'

This sense of wonder, which we have so sadly lost today, was enhanced by the slow approach. But it was possible for only a few people to visit such remote ruins; now bus-loads of people can be driven right to the site, for a road has been built in recent years which leads up past the temple to the adjacent hill, Monte Barbaro, where the town of Segesta once stood, and where excavations have now uncovered one of the loveliest Greek theatres in existence. Even today, however, the site is mostly quiet and unpopulous, so that it is still possible to wander alone over the hillside, sit in the theatre looking out over the hills and sea, and ponder Berenson's words about the temple which he regarded as 'an affirmation of reason, order and intelligence in the midst of the pell-mell, the indifference and the anarchy of nature'. And we can think of Segesta not only in its physical, but in its historical background as well, for unlike the 18th century travellers we now know when it was built and what was happening in Sicily at that time.

Segesta (or Egesta as the Greeks called it) was famed in antiquity for its medicinal sulphurous springs, and these were probably those which are found a short distance to the north near Calametti. It was one of the two main towns of the Elymians, a people about whose origins we know very little. Thucydides said that they were a cross between local peoples and Trojan and Phocian refugees; Dionysius of Halicarnassus, handing

5

down an earlier tradition recorded by Hellanicus of Mytilene, and also followed by Diodorus Siculus, said that they came to Sicily from Italy a few years before the Sikels. Whatever their origin, their lands included most of the modern province of Trapani and part of that of Palermo, and their other important site, a religious one, was at Eryx (the modern Erice). In all probability they were indigenous peoples with some foreign admixture (we know that they were joined at Segesta by people of Cnidian and Rhodian descent) who fairly rapidly became Hellenized, for by the V century they were already using a Greek legend on their coinage, and a century or so before that they had built a sanctuary below the hill at Segesta, which was certainly made under Greek influence. Culturally they must have been more advanced than the Sikels, and they enjoyed the unusual privilege of being allowed to intermarry with the Greeks; in fact they showed a marked ability to absorb the superior cultures, taking from the Carthaginians at Eryx, and from the Greeks at Segesta.

The earliest building known at Segesta is the sanctuary below the hill to the east. This was built over a native occupation level of at least the VIII–VII century B.C. Above this, on the hill near the theatre, must have stood their settlement, later obliterated by the town when it was rebuilt by Timoleon. Of this early settlement very little is so far known, but shepherds still pick up sherds of Greek black- or red-figure ware of the VI century onwards, as well as native pottery, on the hilltop, particularly on the strip of land immediately below the theatre plateau. Some sherds, found in excavations, were inscribed in Greek characters but in another language, and suggest that the writing represents our first hints of the Elymian tongue.

The foundations of the theatre itself were cut into a prehistoric level of the first half of the I millennium B.C. which produced pottery like some from Sant'Angelo Muxaro (p. 129) as well as some brooches of South Pantalica type (p. 192) of the VIII century. A natural cave which existed under the theatre, was carefully respected when the building was planned, and a doorway leads into it from the west part of the *cavea*. Whether this cave was originally a cult centre, we cannot say. The excavators found prehistoric pottery as well as pre-Hellenistic Greek wares and Roman sherds, and it is interesting to note that a track and steps cut in the rock led down to the sanctuary below.

Much of what we know of the history of Segesta is concerned with the continual squabbles with Selinus, for the territories of the two towns met near the upper course of the river Mazaros, and their boundaries were always under discussion. These border disputes began at least as early as the VI century B.C. and were often renewed.

In the wars between the Greeks and Carthaginians Segesta was frequently disputed, and although in their political manoeuvres the Segestans showed themselves to be opportunists, it must be realized that their geographical position, so far west, made it almost essential for them to throw in their lot with the stronger side, whichever that might be; their very survival depended upon this.

At the end of the VI century the Segestans were allied to the Carthaginians, but after the defeat of the first great Punic invasion at the battle of Himera in 480 B.C. they hurriedly changed allegiance in favour of the Athenians who, on several occasions later in the century (in 453 and 426), cultivated Segesta in opposition to her rivals.

In 416 border disputes again broke out with Selinus, which begged help from Syracuse. The Segestans countered by turning for support to their old allies, the Athenians, and an amusing anecdote has been handed down to us concerning their treatment of the Athenian envoys sent to Segesta to report on their wealth and strength. Fearing that their own riches would hardly impress the Athenians, they hastily sent to the other Elymian town Eryx, and to other neighbouring towns, to round up all the available gold and silver drinking cups. These they produced again and again in the houses where the envoys were invited. Needless to say, the envoys were completely deceived, and carried back exaggerated accounts of the great wealth they had seen. It is also possible that the temple at Segesta was hastily begun at this time, again with the intention of impressing the Athenians by the degree of Hellenization the town could boast.

At all events the Athenians sent a fleet to help them, and an armed force whose real scope was undoubtedly to curb the growing power of Syracuse. But their campaign was a disaster, and their defeat at Syracuse and the temporary weakening of the Syracusan power left the coast relatively clear for another great Carthaginian invasion, this time led by Hannibal, son of Giskon. Border disputes were still continuing with Selinus, and Hannibal, fearing that Selinus, if victorious, might hold a strip of land right across Sicily, supported the Segestans, and with their help sacked not only Selinus, but Akragas, Gela, Himera and Camarina as well. After this Segesta actually became subject to Carthage, and was absorbed into the Carthaginian empire. Its independent coinage came to an end.

When Dionysius of Syracuse waged war with the Carthaginians in

397, he besieged Segesta which was relieved by a Punic army led by Himilco, after an attack described by Diodorus, who tells how the Segestans set fire to the Greek tents in the dead of night, and burnt many of their horses tethered outside.

We again hear of Segesta at the time of Timoleon, who inflicted severe losses on the Carthaginians at the battle of the river Krimisos, in 339. Presumably it was after this that Timoleon rebuilt Segesta, together with so many other towns in Sicily. But its prosperity was not to last, for when Agathocles (Timoleon's successor) returned from his campaign in Africa to war with Carthage in Sicily, and had been given a friendly welcome by the Segestans, he suddenly turned against them, killing most of them, plundering their wealth, and selling their women and children as slaves. He accused them of conspiring against him, and although this was probably nothing but a trumped-up excuse, it did not prevent him from putting them to hideous tortures. Men are said to have been bound to catapults and hurled into the air, or placed on a brass bed with recesses for their arms and legs, and then roasted alive when a fire was lit underneath. As Freeman said, Agathocles evidently had an oriental delight in inflicting suffering. Ironically enough, when he re-peopled Segesta, he gave it the name Dikaiopolis (the City of Righteousness).

When Pyrrhus came to Sicily in 277 in his attempt to unite and free the Sicilian Greeks, the Segestans, then independent, joined him, but after he had retired from Sicily they again fell to the Carthaginians, who carried off a prized statue of Demeter, which, restored to them by Scipio Africanus after the final defeat of Carthage, was again stolen by the ubiquitous and insatiable Verres.

During the Roman period the town prospered, and had its own trading port at Castellammare, about 17 kms. away, which gradually rivalled its parent city in importance. The Romans made some modifications to the theatre at Segesta, and must also have carried out alterations to the town itself, but these await discovery by excavation.

The last we hear of the town was when it was sacked by Vandals and so completely destroyed that in medieval times not even its name was remembered.

Although very little remains to be seen of the town walls, there are traces of a tower between the temple and the town plateau. The date of this is probably not older than the late IV century B.C.

There are three other sites to visit at Segesta: the early sanctuary at the foot of the hill (only interesting for specialists), the temple and the theatre. Both the latter are among the most impressive buildings of ancient Sicily.

The Sanctuary is best reached by following the railway westwards from the point where it crosses the main road (113) to Calatafimi, a little south of where the road forks to Segesta. Leaving the railway where it enters the tunnel, you continue westwards; the distance from the road is about half a mile.

Remains can be seen of a large enclosure with a well-preserved *temenos* wall surrounding sacred buildings. Many broken fragments of columns, triglyphs and other architectural elements from at least three Doric buildings were found here, but the site seems to have been much robbed in Arab times. Some of the *echini* were of the earliest Doric type, and fragments of a carved door point to an East Mediterranean inspiration.

The sanctuary evidently goes back to the early VI century, but its life was not long, for it seems to have been deserted by the V century. The conception of a sacred enclosure is a native rather than a Greek one, but the construction itself was carried out under Greek influence, and this is interesting, as it shows that Hellenization had begun at Segesta as early as the VI century.

Under the foundations, and elsewhere in contemporary levels at Segesta, excavations have recovered native Elymian pottery; this was generally painted and incised, and often had handles decorated with stylized human faces. Dating from the VIII–VII century, it continued in use until the sanctuary was built. Similar pottery has been found at Eryx, Motya, and other sites.

A track and rock-cut steps (difficult to find) lead up to the hill, but it is wiser to return to the road which leads right up to the temple and theatre.

The Temple (Plate 5) stands alone on a smaller hill to the west of Monte Barbaro, the site of the ancient city. It is a hexastyle building with 14 side columns, and it has no *cella* or roof: in fact it was never completed. The columns were never fluted, and the bosses used for hoisting the blocks of the steps into position have been left, instead of being chiselled off as they would have been when the final touches were given to the building. The stylobate, too, was left without the intermediate blocks of stone between the columns, which are thus left with what appear to be square bases. The abacuses were also unfinished, with their corners left rough to protect them during construction.

In an early plan by Hittorf and Zanth some stones were shown in the interior, which might have belonged to the lower courses of the *cella*, but these stones were later removed.

It has been suggested that the Elymians built this temple as a shrine, deliberately left open to the sky, and surrounded by Greek columns: a hypothesis which, for many reasons, is unconvincing. It is surely improbable that this temple was the only open 'frame' construction known from the ancient world, and equally improbable that had it been so, the building would show such refinements as, for instance, the slight but deliberate curving of the stylobate and the squared grooves at the base of the columns (perhaps for decorative bronze bands?). Although unfinished the temple shows signs of great sophistication. A. W. Lawrence has suggested that the architect deliberately made it rather squat, 'in keeping with its situation in a wide valley', and D. S. Robertson has described it as 'a carefully planned building rivalling the Parthenon in the subtlety of its refinements'.

It remains to discover why it was left in this condition, and when it was built.

In a most interesting paper published recently, A. Burford has made a very real contribution to the study of this temple. She has drawn attention to a much neglected statement of accounts relating to the contracts for building the IV century temple of Asclepios at Epidauros. From this it appears that the general practice in temple-building was to construct first the peristasis and then to work inwards, leaving all the refinements such as the fluting, and smoothing down the hoisting bosses, till the last. If the stones shown in Hittorf and Zanth's plan really belonged to the *cella*, the Segestans must have intended to continue, and she argues that if they had intended to build a 'frame' only, they would surely have completed it by dressing the surfaces as they proceeded.

Dinsmoor has suggested that the temple was probably begun during the alliance with Athens after 426, and left uncompleted when the quarrel broke out with Selinus in 416, and if A. W. Lawrence is right in thinking the architect was an Athenian, this view may be correct. The alternative view, that it was begun in 416 as a cultural flourish to impress the Athenians (to whom the Segestans had appealed for help), and abandoned after the Athenian defeat in 413, is less convincing.

At all events a Greek architect of outstanding ability was employed, and there is no reason to suppose that the Segestans were not sufficiently Hellenized to want a complete and fully refined building.

PLATE 5. Segesta. (*above*) the Temple (*below*) the Theatre

The Theatre (Plate 5) is unusual in facing north, but this choice was evidently dictated by the desire for it to look out over the hills and sea.

As you approach it you first see the high wall backing the *cavea*. This theatre, like that at Tyndaris, was evidently built in the III or early II century B.C. The wings of the scene building had upper storeys which formed oblique decorative pavilions framing the stage, and the scene wall, as Dinsmoor has shown, was elaborately decorated with pilasters and columns, a feature which, he thinks, may have been due to Italic influence, as it is found elsewhere in the Western colonies. Among the decorative elements found here were *telamones* of the god Pan, a god often connected with worship in caves, and particularly appropriate here where an early cave, perhaps once a cult-centre, was respected by the theatre architect who built a doorway giving access to it from the west part of the *cavea*.

As at Syracuse, the orchestra was provided with an underground passage and steps which enabled actors to surprise the spectators by suddenly popping up from the underworld. As in the late IV century theatre at Athens, the auditorium was in the form of a stilted semicircle with straight prolongations.

The scene buildings show Roman re-handling of about 100 B.C. and Roman cement can be seen in the upper part of the *cavea*. Probably at this time the *proskenion* was rebuilt, or the old one widened and lowered, and a row of small columns was added to the front. (See restoration, Fig. 8).

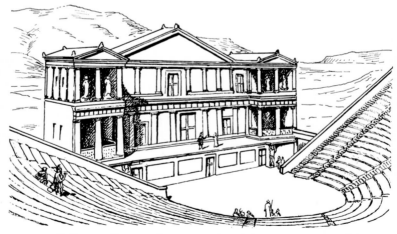

FIG. 8. Segesta. Suggested reconstruction of the scene structure of the theatre (after Bulle)

4 · Erice, Trapani, Lévanzo and Favignana, Motya and Lilybaeum

ERICE (the ancient Eryx)

Access by road, or by bus or cable car-from Trapani. There are now several hotels, and it is more inviting to stay in Erice than in Trapani. There are very few archaeological remains to see, but the town itself is so magnificently situated and played so interesting a role in early history that it would be a great mistake not to visit it.

The distance from Segesta to Erice is about 42 kms. and, although you can take a rather devious way across country via Bruca, it is advisable to return to the road (113) off which you turned to reach Segesta, and to continue along it (passing just below Calatafimi, where one of the great battles in Garibaldi's campaign was fought) towards Trapani. (Apparently the day after that battle, many of Garibaldi's Thousand, though exhausted with fighting, went out to visit Segesta which they must have seen in the distance from the castle at Calatafimi.) Just short of Trapani you turn back right (road 187), and soon afterwards find the zigzagging road up to Erice. If you are without a car, there is a bus service, taking about an hour, or you can take a trolley-bus to reach the hourly cable-car, whose first and last departures it would be wise to check.

Erice, which is still sometimes called by its medieval name of Monte San Giuliano, and which still retains much of its medieval character, stands on the top of a steep mountain well over 2,000 feet high. Virgil referred to it as a mountain of great height, perhaps because he had heard of it from sailors to whom it would give that impression, as it rises almost from sea level. It was the chief sacred site of the Elymians and, unlike Segesta, it was dominated by Punic rather than Greek influence. A number of different legends, often very confused ones, have been handed down about its foundation, and these are mostly concerned with the famous temple of the goddess of fertility identified by the Carthaginians with Astarte, by the Greeks with Aphrodite, and by the Romans with Venus Erycina, worshipped all over the Mediterranean for many hundreds of years, and perhaps descended from the Minoan nature goddess. This temple, and its sanctuary or sacred *temenos*, stood on the ancient acropolis, on the highest part of the hill – the site now occupied by the castle – and must have been visible to passing vessels miles out to sea.

According to one legend the temple was founded by Aeneas, another claims that it was beautified by Daedalus, while another (or an amalgam of others) claims that both temple and town were founded by Eryx, the son of Aphrodite, a local king who gave hospitality to Herakles when he visited Sicily. Herakles was said to be returning from the west, from beyond the ocean, having passed through Tartessos and then through Italy. He swam across to Sicily with his oxen, and travelling westwards, refreshed himself at Himera, and then at Segesta before reaching Eryx where he wrestled with the king or his son who had challenged him to fight. Herakles won, and as a result the place passed into his possession. But he left it to its own people provided that it was given up if any of his descendants claimed it. This legend must have been current at least as early as 514 B.C. because in that year Dorieus, half-brother of the king of Sparta, tried to found a town near Eryx, in the heart of the Carthaginian territory. He wished to call his town Heraclea, after his ancestor Herakles, but he failed in his venture and was killed by the Carthaginians and Elymians.

Very little of the history of Eryx is known, and that little is only fragmentary. We have numismatic evidence of coins with Greek legends going back to the V century B.C. at about the time when the Punic walls around the town may have been built. We have also mentioned its great riches at the time of the Athenian expedition in 415 B.C., when its gold and silver cups were borrowed by the Segestans to impress the Athenian envoys before Athens' disastrous defeat at the hand of the Syracusans. At the end of that century the Greek legends on the coinage were exchanged for Punic ones.

At the time of Dionysius' campaign in western Sicily in 397, the population of Eryx joined him, and their harbour of *Drepana* (Trapani) was used as his naval base. But shortly afterwards the Carthaginians regained the town. A century or so later, in about 278 B.C., it was again attacked, this time by Pyrrhus, during his campaign to free the Sicilian Greeks; he brought powerful siege-engines against the city walls and personally led the hand-to-hand fighting until the defenders were overcome; the victorious army then offered sacrifices to Herakles. A few years later, in 260, Eryx was destroyed by Hamilcar during the First Punic War, and its inhabitants were transferred to Drepana, but even after this Eryx was still sufficiently important as a garrisoned stronghold to warrant a surprise attack by the Romans a few years later. They captured it but subsequently only just managed to hold out on the acropolis hill, when Hamilcar Barca besieged it again and took the rest of the town. But by 241 the Carthaginians had suffered a severe naval defeat and had to sue for peace.

Eryx seems to have been almost deserted in Strabo's time, and Tacitus records that the Segestans applied to Tiberius to restore the temple which was twice depicted on Roman coins, once before restoration, on a coin of G. Considius Nonianus in 60 B.C., and once after its restoration by Claudius. As Suetonius wrote, 'Claudius had the temple of Venus Erycina in Sicily, which had fallen into ruin through age, restored at the expense of the treasury of the Roman people.' In fact the Romans went to great pains to keep the temple repaired and beautiful, and Diodorus says, 'they surpassed all people who had preceded them in the honours they paid to the goddess.' He goes on to say, 'The consuls and praetors for instance, who visit the island, and all Romans who sojourn there clothed with any authority, whenever they come to Eryx, embellish the sanctuary with magnificent sacrifices and honours, and laying aside the austerity of their authority, they enter into sports and have conversation with women [sacred prostitution was practised there] in a spirit of great gaiety, believing that only in this way will they make their presence there pleasing to the goddess. Indeed the Roman senate has so zealously concerned itself with the honours of the goddess that it has decreed that the seventeen cities of Sicily which are most faithful to Rome shall pay a tax in gold to Aphrodite and that 200 soldiers shall serve as a guard of her shrine.'

The Temple of Aphrodite. Today nothing remains to be seen of the temple which may have been destroyed when a Christian church was built over it. Excavations on the north-east side of the castle hill have, however, revealed the remains of a large platform which might once have been the base of the temple. This foundation platform was orientated NE–SW, unlike Greek temples which usually face east and west. So if it really marks the site of Aphrodite's temple it would point, as one would expect, to the non-Hellenic origin of the temple.

Parts of the walls of the sacred *temenos* still exist and contain many architectural fragments of triglyphs, columns etc. belonging to the Roman period, and one triglyph which might have survived from the earlier building. Other remains nearby include the foundations of a Punic house and a Roman bath, etc.

The so-called *Well of Aphrodite* can be seen at the east end of the enclosure, but unfortunately it cannot be closely dated, owing to the repeated re-handling of the site.

It seems hardly credible that so renowned a temple, the scene of offerings and sacrifices for so many hundred years, has disappeared so completely. A few gold and silver rings showing Venus and Eros, but very little else of archaeological interest, have been recovered from the site.

The Town Walls are specially well preserved on the north-east side of the hill. They belong to the Punic defences built in the V century B.C., and have been partly refaced in Roman times. In fact you can see some stones which bear incised Punic characters, and the fact that these characters are sometimes upside down shows that the stones have been re-used. The walls, interspersed with many gateways and posterns, were strongly reinforced with square towers. The upper courses of the walls, and the gateways, are Norman.

The Museo Comunale is in the Palazzo del Municipio in Piazza Umberto I, and contains a small collection of prehistoric, Punic, Greek and Roman material including a IV century head of Aphrodite.

The opening hours are 10–12 and 2–4; holidays 10–1.

TRAPANI

Boats leave the harbour here for the Egadi Islands and for Pantelleria. For Favignana and Lévanzo see page 77.

There is nothing of archaeological interest in the town except the *Museo Nazionale Pepoli* which is on the Palermo road, in Via Conte Agostino Pepoli. Opening hours are: 9.30–4 from Tuesday to Saturday. Sundays and holidays, 9.30–1. Closed Mondays.

It houses a small collection of prehistoric, Greek and Punic objects from the Trapani district and western Sicily. These are in the *Antiquarium* on the first floor. Finds include some interesting bronze figurines (VII–III century B.C.) from Erice. The earliest of these is the figure of a warrior which closely resembles the well-known Sardinian statuettes of the same date.

LÉVANZO AND FAVIGNANA

At Lévanzo and Favignana, in the Egadi Islands off the coast of Trapani, there are important Palaeolithic caves containing painted or incised figures comparable to those at Addaura (p. 61). For permission to visit them it is best to make arrangements with the *Soprintendente alle Antichità* in Palermo, and if you go in May you may be able to watch the tunny fishing as well.

Access is by boat from the quay at Piazza Garibaldi in Trapani, and the latest timetable can be obtained from the shipping office close by. Of the two islands Lévanzo is by far the more interesting, and boats go at least three times a week. Lévanzo is the smallest island of the group and was once, like some of the others, joined to the mainland of Sicily. Only about 9 square kms. in area, it is a bare limestone rock, inhabited by a few fishing families. There is a small hotel.

The caves open from various levels in the cliff sides, and most of them are along the west coast. The most famous of them is the Grotta dei Genovesi (or dei Cervi) about half an hour's walk from the village. About 30 metres above sea level, it consists of an outer room (open to the daylight and containing a rich archaeological deposit) and an inner, dark recess, difficult of access, and apparently without an occupation level, though it, too, contained incised and painted figures. Trial cuttings made in the outer part of the cave revealed two levels: the upper contained remains of domestic animals and pottery including spool handles of the Late Neolithic 'Diana' style; the lower produced bones of Upper Palaeolithic fauna and flint knives (some of Gravettian type with retouching). Although microliths are commonly found in Sicilian sites of this period, none were found here, but their absence may be due to the limited extent of the excavations.

The incised drawings (see Fig. 9) showed various Quaternary animals including *Cervus elephas*, *Bos primigenius* and *Equus hydruntinus*, as well as some human figures wearing bird-head masks like the Addaura ones, but less skilfully drawn.

A second group with painted, not incised figures, may be rather later. They are painted in black or red, and the figures include some of men with their legs apart, and some violin-shaped female figures, treated rather like the pottery figurines of the Mediterranean Neolithic. Mammals and fishes have also been drawn. The date of these is still under discussion, and it has been suggested that they may even be as late as the Neolithic pottery found in the cave; this theory can be proved or

FIG. 9. Lévanzo. Engraved figures of a bull following a cow

disproved only by finding comparable figures in a context known to belong to that date. It is interesting to note that three of the incised human
figures, of which one seems to be dancing, fall stylistically between the
two groups, and one of the painted figures is stylistically comparable
to the incised ones.

Trial excavations have also been made in other caves. In the Grotta
dei Porci, Upper Palaeolithic and a very little Neolithic material was
discovered, and about seven other caves and rock-shelters have yielded
archaeological material which sometimes hints at a long occupation.

Favignana. The whole island is dominated by the Montagna Grossa,
where a number of caves exist at various levels, both near the sea and
inland. More than 20 have been partially explored, but few have so far
proved particularly interesting.

MOTYA (Italian Mozia) (Fig. 10)

Permission to visit the site of Motya on the island of San Pantaleo,
between Trapani and Marsala, must be obtained from the agent of the
Whitaker family to whom it belongs. Apply to Colonnello Lipari, Via
Garaffa 74, Marsala, who will arrange for a boat. This is a very pleasant
and interesting excursion lasting not less than half a day.

The nearest accommodation is in Marsala. The Stella d'Italia hotel is
in the town, and there is a Motel Agip on the road out to Mazara, as well
as a camping site in Via Boeo.

Motya was one of the three main Phoenician sites in Sicily (the others being Panormus and Solus), and it is particularly promising for further excavation because its site on a small island, now all fields and vineyards, has never been built over since the town was destroyed by Dionysius of Syracuse in 397 B.C.; it may therefore produce a fuller picture of a Phoenician town than would easily be found elsewhere.

It is now thought that the Phoenicians did not start acquiring trading sites on a large scale in western Sicily until they had seen the Greeks founding their colonies in the east. They favoured small off-shore islands or promontories with good anchorages, and the island of Motya surrounded by its shallow lagoon provided just the requirements they sought.

The first settlers seem to have established a trading post there at the end of the VIII century B.C., and the fact that their pots are sometimes like those from Al Mina and other places on the North Syrian coast, rather than like those of Carthage, has led to the supposition that Motya was a dependency of Tyre. Later, in the VI century, when the Carthaginian Empire was rising, the contacts with Carthage became more frequent, and in fact Motya was often used as a landing place for armies or supplies during the Carthaginian wars in Sicily.

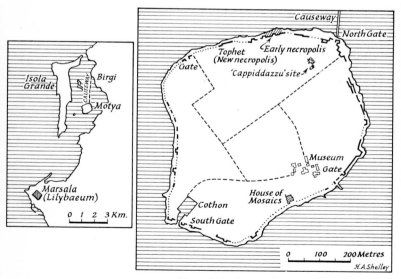

FIG. 10. Plan of Motya (based on Whitaker)

For some time the island remained undefended, and the early cemetery on its northern shore apparently lay outside the inhabited area; in fact it was cut across by the subsequent fortifications. Some of the stelae or tombstones were still found in place marking the burials which were mostly by cremation, and the finds, covering the period between the late VIII and late VII centuries, included amulets, scarabs with pseudo-hieroglyphs, and Phoenician pottery which can be dated from imported Greek pottery of Proto-Corinthian and Corinthian types found with it.

During this period the commercial relations with the native peoples must have been pacific, and Greek traders were also apparently welcomed. In fact, although the people were Phoenician by descent, the Greeks always seem to have played an important role in their lives, and right through the history of Motya Greek influences made themselves felt, in building techniques, coinage, etc., all the more strongly, of course, when relations with the nearer Greek colonies such as Selinus (Selinunte) were amicable. The population must have included some Greeks, for according to Diodorus Siculus, there were temples dedicated to Greek cults in Motya, and after the last violent struggle in 397, Greek citizens, or perhaps mercenaries who fought against Dionysius, were paid for their 'treachery' by being rounded up and crucified.

By the early VI century the Carthaginian Empire was growing, and rivalry with the Greek colonies became inevitable, for both powers wanted to grab as much rich land as they could hope to defend. Strangely enough, the Phoenician cities, unlike the Greek ones, do not seem to have ever had their own armed forces, either on sea or land, but depended on receiving immediate assistance from Carthage.

At all events, it was at about this time that Motya was first enclosed with a defensive wall, and at about the same time the *cothon*, or artificial dock, is thought to have been made near the south gate. This was quite a small dock, only large enough to accommodate boats about 60 feet long, the size of Sicilian sea-going fishing boats today. The sides were lined with stone, and wide quays flanked the channel linking it with the lagoon, a channel which may have been barred by a swing gate. This is the only *cothon* in Sicily, but a bigger version was found at Carthage.

Alterations and rebuilding of the town walls evidently took place in the late VI century, and at about this time, or not long after, the island was linked to the mainland at Birgi, about one mile away, by a causeway made of rubble paved with stones. Owing to the sea level being higher today, this causeway is now under water, but it is still possible for high-wheeled carts to cross it. Birgi is not the nearest point on the mainland,

and at first sight it may seem that the line of the causeway is unnecessarily long: its course may have been chosen because the very shallow water at that point made it easier to construct, or because Birgi, by the late VI or at least V century B.C., was beginning to be used as another burial ground. Here the burials were mostly inhumations, though some traditional cremations still continued. The pottery found in the graves can be dated by Attic black- or red-figure ware and Phoenician glass vessels. This cemetery does not seem to have been used after the IV century B.C.

In the mid-VI century a small shrine was built on the foreshore near the north gate: this was one of the earliest Phoenician monumental buildings in the Western Mediterranean. Inside the same gate (at the 'Cappiddazzu' site) foundations of a large sacred building may have belonged to an early temple, rebuilt several times.

The V century saw the inception at Motya of the atrocious rite of sacrificing infants and small animals, a rite which is well attested in other Phoenician sites. A 'tophet' or sacrificial precinct was discovered not far west of the earlier burial ground, and here stelae, sometimes carved with the figure of a deity, were set up to mark the burials, not only of a few infants, but of birds, dogs, cats and rodents, and even of a monkey, whose small remains were buried in jars. Evidently this tophet was set up at a time when the practice of infant sacrifices was no longer favoured, their place being taken by small animals, and it is interesting to remember in this connection that when Gelon of Syracuse made a treaty with the Carthaginians, after defeating them at Himera in 480, he ordered the abolition of human sacrifice.

Late in the V century, perhaps after Hannibal had sacked the Greek city of Selinus in 409, Motya increased in importance as a port and market (particularly for textiles, dyed with purple from the local molluscs), and the city walls were again rebuilt – this time far more strongly, for they were interspersed with about 20 square towers, bastions with stone battlements, guard-houses, gates and wall stairways. The north gate, leading onto the causeway, was rebuilt with two gateways, one behind the other; each of them had two arches, the inner one with double, and the outer one with triple bars. They were flanked by strong polygonal bastions. These are the walls one can see today here and there around the edge of the island.

But Motya's days were numbered, and these new defences were outmoded only a short time after they were built, for in 397 B.C. Dionysius carried his war against the Carthaginians right into the western limits of Sicily and besieged Motya with a new weapon, the catapult or ballista, said to have been used for the first time. These catapults could throw 'sharp-pointed missiles' (many were found near the north gate) a great distance, and only a defence in depth, such as is found, for instance, at the Euryalus Fortress at Syracuse, could withstand their attack. As Diodorus wrote, 'Dionysius, having put to sword and fire the whole of the territory subject to the Carthaginians, led his entire force against Motya, hoping that if that could be taken, all the other places would fall immediately into his hands'. Marching along the south coast from Syracuse, with a large number of footsoldiers and 3,000 horse, he began to besiege Motya by bringing his ships into the harbour and setting men to rebuild the causeway which the defenders had done their best to destroy. The Carthaginian ships tried to destroy the Greek vessels anchored along the shore of the harbour, but they were foiled by Dionysius who ordered his men to drag his ships across the isthmus and launch them in the open sea. These ships were filled with archers and slingers, and the Carthaginians, greatly outnumbered, decided to withdraw, and sailed away to Libya leaving Motya to its fate.

The story has been well told by B. H. Warmington after Diodorus in his book *Carthage*. He writes: 'Motya must have looked like an Italian city of the Renaissance, for many of the buildings were towers some stories high. In order that the attackers should not be dominated from these, Dionysius built siege-towers six stories high, and while soldiers up above provided cover, teams below attacked the walls with battering rams. When a breach was made the defenders resisted with all the fire for which Phoenicians and other Semitic peoples were famous, making every tall house a fortress as the Greeks sought to move up the narrow alleys. Diodorus continues, 'After the Siciliots had breached the walls and seemed to be masters of the city, they were raked by missiles from men in higher positions in the houses; they accordingly brought up their wooden towers to the houses and equipped them with footbridges which they could push out onto the houses, and thus force a passage, towers and buildings being the same height. . . . Such a determination filled the defenders that the Siciliots were in a very difficult position. As they were fighting from the suspended footbridges they suffered heavily because of the lack of space and the desperate resistance of the Phoenicians who had given up hope of living. Some were killed in hand-to-hand fighting, others, pressed back by the defenders, fell to their death off the bridges.'

The miserable fate of the town and its surviving inhabitants need hardly be described: the usual story of loot, rape, murder and pillage, to which horrors was added the crucifixion of the Greek residents or mercenaries. When Dionysius withdrew from the smouldering ruins, he left the place almost deserted, and although the Phoenicians recaptured the island not long afterwards, they never rebuilt the town; instead they removed the surviving inhabitants to Lilybaeum nearby. (See below).

The Visible Remains (excavated by archaeologists both from Italy and from Britain) include stretches of the walls with their gates, stairways and tower foundations as well as the *cothon*. Near the south coast is the so-called *House of the Mosaics*, probably built in the Hellenistic-Roman period, with an atrium surrounded by a portico, like some of the houses at Solunto. The owner of this house was probably a Phoenician, for the design of the mosaics made with black and white river pebbles (a technique which preceded the use of tesserae) shows oriental inspiration. There are remains of the building, now in course of excavation, near the north gate.

The Museum contains finds from Motya, the Birgi cemetery, and from Lilybaeum. There are funerary stelae, sculptural and architectural fragments, as well as votive inscriptions and small objects of bronze, iron, glass, etc., pottery amphorae, cinerary urns, and other locally made or imported wares from Ionia, Rhodes, etc. There are also a few fragments of pottery of prehistoric type, belonging, one supposes, to the sporadic occupation of the island before the Phoenicians.

The Palermo Museum (Room 3, ground floor) contains a huge torso fished out of the sea near Motya. It is a VI century work with stylistic contributions from Egypt, Syria and Greece.

LILYBAEUM (Marsala)

It is strange that a place known to have been of such importance, first to the Carthaginians and then to the Romans, should still hold its secrets so closely – at least its archaeological secrets. This is largely due to lack of excavation.

As far as we know, Lilybaeum was a small town just beginning to develop on the Capo Boeo promontory, when Dionysius sacked Motya in 397. Diodorus' statement that Lilybaeum was founded only after the fall of Motya is hardly probable; almost surely some small nucleus

must already have existed. But the place must certainly have assumed
a new importance once it had received the remaining population transferred from Motya, and it evidently soon became a prosperous and
valuable Carthaginian naval base, fortified in about 350, and sufficiently
strong to hold out against Dionysius, when he returned to attack it
shortly before the end of his life.

Geographically, although it seems to have had two of its four sides
bounded by the sea, its landward boundary was quite unprotected by
nature, and it must have been fortified not only by walls but by a series
of deep ditches as well. So strong were its fortifications that it was the
one place in all Sicily which was able to hold out against Pyrrhus in 276
when he attempted to free the Western Greeks from all barbarians both
in Italy and Sicily, and to set up a great Greek power there. As Freeman
has written, 'If he had succeeded, the whole history of the world would
have been changed; Rome, if not altogether conquered, could not have
come to be the head even of Italy. As it was, Pyrrhus simply came like a
thunderbolt on Italy and Sicily and did nothing lasting.' One of the
reasons for his failure was his inability to take Lilybaeum, even after
two months of siege, and the good work he might have done came to
nothing. Certainly one is curious to know what the town's defences were
like: perhaps excavations will one day tell us.

Besieged by the Romans in 253 and again, for nine years, between 250–
241, it was never taken, though it surrendered as a result of peace conditions, and the Romans made it into a military port. It was used by
Scipio Africanus, and 150 years later by Caesar in his war against
Pompey, only a few years after Cicero had described it as a *splendidissima
civitas*. Yet today there is almost nothing left, only a few remains of
streets and houses with mosaics and some fragments of fortifications on
the extreme tip of Capo Boeo. The remains from its partly explored
cemetery are in the museum at Motya.

Its one-time glory was momentarily renewed when Garibaldi and his
Thousand disembarked here in 1860.

5 · Selinunte, Sciacca and Heraclea Minoa

SELINUNTE (Greek *Selinus*) (Fig. 11)

Selinunte can be reached by rail, bus or car. The road from Marsala (State road 115) passes through Mazara (once the emporium for Selinus) and then through Campobello, near which are the quarries known as the Rocche di Cusa where some of the great roughed-out column-drums for the Selinuntine temples are still lying. (See p. 99.) Leaving road 115 at Campobello a smaller road runs eastwards towards Menfi, rejoining the main road at a cross-roads from which another road leads south for 5 kms. to Marinella and Selinunte.

If the approach is made by an inland road from Trapani, you reach Selinunte from Castelvetrano where, in the Municipio, is the only large bronze statue known from Selinunte. It is a fine figure of a young man offering a libation, and it has been compared stylistically with the metopes from Temple E (see p. 92) belonging to about 460 B.C.

Accommodation. There are two small *pensioni* down by the sea at Marinella, not far from the ruins, or a Jolly Hotel and several others at Castelvetrano, 14 kms. away.

The site of Selinus is not a dramatic one; it was built on several low hills by the sea, poorly defended by nature, yet for the colossal size of its temples, the quiet remoteness of the moss-grown streets on the acropolis, and the massive strength of its walls, the impact of its ruins is more dramatic than those of almost anywhere in Sicily. The traveller Swinburne, visiting it in the 18th century, left us a graphic description of it. 'As I approached the sea, the face of the country altered to smooth green swells with tufts of lentiscus, but no trees. The river passes through a long line of hills which exhibit the most extraordinary assemblage of ruins in Europe, the remains of Selinus; they lie in several stupendous heaps with many columns still erect, and at a distance resemble a large town with a crowd of steeples; my servants thought they were such, and were quite rejoiced at the thoughts of the very grand city they were coming to.' Instead they found Selinus, much as it is today, except that modern excavations have uncovered many features which were grass-grown in Swinburne's time.

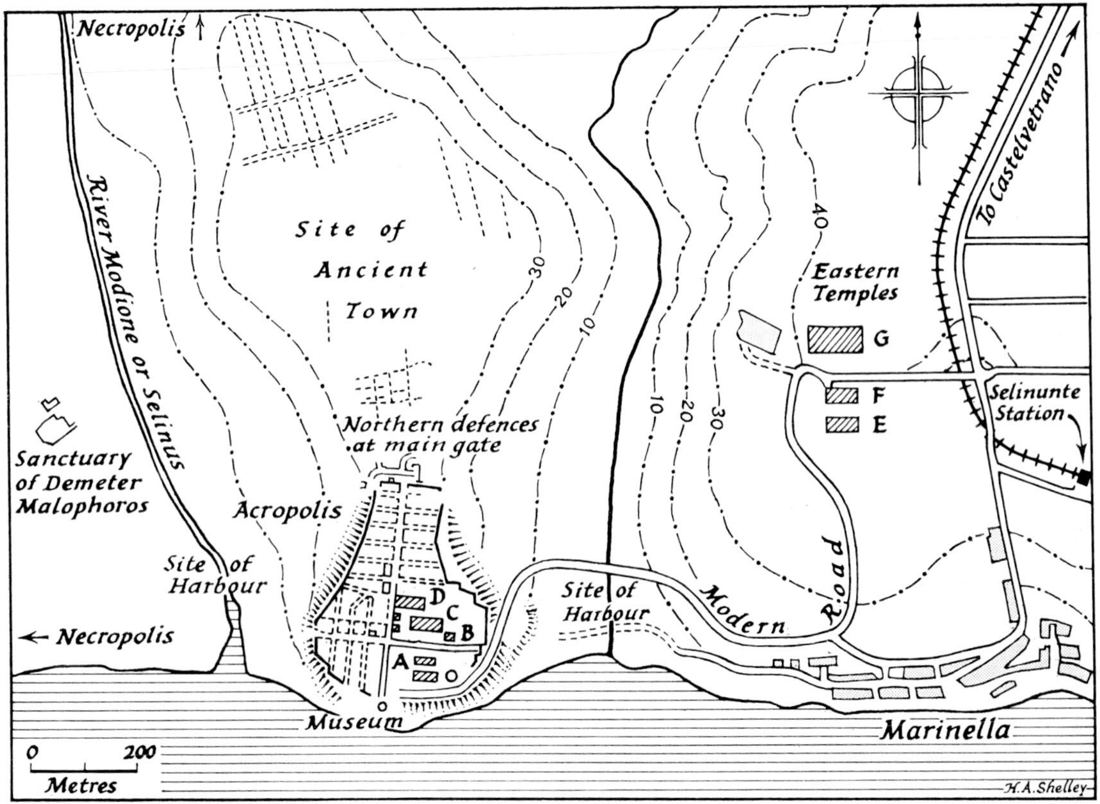

FIG. II. Selinunte

H.A.Shelley

The acropolis, strongly walled and containing many of the temples, stood on a low hill between two small rivers at the point where they flowed into the sea, and the mouths of both the Modione (the ancient Sélinos) on the west, and more especially the Cotone on the east, were useful small harbours in early times before the encroaching sands had largely filled them. To the north of the acropolis lies another hill, the site of the residential part of Selinus, also originally enclosed with a defensive wall. To the east, on rising land, stand three of the great temples, and to the west, across the Modione, are the remains of a very early sanctuary (at Gaggera) dedicated to Demeter Malophoros.

Before describing the visible remains, something must be related of the history of Selinus.

Some modern scholars no longer follow Thucydides' date of 628 B.C. for the foundation of the colony, though it seemed acceptable in the days when the earliest pottery from the site was Early Corinthian. Now, Late Proto-Corinthian ware has also been found, and they think it more probable that Eusebius and Diodorus Siculus were correct when they placed the foundation in 650 B.C.

Founded by colonists from Megara Hyblaea near Syracuse (see p. 199), Selinus was the most westerly of all the Greek cities, and in spite of its poorly defended position, its agricultural wealth quickly enabled it to become one of the most powerful and vigorous Greek colonies, with command over a vast area of land, stretching from the river Mazarus on the west to the river Platani (later to be chosen for the site of Heraclea Minoa) on the east. Its hinterland also extended far to the north, as we know from an archaic inscription in the Selinuntine dialect, found near Poggioreale. Part of these bounds marched with those of Segesta, and continual squabbles broke out between the two cities about boundary infringements.

Selinus (whose name was taken from the wild celery growing there), was placed so far to the west of Sicily that relationships, particularly for trade, had quickly to be established not only with the Sikels but with the Elymians as well, and above all with the Carthaginians with whom the Selinuntines had to live in peace for their very existence. Perhaps it was owing to these non-Greek contacts that the artistic development of Selinus was more vigorous and inventive than that of the more traditional cities of eastern Sicily, a characteristic which is immediately apparent to anyone who has looked at the temple metopes now in the museum at Palermo.

During the first years of the colony there were two main groups of religious buildings, the Sanctuary of Demeter Malophoros in the valley to the west, which may have belonged to an unrecognized native, but Hellenized, settlement in the interior, and a number of small sanctuaries, some of them made of wood and decorated with painted terra-cotta slabs, on the acropolis hill, and undoubtedly belonging to the early colonists. One of these little buildings was soon afterwards replaced by the so-called *Megaron*, in about the year 600. Fifty years later the town was growing increasingly prosperous, and one after another the great temples began to be built. At the same time the Selinuntines started minting their own coinage, choosing the celery leaf as their emblem. The earliest of the cemeteries, some of which yield VII century finds and contain pre-Greek tombs, are not far away at Manicalunga, Timpone Nero, Galera Bagliazzo and Contrada Buffo. They are now being excavated and are producing a great wealth of pottery.

At the end of the VI century the acropolis hill was artificially widened and strongly enclosed with a wall. Inside this area the streets were laid out on a grid plan at right angles to the main street which, starting on the south, ran right across the acropolis northwards to a gate in the defences, and thence continued towards the northern hill where a similar lay-out, differing slightly in its orientation, has been observed in air-photographs. The early *agora* has not yet been identified. (The fortifications between the two hills are much later in date.)

This is one of the most ancient grid plans known, and was followed when the existing Punic streets were made, overlying the earlier ones, in the IV or III century.

The harbour on the east was enlarged and lined with quays and warehouses and a road was built connecting the acropolis and town areas with the temples on the eastern hill. It is unlikely that Selinus ever had a fleet of any size, but it had wide commercial exchanges with other Greek colonies as well as with Chios, Rhodes, Paros (for marble), Etruria, and, from its main harbour at Mazara, with Africa. The Ionian contacts were always strong.

But Selinus, like all the Greek towns in Sicily, ran into political difficulties which led to its downfall. During the first Punic invasion the Selinuntines had trusted in the strength of the Carthaginians, and were fortunate to find themselves independent after their allies had been disastrously defeated at Himera in 480. After this, apart from the inevitable border quarrels with Segesta, they seem to have steered clear of major political pitfalls. But while they were busy erecting temples and beautifying their city, their growing power was causing anxiety to the

Carthaginians who, in 409 B.C., alarmed lest they might defeat Segesta and gain control of a strip of land right across Sicily, seized the opportunity, when Segesta begged them for help, to land a second invasion force, this time under Hannibal, son of Giskon, who immediately besieged Selinus. The Selinuntines seem to have been surprised and unprepared for such a violent threat, for Hannibal's force was indeed formidable. Attacking before help could arrive from other Greek cities, he brought up six siege-towers tall enough to overtop the walls, as well as a number of battering rams, and after only nine days of siege some Iberian mercenaries broke in, and looting, rape and massacre followed. The lovely city was sacked and the walls partially destroyed, and although some of the inhabitants who had fled to Akragas were subsequently allowed to return as tributaries of Carthage, the town never recovered.

At this juncture Hermocrates of Syracuse, who was trying to gain the esteem of the Syracusans by warring against the Carthaginians on his own account, led some of the refugees and others back to Selinus where, Diodorus says, 'he walled in a part of the city'. It is not clear today which walls these may have been. Excavations on the east side of the acropolis have revealed a counter-wall with towers strengthening the original defences, but these additional works are thought to be rather later than Hermocrates, and to date from the early IV century. So we must wait for information from further excavation.

But Hermocrates was killed in Syracuse, and Selinus continued to be under the dominion of the Carthaginians, a state of subjection which was confirmed on the various occasions when the Greek tyrants from Syracuse, Dionysius, Timoleon and Agathocles made treaties with Carthage in 405, 339 and 314 respectively.

In 276, when Pyrrhus captured Heraclea Minoa, Selinus voluntarily joined him in his attempt to liberate the Sicilian Greeks from their Punic enemies, and it is possible that some of the outworks at the north gate were constructed at this time. (See pp. 95–96.)

Again and again the Selinuntine territory was fought over during the First Punic War, and the final end of the town's history came in about 250 B.C. when the Carthaginians thinking it wise to concentrate their strength further west, removed the inhabitants to Lilybaeum (Marsala), and destroyed the city. It is improbable that it was ever rebuilt. The malarial conditions which had always existed, and which were fostered by the choked river mouths, may have discouraged further settlement. This had always been a problem. In fact there was a tradition that as early as the year 444 the Selinuntines had appealed to Empedocles, the scientist and philosopher from Akragas, to help them check a serious epidemic, and he had done so by draining the marshes and swamps near the rivers.

Whatever the cause of its abandonment, we learn from Strabo that by the end of the I century Selinus was no longer inhabited.

It has left us some of the most romantic ruins in Europe and perhaps the most artistic and inventive sculptures in the Greek west.

THE EASTERN TEMPLES (See Fig. 12)

Temple G was one of the greatest temples which ever existed, and it is a tragedy that an earthquake should have caused its complete ruin. Only by climbing and scrambling among the huge tumble of columns and capitals can one now identify its plan and main features. Begun in the second half of the VI century it took so long to build that fashions

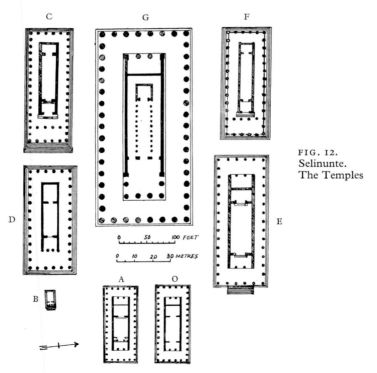

FIG. 12.
Selinunte.
The Temples

changed during its construction, and it was still not finished when Hannibal sacked the town in 409 B.C. Before this event, however, some attempt seems to have been made to use it in its unfinished state, for some of the columns show signs of coloured stucco, and an inscription (now in the museum at Palermo) refers to its dedication to Apollo.

This temple had 8 frontal and 17 side columns, some of which were never fluted, and a *cella* so wide that its roof had to be supported by two rows of columns down the centre: not the large columns of the more usual type, but two tiers of small superimposed ones. Three big doors led into the temple from an open porch (the area of which is too wide to have been roofed). By the time that the builders were constructing the west end, in the V century, they adapted the original plan to conform with changing fashions: instead of the *adytum* they built an *opisthodomos*, and they made the west end of the *cella* into a cult room. The columns along the west front were set more closely together at the corners in conformity with the new practice of angle contraction which had been unknown when the building was started.

This temple offers a fascinating and rare opportunity for students to observe the changing fashions as the work progressed. The first columns erected were those on the east end, and are more tapering than those on the west. Perhaps the architect was growing apprehensive about their adequate strength, and decided to make them more robust as the work continued. Otherwise it is difficult to understand why there was a reversal of the usual custom of making the later columns more tapering. The form of the capitals was also modified, the later ones (*c.* 470) having no hollow between the echinus and shaft.

The total effect is a curious one, for the temple is archaic in style on the east side, and classical on the west. It must have reached a height of 100 feet or more, and dominated the other temples and the whole area around.

In the *adytum* a fragment of the sculptured torso of a giant was discovered, and an inscription, originally on the anta and now in the Palermo Museum, was evidently set up in the middle of the V century. This reads in translation: 'The Selinuntines are victorious thanks to the gods Zeus, Phobos, Herakles, Apollo, Poseidon and the Tyndaridae, Athena, Malophoros, Pasikrateia, and the other gods, particularly to Zeus. After peace had been restored it was decreed that a work executed in gold inscribed with their names, with that of Zeus at the top, be placed in the temple of Apollo, there being 60 talents of gold for this purpose.' (This 'work' was in all probability a shield).

Column drums intended for this temple still lie in their roughed-out state at Cusa. (See p. 99).

Temple F was begun, it is thought, a few decades before Temple G, in the middle of the VI century. It is one of the most archaic of the Selinuntine temples and one of the most interesting, since it had one feature at least which distinguishes it from all other Greek temples. For the spaces between the outer columns were filled with screen walls standing to a height of about 10 feet. Each of these screens had a lintel and vertical pilasters giving the impression of a false doorway, though in the front of the temple they were pierced by real doors. The purpose of this wall may have been to prevent the profane from watching certain secret rites, but whatever its function, it was a wholly revolutionary concept which may conceivably have been inspired by Egyptian architecture, and it is quite likely that the later architect who designed the great temple of Zeus at Akragas (Agrigento) followed and developed this new conception, to which he brought an even more daring and original inventive power.

Temple F had 6 by 14 columns, the front six having a parallel row behind. These columns were widely spaced and crowned with low capitals and expanded echini. The narrow *cella* was unusually long.

The original terra-cotta revetments (a particularly important feature of Selinuntine craftsmanship) were replaced by stone ones early in the V century, when the splendid decorative metopes, showing scenes from a battle between gods and giants, were also added. These are now in the museum at Palermo. (See pp. 57–58.)

Temple E (Plate 6). This is the latest and most classical of those on the eastern hill: dedicated to Hera (or possibly Dionysos), it was begun in the early V century, at about the same time as the Temple of Athena at Syracuse and the temple at Himera, both of which were set up in celebration of the victory over the Carthaginians at Himera in 480.

This structure was designed on an immense scale, and the porches were decorated with fine sculptured metopes of Athena killing Enkelados, the marriage of Zeus and Hera, Actaeon attacked by Artemis' dogs, and Herakles killing an Amazon: all of these are now preserved in the Palermo Museum. (See pp. 57–58.)

In recent years this temple has been much restored, and many of the columns, which had fallen in an earthquake, have been set up again.

PLATE 6. Selinunte
(*above*) Metope
from Temple E
(now in the *Museo
Nazionale* at
Palermo) Actaeon
attacked by
Artemis' dogs
(*below*) Temple E
from the west

THE ACROPOLIS TEMPLES

In the first years of the colony a number of altars and small sanctuaries were set up on the acropolis hill, but about fifty years later these
began to be replaced by larger and more permanent temples, the earliest
of which seems to have been the so-called *Megaron*, just to the south of
Temple C and west of Temple B. This megaron was a very primitive
building without columns, and, together with the megaron in the
Sanctuary of Demeter Malophoros in the valley to the west, is the first
of the pre-Doric temples at Selinus. The entrance on the east led
straight into the *cella* which contained two axially placed bases for
wooden columns supporting the roof. The far end of the cella opened
into a square *adytum*. This building has been rehandled in later times,
and it is not clear which are its original and which its subsequent
features.

There were undoubtedly other temples on this hill which were
destroyed in antiquity, but their foundation platforms may exist. One
of these was a small temple (Temple Y), highly decorated, from which
came the important collection of metopes now in Palermo (see p. 57)
recovered from among the stones re-used in later fortifications.

Temple C (dedicated to Herakles), is the earliest surviving temple on
the acropolis, and it dates from the first half of the VI century. It was
set on the highest point of the plateau and may have replaced an earlier
sacred building. In plan it was very elongated, with 17 side columns,
and a double, 6-column frontal colonnade. Some of these columns were
of the early, monolithic type, while others were built up of drums; the
number of flutes also varied. All these features signify that the building
was continued over many years. The frontal metopes (see p. 58) are in
high relief and have been re-assembled from a great many fragments.
One shows Artemis and Leto on each side of Apollo in a *quadriga*,
another Herakles and the Cercopes, and the third Athena helping
Perseus to kill the Gorgon. These were among the latest elements,
added when the temple was almost completed.

The upper structure was made of wood and decorated with terra-
cottas, and a huge moulded terra-cotta mask of a gorgon decorated the
centre of each pediment. Lion-head water-spouts were also used here,
and are among the earliest known.

Possibly this temple was used for storing the deeds of the Archives,
for nearly a century ago several hundred seals, probably originally

affixed to papyrus documents or tablets, were discovered. These seals portrayed Herakles either taming the bull or with a dolphin and club.

Temple D was stylistically rather more developed and is thought to have been begun in about 535 B.C. It had 6 by 13 columns and the revetments were of stone rather than terra-cotta. The columns were no longer straight-sided but slightly convex, and were given a varying number of flutes.

Temple A is a relatively late one, dating from the first half of the V century. It had 6 by 14 columns, with double contraction on the front and single on the sides, and it contained one interesting feature: inside the wall dividing the *pronaos* from the cella, two round stairways led up to the roof-space. Such stairs are also known in temples at Agrigento and Himera, but they are square, not round. *Temple O* appears to have been very similar.

Temple B is a very small Hellenistic building consisting of a single room with a four-columned porch in front. It is thought to have been built not long before Selinus was finally abandoned in 250 B.C.

THE ACROPOLIS DEFENCES

It has already been mentioned that the original layout of the streets on the acropolis and the earliest defensive walls, both there and on the northern hill, went back to the late VI or early V centuries B.C.; but much that is visible today is the result of subsequent rebuilding, either to strengthen the defences according to the developing requirements of warfare, or to patch up, sometimes very hastily, what had been destroyed.

Perhaps the finest stretch which may belong to the original walls is the high, stepped wall on the east side of the acropolis. Rising to a height of about 35 feet, it is stepped back from the outer façade, and must once have been topped by a vertical wall.

Further north on the same side the acropolis has been strengthened with a counterwall and towers, thought to date from the early IV century.

The North Gate Defences, a complex system of ditches, bastions, posterns and secret gateways, deserves more intensive study than it has so far been given, for as an example of military architecture it is of the first importance.

Remains can be seen of a long covered gallery running parallel to the north wall of the acropolis. This was associated with three semi-circular towers, one on the west, one defending the north-east angle of the acropolis, and the third, containing an artillery storeroom beneath, built to the north of the gallery. These defences also included a deep ditch with passages into both walls, which served to isolate the acropolis from the land behind.

These secondary defences were once thought to have been built by Dionysius and Hermocrates, but more recently it has been realized that they are later, and belong in fact to the first half of the III century B.C. probably soon after Agathocles (who may have been responsible for the somewhat comparable tower complex at the Euryalus Fortress at Syracuse), or even to the time of Pyrrhus, when the most up-to-date ideas on fortification current in the Eastern Mediterranean were beginning to reach Sicily.

The Sanctuary of Demeter Malophoros (Fig. 13)

On the far side of the river Modione (about 20 minutes' walk westwards by a footpath from the acropolis) are the remains of one of the most interesting sanctuaries in the Greek world, dedicated by the early colonists to the goddess of fertility (Malophoros means 'apple-bearer', i.e., fruitful), a most appropriate divinity, for people who were primarily farmers, to propitiate.

At first, no doubt, these people worshipped and made their offerings to the goddess round open-air altars, but soon these were replaced by a more permanent sacred site, consisting of a *megaron* temple surrounded by a high-walled *temenos*. Some scholars think that this *temenos* was used as a *hekataion*, or stopping place for the funeral processions making their way westwards to the cemetery of Manicalunga.

The remains visible today comprise many elements of this early structure, but during the many centuries following its initial dedication building activity was continued, to such an extent that it has not always been possible to disentangle the original buildings from secondary modifications.

The easiest way to understand the complex is to find the *propylaeum* (5), a covered entrance with a colonnade at either end and steps outside, which in fact was added to the *temenos* in the late V century. To the right (6) stood a long portico built against the *temenos* wall, with seats for the public, while outside were altars where sacrifices could be offered.

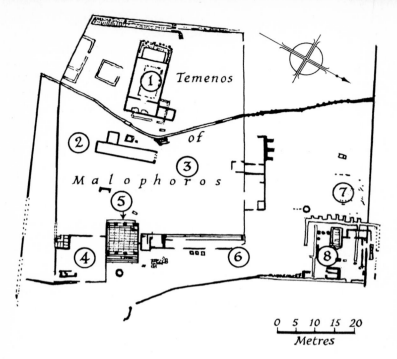

1. *Megaron in original temenos preceded by atrium.*
2. *Large altar.*
3. *Main temenos*
4. *Sacred enclosure of Hecate Triformis.*
5. *Propylaeum*
6. *Portico.*
7. *Stelae*
8. *Temenos and Temple of Zeus Meilichios.*

FIG. 13. Selinunte. The Sanctuary of Malophoros and secondary deities (after Gabrici)

Entering the *temenos*, you first see a small altar and then a very large one (2) facing east: this was the main sacrificial altar and in fact quantities of ash and burnt animal bones were found inside. Between this and the main temple (1) are a well and a stone canal for leading water from a spring to the *temenos*.

The *megaron* itself is thought to have replaced an earlier one in about 580, not many decades after the first one had been built. It was divided into a short ante-room, a long *cella*, and a short *adytum* which was opened in the Hellenistic period, when other slight modifications were made. The cornice of this *megaron* is one of the earliest known in Doric architecture.

Behind the *megaron* the south wall of the *temenos* has been reinforced from time to time in an attempt to keep back the invading sands.

Two other sacred precincts outside the *temenos* of Malophoros are dedicated to the secondary divinities Hekate Triformis (Triple Hekate) and Zeus Meilichios, both of whom were worshipped in the colonists' original homeland at Megara Nisaea and perhaps at Megara Hyblaea as well.

The precinct dedicated to Hekate Triformis (4) was reached from the *propylaeum*, and contains two small buildings and an altar. The other divinity, Zeus Meilichios, was worshipped in another precinct to the north of the main complex (8). When this was excavated many years ago it was found to be so cluttered with secondary elements, and so altered by rebuilding and additions, that it was not easy to interpret. However, it is now thought that what remains today is largely Hellenistic in date, though following the earlier layout.

The precinct was enclosed by a portico on two sides, with columns of different types, probably belonging to different phases of the building. Inside was a very small structure with an Ionic architrave supported on Doric columns. On the outside, to the west, the worshippers had set up a number of stelae (7). These are most unusual in being carved with pairs of human heads set side by side: a conception which may be native, though the stelae bear Greek inscriptions. Some of these are in the Palermo Museum (see Fig. 14).

FIG. 14.
Two-headed stone
stela from the
Sanctuary of
Malophoros

An enormous number of finds were recovered from the Malophoros *temenos:* no fewer than 12,000 terra-cotta votive figurines of goddesses or female donors, many made from the same mould, and ranging in date from the VII to the V century. A great deal of Early Corinthian pottery and some Late Proto-Corinthian were also recovered. From near the entrance came an archaic bas-relief of Pluto abducting Persephone (or perhaps a silenus and a maenad, for this was a common subject in the VI and V centuries). There were also some small sculptured *arulae* (altars) including an impressive early V century one with the figures of Eos and Kephalos, now in Palermo.

Another VI century *megaron* has recently been found a few hundred yards to the north-east.

The Rocche di Cusa (the quarries for the temple columns) are reached from Campobello. Leaving the town on road 115 for Mazara, you turn left after about 400 yards and follow the Principe-Torre Cusa track (rough, unless it has been recently repaired) for about 4 kms. till you reach an iron gate leading into the quarries, which are thickly overgrown with trees. Here you can see some of the column drums which had been cut and left ready to be transported to the temples. The work of cutting and carrying these drums was interrupted by Hannibal's sudden threat to the town in 409 B.C. and some roughed-out blocks were abandoned in various stages of completion while others were dumped beside the road to Selinus. The quarrying of the drums was evidently begun by making a circular incision in the rock. Then the rock was cut back for several feet around the incision to allow working space so that the groove could be deepened, and this process was continued until the drum could be extracted; after that it was presumably encased in a wooden frame and transported in ox-carts with solid wooden wheels.

SCIACCA

Leaving Selinunte for Heraclea Minoa and Agrigento you rejoin the main road (115) and continue eastwards for 37 kms. to *Sciacca*. This is a pleasant walled town on the sea with plenty of character; it would make an excellent centre for visiting both Heraclea and Selinunte, and is well provided with hotels (Grand Hotel Delle Terme is luxury class, while less expensive are the Garden, Eden, and others, including a Motel Agip, and a camping site at Sirene on the sea just to the west of the town).

Sciacca was one of the forts established by the Selinuntines, and was renowned for the therapeutic qualities of its hot sulphur and salt springs for which the town is still much frequented. These hot springs are the earliest known to have been used by the Greeks, and in Roman times, in fact, they were known as *Thermae Selinuntinae.*

Dominating the town is Monte San Calogero (*Mons Kronios*) where, below the Sanctuary of San Calogero, 3 to 4 miles outside Sciacca, are some natural caves filled with hot vapours which, according to legend, were arranged for human use by Daedalus himself. (These are now known as the *Stufe vaporose di San Calogero.*) A highly interesting discovery has been made here in recent years. Two deep underground galleries were explored by a team of speleologists and archaeologists who, equipped with breathing apparatus to overcome the fumes, managed with great difficulty to get down to a depth of nearly 200 feet, though this was still not the bottom. Down here they came upon a number of huge four-handled jars of Copper Age date (III millennium) and one group of three pots of particular interest, for one contained decomposed organic material (perhaps grain?) and was accompanied by a carefully selected collection of little bones, all exactly similar and thought to be the arm bones of very young children. Without a doubt these were sacrifices made by anxious prehistoric people in an attempt to placate the terrifying gods of the underworld. In those times these galleries must have been open, but now, having been closed from outside (perhaps the work attributed to Daedalus?), their vapours are more concentrated, and the finding of these pitiful offerings is all the more dramatic when one realizes the difficulties and dangers encountered by their discoverers.

Just how terrifying and capricious such underworld gods must have seemed in volcanic areas such as these, can be illustrated by a much more recent happening. In 1831 the crew of a British ship passing the coast of Sciacca was surprised to find an island which appeared to be uncharted, and hastily sent someone ashore to raise the Union Jack and claim it as a possession. The Sicilian authorities, understandably angry, protested strongly that since the island had come up off the coast of Sicily it could not be claimed by a foreign power. Six months later, fortunately before relations had become too seriously strained, the island tactfully saw fit to sink quietly under the sea again, not however before an engraving had been made to record its short presence.

Another equally strange volcanic site, this time connected with the Palici (the gods of the native Sikels), can be seen near Mineo, not far from Caltagirone. Here in antiquity two jets of carbonic acid gas (now only one) broke from the surface of a small lake and released such powerful fumes that small birds were asphyxiated as they flew over the water. This place was regarded with awe and reverence by the Sikels who made it the focal point of their national sanctuary. The Palici were looked upon as the special protectors of the Sikel peoples and of oppressed slaves, and their name was given to the town of *Palica* founded nearby in 453 B.C. by the nationalist leader Ducetius.

HERACLEA MINOA (Fig. 15)

Heraclea Minoa stood on the bank of the river Halykos, the present Platani, at the point where it runs into the sea at Capo Bianco, about 40 kms. west of Agrigento. It can only be reached by car, unless you walk 6 kms. from the cross-roads where the State road (115) from Ribera to Agrigento is joined by the road to Cattolica Eraclea immediately after crossing the river Platani. Alternatively you could take a train to Montallegro and walk 11 kms. from there.

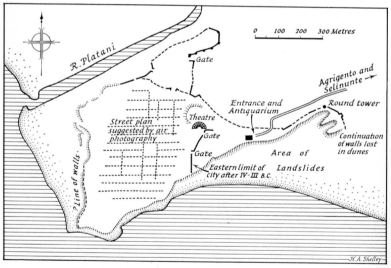

FIG. 15. Heraclea Minoa

Once you leave the main road the countryside is strangely deserted; composed mostly of marls and clays, it has suffered from such massive landslides that the original topography of the ancient town area would hardly be recognizable to one of its original colonists. It was probably owing to these landslides and coastal erosion that after the town was abandoned in the I century BC. it never grew up again, and for this reason it offers a particularly rich field for excavation. Less than a century ago the site was described as 'wholly deserted and scarcely any ruins remain to mark the spot'. It is very different now. Excavations and air-photographs are gradually recovering the urban lay-out and many of its buildings; its theatre and much of the town walls are now uncovered, and a resident custodian has been installed to take charge of the small but interesting Antiquarium on the site.

According to Herodotus, the town was founded as a Selinuntine colony in the VI century B.C., in all probability in an attempt to check the ever-growing power of Akragas, not very much further to the east. The settlement was at first simply called *Minoa*, a name which Diodorus claims was given to it to commemorate Minos, the legendary Cretan king, who was said to have pursued Daedalus from Crete to Sicily many centuries earlier. He landed at the mouth of the river Halykos, and there founded his city. Another legend would have it that Minoa was founded after Minos' death, by his followers. In either case the name may have existed long before the Selinuntines founded their colony, and they probably adopted the ancient name for it.

These hints of contact with the Aegean world in Mycenaean times are strengthened by a particularly interesting find recorded by Diodorus. According to him, when Theron (the victor of the great battle at Himera in 480 B.C.) was tyrant of Akragas, he found the tomb containing the bones of Minos at Minoa. This tomb was described as a double building, an underground burial chamber with a temple of Aphrodite above. This is far from being a common type of tomb, but in recent years a very similar building has been excavated at Knossos in Crete, and as Dunbabin has written, 'The discovery of the Temple tomb at Knossos provides the most convincing proof that the tradition of a Minoan colony in Sicily is genuine.'

Daedalus was welcomed at the court of the local king Kokalos, and he built for him a new fortified stronghold at Kamikos, a site which has convincingly, though still only tentatively, been identified with the modern Sant'Angelo Muxaro (p. 129) where large and unusual tholos tombs have produced finds of Eastern Mediterranean inspiration. These tombs are much later than Mycenean times, but both their form and their contents may reflect a lingering Cretan tradition. For various reasons, therefore, we cannot rule out the fascinating possibility of direct contacts between Sicily and Crete in the II millennium B.C. Further excavations may be able to prove them.

The additional name Heraclea (after Herakles) was appended at a later date, but precisely when is not known; possibly it was given by the Spartan colonists under Euryleon at the end of the VI century for Herakles was the mythical progenitor of their stock, and they may well have wished to commemorate him.

But the name is not clearly attested until 314 B.C., so it seems more reasonable to think that it was added not long before that date when, according to coin evidence, some of the people from the ancient Cephaloedium (Cefalù), who worshipped Herakles, settled at Minoa after the treaty made with Carthage by Timoleon in 339 B.C.

Throughout its life the town was almost continuously a bone of contention either between Selinus and Akragas, or between Greeks and Carthaginians, for it stood on the approximate border of their territories. Its early phases are still but little known, as the excavations which have now been in progress for some years have not yet uncovered the levels of that date, though sporadic early finds have come to light.

After the site had been seized by Euryleon in about 508 B.C. it passed into the possession of Akragas who still evidently held it in Theron's time. But after 409, when many Greek parts of Sicily were greatly devastated during the second big Punic invasion, Heraclea was destroyed and depopulated, and not long afterwards, when Dionysius concluded a peace treaty with the Carthaginians, Heraclea was allotted to their zone of influence which, as again in Timoleon's time, was delimited by the river.

Diodorus refers to it in 357 as a small town subject to Carthage (its Punic name was Ras Melkart), but in 345, after a period of internal strife, the democracy was restored by Timoleon who subsequently, after the battle of the river Krimisos and the treaty with Carthage, agreed that Heraclea should remain in Carthaginian territory, provided the inhabitants could transfer to Greek areas of Sicily if they so wished.

The prosperous conditions which Timoleon had initiated lasted on until the end of the century, when Agathocles, tyrant of Syracuse, renowned for his cruelty, seized the city (which had since become independent with a mixed Punic and Greek population) and brought it once again into subjection.

It was during the latter half of the IV century that Heraclea, like so many Greek towns in Sicily, reached its maximum importance, with new town walls interspersed with towers and gateways, and a theatre, and it was at this time, too, that the eastern limits of the original town were brought further west, and the houses which had been in that part of the town were abandoned, apparently as a result of the extensive damage brought about by landslides and erosion.

Heraclea was again disputed at the time of the first war between Carthage and Rome, and in 262 B.C. Hanno the Carthaginian made it his base after landing from Africa with, according to Philinus, 50,000 foot-soldiers, 6,000 horses and 60 elephants. His immediate aim was to relieve Akragas, then being besieged by the Romans. Thereafter Heraclea changed hands several times until 210 when it finally fell to the Romans.

Even under Roman rule the unfortunate town was not destined to be peaceful, and much of its remaining history was restless and violent, owing to the two Slave wars. By 136 B.C. conditions for the slaves, who mostly worked on the great corn-growing estates, were intolerable: they rebelled, and Heraclea suffered so extensively that it became semi-deserted and had to be re-peopled. This was done under the direction of Publius Rupilius, known subsequently for the laws he introduced for governing the province. The town seems to have been greatly rebuilt, and the lay-out of the road system, shown by air-photographs, belongs to this time. New reinforcing walls were also added to the town's defences.

But thirty years later the slaves again rebelled, and the town was damaged once more. However, it seems to have been flourishing not very long afterwards, for Cicero, who went there to collect evidence against the iniquitous praetor Verres, mentioned it as one of the *civitates decumanae* and made no hint that the town was in decline. Yet only seventy years or so later, at the end of the I century B.C., it no longer existed. There is no reference to it either in Strabo or in the Antonine Itinerary, and the absence of any Arretine ware from the excavations bears out the fact that the place was no longer being lived in.

The Town Walls belong to four main phases, the earliest of which has not yet been dated, though it was probably a considerable time before the second and most important phase of fortification which belongs to about the years 320–313 B.C. when a strong wall, interspersed with towers, gateways and posterns, was built around the town. The old wall was reinforced, new stretches were added, and the eastern limit of the town, undefended by natural features and particularly vulnerable, was strengthened by an impressive length of walling and a tower. This wall was made in the so-called 'dual technique', with its lower courses made of masonry, and the upper of sun-dried bricks. Some of these bricks contained sherds of prehistoric pottery from an unidentified site nearby, perhaps completely lost in the landslides. Walls of enormous strength, and built in the same manner, can be seen at Capo Soprano, Gela. (See page 148.) The southward continuation of this wall has been destroyed by erosion.

A little later (phase 3) the tower was reinforced, and a strong round tower was added when this eastern outpost seems to have been designed as a separate unity. At about this time the town was contracted, and a new eastern delimiting wall was built, running south from the area of the theatre which must only recently have been finished. This wall (which cuts through the late IV century occupation belonging to the time when the town still stretched further east) was evidently strengthened in the First Slave War (phase 4), and then partly dismantled and built over after the Second Slave War. It had two gates, one near the theatre and another a little further south, and a postern which was later blocked up. These gates correspond with the streets shown on air-photographs and shown by excavation to belong to the period of re-population after the first of the Slave Wars. Some of the houses were built with masonry and sun-baked bricks, and overlay others of the III–II century B.C. It is possible to see some of these superimposed buildings which have been preserved by the excavators.

During the time of the Slave Wars parts of the walls to the north of the theatre were also hurriedly altered with re-used material.

The Theatre dates from the very end of the IV century B.C. (about 320–300). It is partly cut into very friable rock which weathers so badly that the seats have had to be protected with a plastic covering.

Rehandled and enlarged soon after its construction, it seems to have continued in use at least as late as the rebuilding of the town by Rupilius after the First Slave War, for, as we have already noted, it was integrated in the urban lay-out revealed in air-photographs, but not long after that, perhaps owing to the damage inflicted in the Second Slave War, it fell into disuse, and buildings of Cicero's time overlay it in places.

For its plan the same geometric principle was adopted as in the late IV century theatre at Athens, and in fact the Athenian theatre, with its semicircular *cavea* and prolonged sides, was the model not only for this theatre but also for those at Segesta and Tyndaris, as well as others outside Sicily. The Heraclean theatre also contains structural features comparable to other late IV century theatres such as Epidauros.

The *cavea*, which is divided into nine sectors, had seats provided with backs and armrests, and the priests of Dionysus and high government officials normally must have sat in the front row.

In the orchestra two superimposed foundations for stage buildings were discovered, the upper one still retaining the holes for the posts which once supported the stage podium; recently parts of the scene building have also been recovered.

On the hill above the theatre traces of a Hellenistic sanctuary have recently been found, and in the last few years an archaic and a Hellenistic cemetery have been recognized; the archaic one is expected to be excavated shortly.

A new *Antiquarium* has recently been built on the site. It houses interesting finds from Heraclea.

FIG. 16.
Coin of Akragas
with eagles devour-
ing a hare

6 · Agrigento and Sant'Angelo Muxaro

AGRIGENTO (Greek *Akragas* and Roman *Agrigentum*) (Fig. 17)

There are plenty of hotels of all categories in the town. The quieter ones are outside. The small Hotel Vittoria at San Leone on the coast can be recommended, as well as the Hotel del Viale off Viale della Vittoria.

'One hundred and eight years (to the best of one's reckoning) after the foundation of their own city, the people of Gela founded Akragas, giving the city its name from the river Akragas and making Antonous and Pystilus the founders; the constitution was the same as that of Gela.'

This very precise information is given us by Thucydides, and since Gela is known to have been founded in 689, there is no reason to doubt that Akragas was founded in 581. This was the official date when the independent colony was set up; but for a long time before that Geloan merchants had been trading with the native peoples, and had evidently established trading rights along much of the south coast, for it is otherwise difficult to explain why the citizens of Megara Hyblaea had to go so far west as Selinus to find a site for their new colony in 650. At least since the mid-VII century these Geloan traders must have been frequenting the site, carrying on their commercial activities (for which they probably used the small harbour at San Leone) and prospecting for the possibilities of establishing a colony there.

The two leaders brought colonists from Gela itself and from Rhodes, Crete and other islands nearby. The Rhodian element was the most evident, for not only did it introduce new religious cults, but it also left a deep imprint on the artistic achievement of Akragas: in fact Polybius even went so far as to refer to Akragas as a Rhodian colony.

From almost the first years the town seems to have been carefully planned. The acropolis occupying at least the eastern end (Rupe Atenea) and probably the whole of the long rocky hill where the present town stands was the first part to be defended by a wall. On the highest point, according to Polybius, the Akragantines built a *temenos* enclosing temples (or perhaps altars only at first) dedicated to two Rhodian

deities, Zeus Atabyrios and Athena Lindia. These temples have tenta-
tively been identified with those underlying the Cathedral church of
San Gerlando and the church of Santa Maria dei Greci respectively.
Little is known of the former; the latter seems to be the temple built by
Theron in 488.

South of the acropolis hill the land slopes gently down towards the
sea, and about half way to the coast a long rocky scarp, delimited on its
west end by the river Hypsas and on the east by the river Akragas, (the
scarp along which the great temples were later to be built) was chosen
as the southern limit of the town. Strong walls, punctuated with square
towers and many gateways, linked the two ends of the scarp with the
acropolis ridge, and these walls, even if rebuilt here and there at subsequent dates, are substantially those one can see today. Probably they
were largely built by Phalaris, the first of the known tyrants of Akragas,
who ruled the new colony from 571 to 556. Although in his time the main
settlement was undoubtedly on the acropolis, it is possible that the street
layout had already been designed, and roads made to link the acropolis
with the coast at San Leone (passing through Gate IV) and with the
several sacred sites which are known to have existed in the early years of
the colony. An early Sanctuary to the Chthonic deities (the powers that
live under the earth) has been excavated just inside the walls on the south
(see Fig. 17) and found to contain shrines and round and rectangular
altars with *bothroi* for the libations. This, sometimes called the sanctuary
of Demeter and Persephone (or Kore) from the two fertility goddesses
often associated in Sicily with the Chthonic deities, certainly went back
to the first years of the colony or possibly even before. Another sanctuary,
whose dedication is unknown, stood to the west, and yet another, below
the east end of Rupe Atenea. Here two artificially enlarged natural caves
contained VI–V century terra-cotta ex-voto offerings to Demeter and
Persephone. The Chthonic deities had been worshipped in Sicily for a
very long period of time (presumably these gods were thought to cause
such phenomena as the sulphurous fumes at San Calogero at Sciacca,
or the volcanic eruptions of Etna and Stromboli, and even earthquakes
and deluges), and as time went on and the Greek prospectors and
colonists arrived, these deities became associated with the two goddesses
of fertility, Demeter (Mother Earth, the giver of crops) and Persephone,
queen of the underworld, and even after the worship of Zeus and the
Olympians had been introduced, the old and new religions continued
side by side, and as late as the plays of Aeschylus, and even later, it is
clear that they were inextricably mixed.

Apart from his contribution towards the building of Akragas, Phalaris seems to have extended his city's territory by warring against the Carthaginians and possibly against the native Sikans in the interior. His cruelty reached legendary proportions and he is said, by Pindar, to have set up on the acropolis a great brazen bull in which he roasted his enemies alive. The custom of putting statues of bronze bulls on high places is a Rhodian one, for some are known to have stood on Mount Atabyris in Rhodes. There are various stories about what happened to Phalaris' bull; some say it was carried off by the Carthaginians, and others that it was sunk in the sea.

After the death of Phalaris the work of building streets and temples continued. Some of the temples were small archaic buildings whose remains have been found along the southern scarp, but at least two of the very big temples were begun at the very end of the VI century, the temples dedicated to Herakles and Olympian Zeus, the latter at least being one of the most revolutionary architectural designs ever conceived.

The next tyrant about whom much is known from written records is Theron whose tyranny lasted approximately from 489 to 472, and who initiated a long period of prosperity for Akragas. In character he was quite the opposite of Phalaris, and Pindar, who was certainly rather naive in his appreciation of tyrants, but who did, at least, have personal experience of Theron's qualities, described him as the 'bulwark of Akragas, hospitable and bountiful, whose good deeds to others outnumbered the sands on the sea-shore'. By giving his daughter in marriage to Gelon of Syracuse, Theron made a valuable political link which stood him in good stead when the two tyrants combined to inflict an overwhelming defeat on the Carthaginians at Himera in 480, nine years after his tyranny had begun.

After this victory at Himera, vast numbers of disbanded soldiers and captives were set to work either to build new temples (the temples of Athena Lindia and that of Demeter, under the church of San Biagio, were begun at this time) or to continue with the building of those already started, particularly, no doubt, that of Zeus. Labour cost little or nothing (some citizens are said to have owned as many as 500 captives) and the opportunity was not lost, since a building campaign was initiated which provided not only for the temples and public buildings, but also for aqueducts and waterworks, including, it seems, a large artificial fishpond, with decorative swans and water-fowl, which was contrived in the south-west corner of the town, inside the walls.

FIG. 17. Agrige

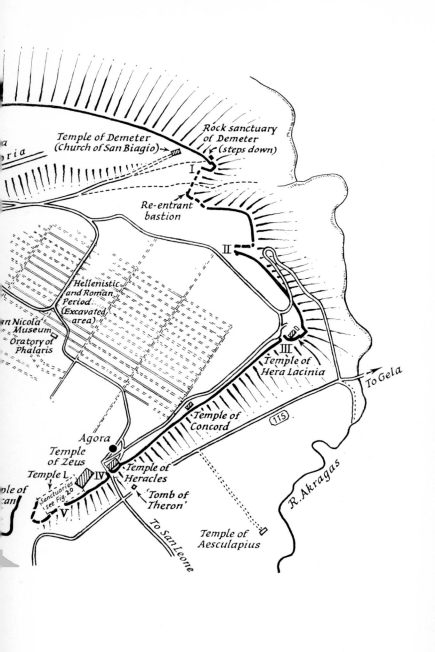

Temple of Demeter
(Church of San Biagio)

Rock sanctuary
of Demeter
(steps down)

I

Re-entrant
bastion

II

Hellenistic
and Roman
Period
(Excavated
area)

an Nicola
Museum
Oratory of
Phalaris

III

Temple of
Hera Lacinia

To Gela

Temple of
Concord

115

Agora

Temple
of Zeus

Temple L

IV

Temple of
Heracles

'Tomb of
Theron'

Sanctuaries
see Fig. 20

V

To San Leone

Temple of
Aesculapius

R. Akragas

After Himera the Akragantine territory, already large, was extended to reach the north coast, while to the east and west it stretched from near the present town of Licata to the river Platani. Shortly after this Theron won another victory, over the Motyans. The city became fantastically rich and splendid, and Pindar, who lived for some years in Akragas, acclaimed it as 'the most beautiful of mortal cities that lives upon the hill of fine dwellings above the banks where sheep graze beside the river'. From the temple ridge at dusk, before the lights in the modern town are lit, it is not difficult to imagine Akragas as it once was.

All through the V century the arts flourished, and a local school of sculpture was developing, less strongly Rhodian by now, and more Attic in style. This was the period of the great works of art such as the lovely head of Athena, originally wearing a bronze helmet, found near the Temple of Zeus. Architects, coin designers and poets were given full rein for their creative powers, and both Pindar and Simonides lived in the city. The new temples built during this century included those to Hephaestus, Hera Lacinia, Asclepius, the Dioscuri, and the temple of Concord. The whole atmosphere must have been imbued with confidence and hope, and perhaps this euphoria may have been partly responsible for the lack of modesty which inspired Simonides to write for his own tombstone, 'He left his glory to all Hellas.' Another exceptionally brilliant man living in the town at the time was Empedocles, philosopher, poet, democratic reformer and engineer. It was he who is said to have drained the malaria-infested harbours for the Selinuntines.

The Akragantines enjoyed their great wealth with almost nouveau-riche exuberance; it was said that people 'gave themselves to delights as if they would die tomorrow, while they built their houses as if they would live for ever'. They used gold and silver lavishly, and even slept, we are told, on ivory beds; and they built costly tombs for their pet animals and favourite horses. There are frequent references to fine horses and horsemen, and Akragantine competitors were successful in the chariot races at Olympia. One of these victorious charioteers was escorted into the town on his return by no less than 300 charioteers, their chariots drawn by white horses.

Individual citizens grew so rich that one of them, a distinguished man called Gellias, was able, on one occasion, to give lodgings and a change of clothes to 500 horsemen, caught in a violent storm on their way from Gela.

Much of this money must have come from rearing horses, particularly race-horses, and from the fertile farming land surrounding the town.

'No country produced finer or more extensive vineyards. Almost the whole territory was planted with olives of which the finest were exported and sold at Carthage, as Libya was not cultivated at that time. The Akragantines, receiving money in exchange for their native products, piled up immense riches' (Diodorus).

Relations with Syracuse, once so cordial, had deteriorated and at least on one occasion war broke out between the two and the Akragantines lost: after this they wisely avoided military engagements. The Syracusans were at the height of their power, and soon afterwards, in 415, gained their overwhelming victory over the Athenians, so eliminating the main supporter of some of the Greek cities in western Sicily. The Carthaginians seized the opportunity to intervene in one of the many border squabbles between Segesta and Selinus, for they appreciated the danger that would menace their territory if Segesta were defeated and Selinus dominated a strip of land right across Sicily. They landed a great invasion force and completely wiped out both Himera and Selinus. We hear from Diodorus that some of the Selinuntine refugees, 2,600 men, women and children, were received at Akragas 'with all possible kindness, for the Akragantines, after portioning out food to them at public expense, divided them for billeting in their homes'. Little could these poor people imagine that they were to enjoy only three years of peace.

Anxiety for their own safety now dominated the thoughts of the Akragantines who re-ordered their army and strengthened their defences. After a short respite, the Carthaginians, under Himilco and Hannibal son of Giskon, set siege to the city from their camp on the southwest. Even then the confidence of the citizens seems to have been little shaken, and Diodorus records with some amazement that while the siege was taking place 'they passed a decree about the guards who spent the nights at their posts, that none of them should have more than one mattress, one cover, one sheepskin and two pillows', evidently rigorous conditions compared with their normal standards.

For eight months the siege dragged on and many of the Carthaginians, including Hannibal himself, died of disease or weakness, for they had difficulty in obtaining provisions. They destroyed many of the temples and other buildings on the south of the town, and when reinforcements arrived to relieve them, the mercenaries in the Akragantine army mutinied and deserted, and the city's defences broke. Orders were given for the town to be evacuated, and soon afterwards the Carthaginians sacked it. Gellias and many other citizens took refuge in the temple of

8

Athena on the ridge, but when they saw that there was no hope left, they set fire to it and chose to die in the flames rather than fall ignominiously into the hands of the sacking and looting enemy. The city was, however, allowed to stand, but it was robbed of many lovely works of art which were shipped off to Carthage. The magnificent temple of Olympian Zeus, which had been nearly a century in building, was left incomplete and apparently roofless.

Some years later, when Dionysius of Syracuse made a treaty with the Carthaginians, some of the people of Akragas were allowed to return to their town on condition that they should be subject to Carthage and that they should not reconstruct their fortifications. In time they managed to regain their independence, but the city was so reduced in wealth and population that in 340 B.C. Timoleon, as part of his programme of restoring Greek towns and giving them democratic government, sent new colonists to rebuild the town, a work which continued till the end of the century. So began the second period of prosperity for Akragas.

The new urban developments included streets laid out on a grid plan which may have followed the VI century layout, the improvement and reconstruction of public buildings to the west of the main street leading to Gate IV, and the main residential area to the east. The city walls were restored and the defences of Gate VI redesigned. The *agora* at this time was evidently just inside Gate IV (it was paved and its extent has now been identified), and it was still in that place when Cicero described it in the I century B.C. It is strange that the theatre, which must surely have existed at some period at Akragas, has not yet been identified.

This rebuilding of the town was carried out over many years, and the town's territory was again extended between 286–280 under the tyrant Phintias who was responsible for the sacking of Gela. In 276 it was taken by Pyrrhus, liberator of many Greek cities, but when he withdrew from Sicily, having failed in his attempt to take the Carthaginian stronghold at Lilybaeum, Akragas fell under Carthaginian rule, and in 261, during the First Punic War, their commander was allowed to fortify the acropolis hill. But he was forced to capitulate to the Romans after a long siege, and although the town changed hands several times in the following years, by 210 it was permanently in Roman hands. Its defensive system seems to have been abandoned after the damage incurred during the Punic Wars, but rebuilding continued and many Roman houses and other buildings can be seen in the large Hellenistic-Roman area uncovered near the church of San Nicola. Twice the town, now known as Agrigentum, was repopulated, once in 207 and again in the time of Augustus, and its inhabitants enjoyed a peaceful and prosperous existence, cultivating corn, wine and fruit, and producing sulphur and textiles. Both Strabo and Ptolemy mention it as an emporium, and many richly ornamented houses reflect its fortunate conditions in Imperial Roman times. But gradually after the III century it began to decline. It shrank in size and importance. With the coming of Christianity the temples became obsolete: only the temple of Concord was saved for posterity by being adapted as a church, like the temple of Athena at Syracuse. When, in the 9th century, the Arabs invaded the land, they found only a relatively insignificant settlement on the long high ridge.

The buildings will now be described, starting at the east end of the acropolis and following round in a clockwise direction.

Temple of Demeter (Church of San Biagio). This temple, which is partly incorporated in the medieval church, originally stood in a sacred *temenos* which included some little circular altars, one containing a *bothros* full of offerings to the Chthonic deities: some fragmentary busts of Demeter and Persephone make the attribution certain. The temple, which may have been one of those built by Theron as a thanksgiving for his victory at Himera (for its date should be about 480 B.C.) consisted of a *cella* and *pronaos* with two columns. Some fine lion-head spouts from this temple can be seen in the Museum.

The so-called Rock Sanctuary of Demeter (Fig. 18) is reached from the temple above by a path and steps down the cliff side. What you first see when you reach the site is a stone-built enclosure on two levels, divided into several chambers containing troughs. The high back wall of a long narrow building (D) runs parallel to the rock face, and behind it are two caves (A and B) which, at the time of their discovery, were found to be filled with terra-cotta ex-voto offerings and busts of the Chthonic deities Demeter and Persephone. This building, which lies outside the walls of the Greek town, is regarded as the archaic predecessor of the temple of Demeter, but the site badly needs re-examining, for its true character is not yet clear. Unfortunately the first discovery of the sacred caves, which are partly or perhaps wholly artificial, was made by 19th century treasure-seekers, and the accuracy of the subsequent descriptions of the site leaves much to be desired, for the objects recovered were not kept distinct from those found at a later date in

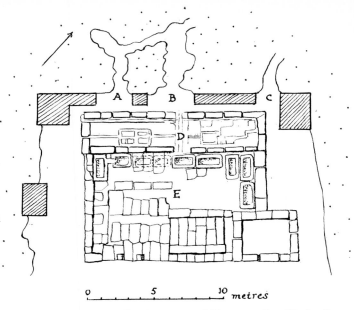

different archaeological levels. What seems clear, however, is that there is no foundation for the belief that the caves were other than *favissae*, destined for the reception of ex-voto offerings over a long period of time.

In front of these caves the long narrow building (D) with two doors opening into the *favissae* had originally a false-vault roof with a Proto-Doric cornice of so rudimentary a character that it suggests an early date (perhaps VII century) and is reminiscent of the cornice of the Demeter Malophoros Sanctuary at Selinunte. These features, therefore, hint at a pre-colony date for this part of the building, even though it was already partly Greek in inspiration. This supposition was supported by the discovery of prehistoric pottery of the VIII–VII centuries as well as of Geometric and Proto-Corinthian sherds, at the base of these walls and in the neighbourhood of the *favissae*. There is therefore a strong presumption that this rear building was erected before the colony was officially founded, and served as a sacred site to the goddesses probably until the town was sacked by the Carthaginians in 406. It contains some re-used stones and has evidently been rehandled.

The whole of the building in front (E), together with the water troughs which were fed by water artificially conveyed by pipes inside the cliff from C into Cave B, must be later, and the technique of some at least of the masonry is comparable to structures of Timoleon's time. This later building has nothing whatever to do with the Chthonic deities: as Professor Zuntz has written, 'Persephone could not have resided in a hydraulic system.' But it may have replaced an earlier sanctuary which needed water for ablutions, or alternatively, and perhaps more convincingly, the whole of the frontal part of the building, together with the water-pipes in the cliff, and the troughs, may have been set up as a Nymphaeum in Timoleon's time, after the monument had not been used as a sacred place for many years. The building of a Nymphaeum would not have been regarded as a profanation of a one-time sanctuary. At the same time the early building (D) was partly rebuilt.

The curious asymmetry of the frontal part of this complex is apparently due to its having slipped forward out of place. The façade was originally parallel to the cliff face.

Close to the sanctuary, but above it, the remains of Gate I offer nothing of interest today, but by following a track round the edge of the cemetery you can see some interesting fortifications which were designed to block the head of a small valley penetrating the line of the walls. A V-shaped re-entrant bastion can be seen, and the lower courses of a strong tower which defended it outside.

Another natural obstacle, this time a deep cleft in the rock, called for additional defences at Gate II, from which led the road to Gela, in which you can still see wheel tracks. Here the two sides of the cleft were cut back to form vertical walls, and the masonry walls were then built along the edges. The north side, which is about 150 feet long, had several re-entrants, while the south side was strengthened by a tower near the gateway which was at the head of the gully. Originally there was yet another sanctuary to the Chthonic deities nearby, with finds showing that it was venerated from the V century to the Roman period.

Temple D (erroneously attributed to Hera Lacinia). This is a classic Doric building with a colonnade surrounding a *pronaos*, *cella* and *opisthodomos*. Built in about 460–440, it shows signs of burning here and there in the structure: probably caused during the Carthaginian sacking of Akragas in 406.

The six frontal columns and thirteen side columns are evenly spaced round the whole building, in spite of the fact that the side columns were smaller in diameter and set more closely together. On each side of the door leading from the *pronaos* into the *cella* there were stairways giving access to the roof space.

The Romans carried out restoration work here, and built a new roof with terra-cotta tiles replacing the earlier marble ones, and a ramp sloping up to the entrance on the east. Outside the east end of the temple the remains of its large associated altar have recently been restored.

Gate III and its tower have unfortunately been much damaged by the cutting of tombs of the Byzantine period, but outside the walls some deep ruts can be seen in the ancient road which left the city from that gateway.

Between this temple and the Temple of Concord you follow the ancient walls, in some places not built with masonry but cut out of the rock with two vertical sides. The inner face is full of arched burial recesses of the Byzantine period and near the temple of Concord are many other graves of the same date.

Temple F (Concord). (Plate 7.) This is quite erroneously called the Temple of Concord, because many years ago a Latin inscription of Imperial Roman date was found nearby and was thought to refer to this temple.

It is one of the most classic and perfectly preserved Doric temples in existence, and owes its preservation to the fact that, like the Temple of Athena in Syracuse, it was converted into a Christian church in the 6th century. The spaces between the columns were filled with walling; the division between the *cella* walls and the *opisthodomos* was destroyed, and the *cella* walls were cut into a series of arches flanking the nave.

In spite of this the main structure and many of the features of the building can now be observed in greater detail than in almost any other temple. Its colonnade, freed in the 18th century of its interwalling, has 13 columns along the sides and 6 at each end. Inside, the *cella* still stands to its full height and even retains its cornice: a rebate evidently received the timbers of a wooden ceiling.

The inner gables of the walls separating the *cella* from the porch and *opisthodomos* are almost intact, and in each a central doorway with slanting sides and an ogival arch over the lintel may have served to distribute the weight above, but also allowed access to the attic room over the *cella*, reached from stairways of characteristic Akragantine type, on each side of the entrance from the *pronaos* to the *cella*.

PLATE 7. Agrigento. (*above*) The Temple of Concord (*below*) and one of the giant *telamones* re-assembled from fragments, in the Temple of Zeus

To appreciate the many structural refinements of this temple you need to spend some time observing such details as the curvature of the platform, the entasis and the inward slant of the columns, and the 'double contraction' on all sides of the colonnade. It was this last feature which led Dinsmoor to propose a date of about 430 for the construction of this temple, for it was at about that time that the practice of setting the columns closer together at the angles (to overcome the problem of the corner metopes) reached Sicily from Greece.

Another feature of this temple – a unique feature in a Sicilian temple – is the complete preservation of the entablature on the two ends, the frieze of plain metopes and triglyphs, and the mutule cornice.

Like all other stone temples, as distinct from marble ones, (and owing to the absence of marble all the Sicilian temples were made of local stone), this temple must originally have been covered with white stucco below the capitals, and brightly painted above. The metopes which, unlike the carved metopes at Selinunte, appear to be plain, may have been painted with mythological scenes pertaining to the deity to whom the temple was dedicated, and the same may apply to the pediment which is unlikely to have been left undecorated. The roof was presumably tiled with coloured marble tiles. In view of all this we can perhaps count ourselves lucky to see the temple when the patina of over two thousand years has enriched and beautified the texture and colour of the local limestone, now no longer covered with garish stuccoes.

To the west of this temple most of the ancient town walls have tumbled over the scarp, and a number of tombs, foundations and house walls which can be seen belong for the most part to late Roman or post-Roman periods.

Further west, the garden of the Villa Aurea contains rectangular graves in the rock, as well as two hypogea, and outside it, near the north-east corner, a sepulchral street passes through an area of early Christian graves and thence to the original entrance to the Catacombs, now blocked by the modern road. Dating from about the 3rd or 4th century, these in many respects resembled the more extensive series at Syracuse.

The Temple of Herakles. The attribution of this temple to Herakles is not certain, being based on the fact that Cicero mentioned that a temple so dedicated stood near the *agora*. The latter, described by Livy, in his account of the Roman capture of Akragas, as being near the south Gate, has now been identified.

Built, like the temples of Hera and Concord, on an artificial platform, it is the earliest of the large temples in Akragas, and is thought to have been begun in the last decades of the VI century, only shortly before the temple of Olympian Zeus nearby. It is unusually long – well over 200 feet – and required more than the normal number of side-columns: in fact it had 15 of these, and 6 at each end. Inside the colonnade it was divided into *pronaos*, *cella* and *opisthodomos*, and there were stairways leading from the *cella* entrance to the attic or roof-space. This is the first instance of this feature which subsequently recurs in many temples in Akragas.

This temple has been partially restored in modern times, for in 1924 eight of the fallen columns on the south side were re-erected. The Doric columns have very wide echini with a hollow moulding where they join the top of the column: it is thought that this is the first instance in Sicily of echini with the very rigid profile, which are found on the Greek mainland. Another innovation in this early temple was the attempt at 'angle contraction', a device which was still only partly understood in Sicily at that time.

The unusually wide *cella* must have presented some difficulty to roof, and the suggestion has been made that the architect had to resort to the use of braced beams.

Remains of two entablatures have been found in this temple, different both in the style and the size of the lion-head spouts; one dates from about 470–460 and the other from twenty years later, neither being the right date for the temple, so for the present their exact relation to the building is obscure. Perhaps, as Dunbabin suggested, the original sima was painted with a lotus and palmette design like that of Temple C at Selinus.

Traces of fire may be attributable to the sacking of the city by the Carthaginians, and for a long time after this the temples must have been left in their ruinous condition. But the Romans repaired and used the temple of Herakles, and Cicero speaks of a bronze statue of the god which stood inside and which the predatory Roman praetor Verres tried to acquire by sending men to wrench the bolts from the doors and lever the statue off its pedestal with crowbars. Fortunately a general alarm was given and the men were beaten off. The statue must have been greatly prized by the citizens, and in fact Cicero says, 'I do not know that I have ever seen a lovelier work of art . . . so lovely that its mouth and chin are quite noticeably rubbed from the way in which people, when praying or offering thanks, not only do reverence to it, but actually kiss it.'

Before continuing westwards, mention must be made of two interesting mouments standing outside the walls to the south.

Not far outside Gate IV (of which nothing remains) is the so-called: **Tomb of Theron**. This has nothing whatever to do with the tyrant and is a tomb of Roman date (about 75 B.C.), belonging to a large cemetery extending for some distance along the south side of the scarp, outside the walls. Built on a square podium, the upper part of the building has a Doric entablature with engaged Ionic columns at each corner, and false doors in between. Such a mixture of styles is not uncommon in Hellenistic architecture, and while comparable to certain tombs of the Roman period in North Africa, this tomb is thought to have been inspired by monuments in the Hellenistic tradition of Asia Minor. According to some scholars, it may originally have had another floor above the two remaining ones.

To the east of this, and reached by a track leading south from the main road (115), there are the ruins of the small but interesting **Temple of Asclepius** mentioned by Polybius when he described the Roman siege of 262. Its identification is verified by the presence of a medicinal spring nearby.

Above very strong footings, carefully cut and laid, three steps give access to the small Doric temple which is quite unlike any of the other temples. It has solid walls instead of a colonnade, and set into the outer face of the end wall are two fluted half-columns suggesting a false portico, and perhaps imitating the half-columns in the outer wall of the Temple of Zeus. Inside, a *pronaos* leads into the *cella*, and between them is a well-preserved stairway. Only a few elements of the entablature are known, including part of the frieze and a few lion-head spouts. These elements do not agree with the late V century date usually assigned to the temple.

Within the temple, according to Cicero, there was 'a beautiful statue of Apollo, on whose thigh was inscribed the name of Myron in small silver letters'.

To the west of Gate IV, stand the ruins of the largest of all the temples:

Temple of Olympian Zeus (*or the Olympieion*). (Fig. 19.) Sacked by

the Carthaginians in 406 while still apparently incomplete, and subsequently damaged by earthquakes, the temple, by then reduced to a
huge pile of tumbled stones, was still further despoiled when it was
used as a quarry for stones to build the jetties at Porto Empedocle in the
18th century.

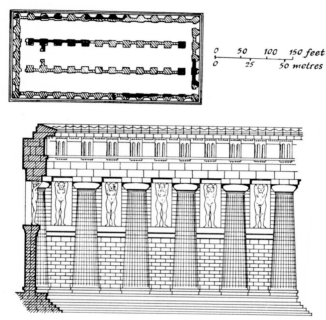

FIG. 19. (*above*) The Temple of Zeus. Plan. (*below*) Temple of Zeus.
Reconstruction of the façade, showing the probable position of the giant
telamones (after Prado)

In front of its eastern end one can still see the remains of its big altar,
with its foundation piers and the blocks for the substructure of the
steps which once led up to it.

In spite of its present condition, this temple is particularly worth
studying, for its design was wholly new and original and must have
stirred public admiration and wonder at its revolutionary break with
the accepted architectural canon, quite as much as did, say, the Crystal
Palace 2,400 years later. It was indeed a tragedy that Akragas was sacked
before the completion of the temple.

It has often been argued in the past that it was begun in 480 by Theron, in gratitude for his victory at Himera, but now its very archaic plan and certain other features have led to the belief that it may be earlier, and probably dates from the late VI century, like the temple of Herakles nearby. From the outset it was planned on a colossal scale as one of the most grandiose temples anywhere in the Greek world: a conception which was quite consonant with the tastes of the Sicilian Greeks, who aspired to build larger and grander temples than those in their land of origin.

Fortunately, although an earthquake destroyed the temple, the various architectural elements still remained in their correct order on the ground, and the study of these elements, together with a most useful description of the temple by Diodorus Siculus, has made it possible to reconstruct, with a fair degree of certainty, not only its plan, but its elevation and some of its details.

A massive platform about 350 feet long was first constructed on foundations nearly 20 feet deep, and around this was built, not the normal colonnade of free-standing columns, but a series of Doric half-columns of enormous size (13 feet in diameter) engaged to about half their height in a continuous screen wall. The top of this wall was finished with a shelf or belt-course upon which, in the 'window' between each column, stood a giant *telamone* supporting the architrave with the help of invisible iron beams from column to column. These *telamones* (Plate 7), over 25 feet tall, were made up of blocks of stone which were then covered with plaster, and probably painted. They are male figures, alternately bearded and beardless, with their feet together and their arms raised and bent to bear the weight of the architrave between the columns. Stylistically the heads of these Atlas-like figures belong to about 470 or so, and evidently the building was quite well advanced by the time. In fact, since the victory at Himera, hundreds of captives and disbanded soldiers had been put to work on it.

Such an elevation was wholly revolutionary, though it may have been influenced by Temple F at Selinus, which in its turn might have been inspired by Egyptian architecture. But not only was its design revolutionary: the way in which it was built was equally untraditional. The capitals and *echini* were built with large blocks of stone, and, as Professor Lawrence has written: 'Instead of building up columns with drums and spanning each intercolumniation with a single architrave block, the entire construction was achieved with comparatively small blocks, and the stucco coating would have concealed the joints.' By adopting this method the transport and labour costs were, no doubt, reduced, but unfortunately it also meant that it was easier to despoil the temple for building stone.

There seem to have been two entrances leading into the side aisles, which, as we have said, must have been lit from the 'windows' in which the *telamones* stood: these entrances were placed at each side of the five frontal columns. Inside, a very long and (in proportion to the width of the building) narrow *cella* was divided into three in the usual way. But here again the structural methods adopted were quite new, for the *cella* wall was extremely thin and punctuated at frequent intervals by big square pillars which were so set that they projected into the *cella* to diminish its span for roofing. There cannot be any other explanation for this feature: the *cella* was surely meant to be roofed, even if the work was interrupted by the Carthaginian attack before it was begun. This is what Diodorus wrote: 'Although all other men build their temples either with walls forming the sides or with rows of columns, thus enclosing their sanctuaries, this temple combines both these plans; for the columns were built in with the walls, the part extending outside the temple being rounded and that within square [he is referring to the rectangular pilasters behind each half-column]. The circumference of the outer part of the columns which extends from the wall measures 6 metres, (the flutings are so wide that the body of a man can be contained in each of them), while that of the inner part is 12 feet. The porticos were of enormous size and height, and in the east pediment they portrayed the battle between the Gods and the Giants in sculptures which excelled in size and beauty, and in the west "the Capture of Troy", in which each one of the heroes may be seen portrayed in a manner appropriate to his role.'

A few fragments of these sculptured scenes are heaped together near the south-west corner of the temple. The head of Athena was found near the temple, and in the *cella* a male torso which may have been one of the figures in the scene of the Gods and Giants. Only one *telamon* still remains today: assembled from various fragments, it lies on the ground among the temple ruins. The heads of three others are in the museum. It is interesting to note that what appears to be a representation of one of these *telamones* has been found on a vase from Akragas.

To the west of the Temple of Zeus (Fig. 20) is the most interesting of the Akragas gates (Gate V), excavated a few years ago. Defended by a massive projecting tower, the very narrow entrance was probably closed by a double gate, one behind the other. From this point westwards the city wall is well preserved with its towers and posterns; not all of it belongs to the same date and it must have been rebuilt in places at the time of Timoleon and again in the Punic Wars.

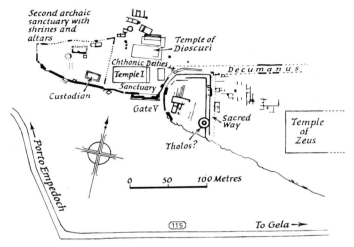

FIG. 20. Agrigento. The area to the west of the Temple of Zeus

The Sanctuary of the Chthonic Deities and the nearby Temples.
(Fig. 20). This is the earliest sacred site at Agrigento and it goes back to the VII or VI century, perhaps before the official founding of the colony. Originally the area was enclosed in a sacred *temenos* and it partly overlay an earlier Sikel site which is also thought to have been a religious one. Inside this *temenos* were altars, often arranged in pairs with one square altar and one round, and other small sacred buildings which were put up as necessity required. There are two simple shrines of archaic type with *cella*, *adytum* and short *pronaos*, as well as two enclosures each containing a couple of altars, and a number of *bothroi* and *favissae*, found full of ex-voto offerings.

By the mid-VI century a temple was begun here and another was started fifty years later; neither was finished, and in fact the foundations of one slightly overlie the other. They stand to the north of the so-called **Temple of the Dioscuri** (or Castor and Pollux) which, in its present form, is only a delightful piece of 19th century landscape gardening. Originally a temple of classical type built in about 480–460 (perhaps one of those built after the battle of Himera), it is now only a pastiche of architectural fragments from later buildings.

Some of the elements assembled here may have come from **Temple L** of which only the platform and some column drums now remain, as well as its altar not far to the east. Its original date is unknown, but it was certainly restored much later.

Excavations should be able to establish the sequence of this confusion of buildings which range from VII or VI century right through the Roman period.

Another sanctuary has lately been discovered to the west, but is so damaged that neither its date nor its dedication is known. Inside it are some small shrines and an altar.

The Temple of Vulcan (*or Hephaestus*) is situated on the far side of the railway, and is hardly worth visiting unless you are particularly interested, as it is difficult to reach. To do so you take a path from the north edge of the Sanctuary of the Chthonic Deities and, after crossing a valley and reaching the railway line, turn back along this until you find the temple. Built in about 430, only two columns still stand, and as they were only partially fluted, one may infer that the temple was never completed. Parts of its decorated double cornice show Ionic influence. Its *cella* was partly built over a small archaic temple of the early VI century; this had painted terra-cotta revetments, fragments of which are in the museum.

Gates VI-IX are interesting only to students of military architecture. Some had double gateways, one behind the other; nearly all had towers protecting them, and some had additional outworks. Not all of them are as originally planned, for some, at least, have been redesigned at the time of Timoleon or later.

The Area round the Church of San Nicola. On the east side of the road passing the medieval church of San Nicola, a very extensive area has been excavated. This development, initiated in the late II century B.C., a few years after the Roman conquest of Akragas, continued until the 4th or 5th century A.D. Some of the houses are of Hellenistic type with a peristyle; others are of Italic type with an *atrium* surrounded by porticos and rooms, and they sometimes have a stair leading to an upper

floor. These houses line the many parallel streets running north and
south at right angles to the main roads, or *decumani*. Many of the late
Hellenistic houses have mosaic pavements made with white tesserae;
the brightly coloured mosaics are of Imperial Roman date.

Test excavations under these houses show that after the town was
sacked in 406 the area was deserted for many years, and people returned
to live there at the time of Timoleon's rebuilding.

The so-called Oratory of Phalaris stands to the west of San Nicola.
In certain respects it resembles the so-called Tomb of Theron, for its
architecture is stylistically mixed. It has a hollow rectangular podium
reached by steps on the east side, and above this podium stands a small
temple with Ionic columns supporting a Doric entablature. According
to an inscription this building was dedicated to a woman of the Teretina
tribe by her son. It is in fact a small late Hellenistic shrine or temple of
the II century B.C. connected with a Graeco-Roman sanctuary which
seems to have been the successor of an earlier sacred site perhaps
dedicated to the Chthonic deities. In fact its development can be
traced from the VI century B.C. to the building of the medieval church.

At about the same time as the little temple was built, a semicircular
theatre-like structure, thought to be a *comitium* for public meetings, was
constructed nearby. It has 24 rows of seats divided by water channels
into sections.

The Museo Nazionale a new building near San Nicola, which can be
visited on application but is not yet officially open (Spring 1967). It
houses a very important collection of finds from the prehistoric period
onwards. Its opening hours will be established shortly.

The Temples on the Western Hill of the Acropolis. The Doric
temple underlying the church of S. Maria dei Greci is thought to have
been dedicated to Athena, but this is uncertain. It had a *cella*, *pronaos*
and *opisthodomos*, and 6 by 13 columns. It also had the usual stairs to
the attic. Its date is about the second quarter of the V century, and it
may be the temple built by Theron on the acropolis in 488.

Another temple, thought to be that dedicated to Zeus Atabyrios, is
now covered by the Cathedral church of San Gerlando.

SANT'ANGELO MUXARO

If you are staying in Agrigento, and have a car, an interesting excursion can be made to Sant'Angelo Muxaro, 30 kms. to the north. You take the State road (118) to Raffadali, where you fork right. (If you are particularly anxious to visit all the tombs possible here, it would be wise to make arrangements with the *Soprintendenza alle Antichità,* whose offices are by the new Museum at Agrigento.)

It has convincingly been argued that this site may be identified with the ancient capital and stronghold of *Kamikos,* where the legendary king Kokalos reigned in the II millennium B.C. Of the stronghold there is nothing to be seen, but there are the finest 'tholos' (dome-shaped) tombs in Sicily. These tombs are not far from the village and you should ask there for the biggest of them which is known as the Grotta Sant' Angelo (or the Tomba del Principe). This group of tombs is the most important cemetery in western Sicily, rivalling the great Pantalica one near Syracuse (p. 192).

Kokalos originally had his capital at *Inykon* which, although not definitely identified, was possibly on Monte della Giudecca, a little to the north-east of Cattólica Eraclea, where some remains of walls and towers enclose the hill-top, thickly scattered with potsherds. Subsequently Kokalos moved his capital 12 kms. further east, and this new stronghold was said to have been designed and fortified by Daedalus who had fled to Sicily from Crete, and it was also said that he made the entrance so narrow that only three or four men were needed to defend it. Daedalus was pursued by Minos, King of Crete, who was received at Kamikos, but Kokalos's daughters then drowned him in scalding water, and he was buried at Heraclea Minoa (see p. 102).

This legend was already current in Crete in very early times, certainly before the Greeks began colonizing the West, and in fact the name Kokalos appeared on the Mycenaean inscribed tablets from 'Nestor's Palace' at Pylos.

The cemetery, on the south and west sides of a small terraced hill overlooking the Platani valley, was excavated by Orsi who did not, however, write more than a preliminary report. He found that there were two groups of rock-cut tombs; the earlier ones (XI–IX century), nearer the foot of the hill, contained bronze razors and daggers of North Pantalica type, and pottery comparable to that from Cassibile, and the later tombs, further up the hill, were quite different from most Sicilian ones, not only for their unusual size, but also for their 'tholos' roofs.

9

PLATE 8.
Sant'Angelo Muxaro.
One of the gold bowls. (Now
in the British Museum)

One of these, with a diameter of about 28 feet, was made into a chapel in the Byzantine period and dedicated to Sant'Angelo. Some of them had a funeral bench around the inside where the corpses were laid, though in others the body was laid in the ground and surrounded by pottery vessels. These tombs were used over many centuries, probably from the VIII to the middle of the V, and evidently succeed the other group.

The finds can be seen in the museums at Syracuse, Agrigento and Palermo, and one of the most important is illustrated in Plate 8. It is the only remaining one of four gold bowls, and is decorated with a procession of bulls in relief. One is tempted to imagine some local king between the VIII and VI centuries wishing to recall the Cretan origin of his dynasty both in his 'tholos' tomb and in his bull-decorated riches. According to at least one authority, these bowls may be Phoenicio-Cypriote work of the VII century.

The pottery is quite different from that in East Sicily, and includes pots with concentric circles and geometric motifs. There are also tall-footed cups and big jugs, often red, and some painted in imitation of Corinthian and Rhodian wares of the orientalizing phase (late VII–early VI). The imported wares begin about the date of the foundation of Akragas in the early VI century.

The gold bowls were not the only signs of wealth. There were also two gold rings, one of which, at least, is known to have come from one of the later tombs. They are incised with a wolf and with a cow suckling her calf, and in no way resemble either archaic Greek gold-work or anything local. Perhaps here again we have a far distant echo of the Mycenaean world.

7 · Caltanissetta, Enna, Realmese, Aidone (for Morgantina), Piazza Armerina and Caltagirone

Leaving Agrigento by road (122) or by rail, the distance is about 70 kms. to **Caltanissetta** where a new museum is now (1966) in course of arrangement. It will contain finds from some of the prehistoric and Hellenized Sikel settlements in the district, including those from Sabucina from where came the terra-cotta model of a small shrine shown in Fig. 21, a fascinating native interpretation of a Greek prototype, dating from the late VI century B.C.

FIG. 21. Terracotta model of a shrine. Native work of the VI c. B.C. from Sabucina

From Caltanissetta the railway and road (122) continue to Enna. **Enna** was known until the last century as Castrogiovanni (an intriguing corruption of the Arab name Casr-janni which came from the Roman name Castrum Hennae), and it is worth visiting for its dramatically impressive position, dominating miles of countryside from a height of over 3,000 feet. This countryside was once richly wooded and fertile, so fertile that it was said that the hunting dogs lost the scent of their game for the fragrance of the flowers. It is small wonder that the site was chosen as the seat of the cult of Demeter and Kore or Persephone – the most venerated of all deities among the Sicilian Greeks. According to the ancient myth brought from Greece to Sicily, Persephone was carried off by Pluto, god of the netherworld, and Demeter wandered the world over to find her. Finally Zeus ordained that Persephone should reign for half the year as Queen of the Netherworld, and spend the other half with her mother in Sicily. In the earliest forms of the myth there is no mention of Enna, but later poets and writers such as Callimachus, Cicero, Livy, Ovid and Claudian speak of Enna as the specially holy place of the goddesses. Just to the north of the castle there is a rocky spur, the Rocca di Cerere, where once stood the Temple of Ceres (Demeter), containing, according to Cicero, huge statues of the goddess (reproduced on the local coinage), and of Triptolemus.

The position of the town, described as *inexpugnabilis* by Livy, made it an obvious choice for early settlement, and the Sikel town there was already receiving cultural influences from Gela by the VII century. It passed into Roman hands in 258 B.C. and was the main centre of the First Slave War in 134 when it managed to hold out for two years before it fell.

A small archaeological collection is housed in the Museo Alessi which is in a modern building behind the apse of the Cathedral (Piazza del Duomo) where the Cathedral treasure is also kept.

A very short distance to the north of Enna is *Calascibetta* which also has a small collection of archaeological material in the Municipio. There are several important prehistoric cemeteries in the neighbourhood and perhaps the most accessible is that of **Realmese,** in the Cozzo San Giuseppe district. To reach it, follow the Petralia road for $1\frac{1}{2}$ kms. and, just beyond a wood, fork right into a newer road from which a lane leads off to the left towards the cemetery. There are over 300 rock-cut tombs here, generally round but occasionally square in plan, and they date from about 850–730 B.C. (contemporary with the third phase at Pantalica). They contained finds which include fibulae of the looped, Pantalica South type, and pottery which is more like that from Sant' Angelo Muxaro than Pantalica.

Not far away, in the *Valle Coniglio*, there is another, rather later cemetery (VII to V century), with rectangular chambers.

From Enna continue southwards for Aidone (Morgantina) or Piazza

Armerina, by taking Via Pergusa, and passing Lake Pergusa before joining the main road (117 bis). The lake, now shorn of its wooded Arcadian charm, and far from romantic, was the fabled scene of Pluto's rape of Persephone, an honour which it disputes with the far lovelier Fonte Ciane (the source of the Ciane river), just outside Syracuse.

MORGANTINA

The ancient city of Morgantina has been identified in recent years from ruins (now being excavated by the University of Princeton), on the Serra Orlando ridge, a short distance outside Aidone. Coming southwards from Enna, the village of Aidone is reached by a smaller road forking off the main road (117 bis), about 4 kms. north of Piazza Armerina, and to find the site you must continue eastwards on the same road for another 5 kms. Just after passing another road on your left, look for the signpost or ask for the '*scavi americani*'. (The site is not easy to find, and as the track is rough it is better to walk the last few hundred yards).

Morgantina is situated on an oblong ridge dominated by a small knoll called the Cittadella – the acropolis. It is not exactly known who were the founders, but to judge from the earliest pottery it is thought that they were Chalcidians from Catane, who settled on the Cittadella hill, alongside the native Sikels, in the first half of the VI century B.C. The Cittadella had already had a very long history before that time, for below the earliest defences put up by the colonists, the excavators have found at least three prehistoric levels (starting with the Early Bronze Age of Castelluccio, followed by the Thapsos period with late Mycenaean XIII century ware and Ausonian pottery of the XII century, and then by VII century pottery of Sant'Angelo Muxaro type). The co-existence of the Sikels and Greeks is interesting. As the excavators have written, 'while the main acropolis area in the second quarter of the VI century saw the rise of a small but well-organized Greek city, the outskirts of the lower Cittadella were still occupied by the indigenous people whose huts were not destroyed till the third quarter of the century.' This hill-top had its own defences, but soon, by the late VI century, the town had spread over much of the ridge as well, and walls were built to protect it. Not much more than fifty years later, however, it was destroyed, almost surely by Ducetius, the Sikel leader, the only man who ever attempted to unite the Sikels to free themselves from Greek domination.

Then, like so many other towns in Sicily, it was rebuilt in the late IV century at the time of Timoleon and Agathocles, and continued to develop, always under strong Syracusan influence, under Hieron II. From the outset of this new colonization Morgantina had been designed anew, with its streets laid out on a grid plan, defences with towered gateways at the cardinal points, and posterns between them leading to springs of water. A number of public buildings belong to this time. *The agora*, an exceptional structure built on the slope, with flights of steps forming three sides of a polygon, was first laid out in about 300 B.C. and continued subsequently, but it seems to have been abandoned before completion. The steps served admirably as seats for public meetings which were addressed from a podium, or speaker's platform, recently discovered. On the east side, for a length of 100 metres or so, there ran a long stoa with piers down the centre and pairs of rooms at each end. This building was stuccoed and painted, and in all probability it had an upper storey, but the colonnade planned to run along the front may never have been built. Another stoa, on the west side, was also abandoned before completion.

Other public buildings included a theatre (at the foot of the hill to the west of the Agora) built in the III century B.C. and bearing a dedicatory inscription to Dionysos incised on the front of one of the seats; a IV century sanctuary of Demeter and Kore, and many Hellenistic houses. One, the 'House of Ganymede' (so called from a III century B.C. mosaic showing Ganymede being carried off by the eagle of Zeus), is of particular importance for the very early date of the mosaics.

The town defences had evidently fallen into a bad state by the III century, for there are clear signs of hurried patching and rebuilding just before the outbreak of the First Punic War, but the town continued to thrive, minting its own coins and erecting a number of important buildings which are now being uncovered. A huge public storehouse, probably for grain, belongs to the mid-III century B.C. and other structures date from between that time and the I century B.C. when the city, which had by now been for some time in Roman hands, ceased to exist.

Ruins of many of the buildings mentioned above are visible today, and from the excavations which are still continuing it should soon be possible to obtain a clearer outline of the history of Morgantina and of its lay-out.

PLATE 9. Piazza Armerina. Detail of one of the mosaics in the Roman Villa

THE ROMAN VILLA AT CASALE NEAR PIAZZA ARMERINA (Fig. 22 and Plate 9)

To reach the villa you should follow the road signs from the town, and after going westwards for 6 kms. you will find the entrance and ticket office.

Hours of visiting. Winter 9–1 and 2 till dusk. *Summer* 9–1 and 3.30 till dusk. Sundays 9–1.

Hotel accommodation. In Piazza Armerina there is a Jolly Hotel and a smaller one, the Gangi.

This is one of the best-preserved large country houses of late Roman date, and is particularly famed for the splendid mosaic pavements which decorate almost all the rooms.

Described as one of the most outstanding monuments in the whole Roman world, it consists of four united groups of buildings on different levels (according to the slope of the hillside), in a peaceful and wooded countryside. Its existence had been known for a long time, but it is only in the last twenty years or so that it has been excavated and preserved, and even now the outbuildings and servants' quarters still remain to be uncovered.

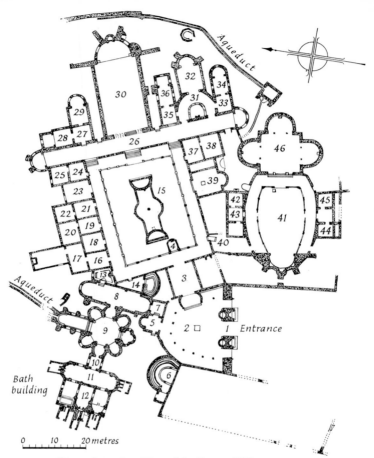

FIG. 22. Piazza Armerina. Plan of the Roman Villa

The original building on the site seems to have been a fairly simple one of the 2nd century A.D. but this was rebuilt and enlarged to make a luxurious hunting lodge at the end of the 3rd century, and it is thought that the new owner may have been the Emperor Maximian, though some scholars are hesitant about this attribution.

Maximian was a man of humble Pannonian origin who rose to imperial status after having served in the army and been promoted by Diocletian who gave him the name Herculius (under the divine protection of Hercules) and made him co-regent. He had many military successes, particularly in Gaul, and was an Emperor from 286 to 305.

Certainly this villa, or palace, is opulent, and there are various reasons for attributing it to the period of Maximian, although some scholars have argued for a rather later date. The mosaics are stylistically comparable with the Tunisian and Algerian mosaics of about 300 A.D., and African stone has, in fact, been used for the tesserae; the hair styles and the cut of the men's beards were fashionable at the same time; the cylindrical cap worn by some of the state and military officials was an Illyrian type popular in Diocletian's time, and the baton with mushroom-shaped handle carried by some of the officials also belongs to the time of the tetrarchy. The column capitals present in several of the rooms belong to a type which was mass-produced in Diocletian's time and were used in his palace at Split, and their presence in several parts of the building here argues for one consistent plan for the whole palace – a palace whose presiding spirit was that of Hercules, symbolizing the reigning monarch and his achievements, in conformity with a panegyric of 289 offered to the Emperor Maximian Herculius, likening his victories to the labours of Hercules. It is interesting in this connection to note that the *Liber Pontificalis* refers to Constantine's properties in Sicily (*in territorio Catinense*) and these properties he may well have inherited from Maximian's son Maxentius after he had defeated him in 312. The road linking Catania with Agrigentum at that time passed close by the villa.

There is therefore strong presumptive evidence that Maximian was the owner, and the *Adventus Augusti* scene in the mosaics in the room (3) leading into the great Portico shows a ritual welcome and ovation suitable only for an Emperor.

The Entrance leads into a colonnaded *atrium* (2). On the left are remains of a big latrine (6). The little *aediculum* (5) which was designed to hold a statue of Venus, leads into the long apsidal room (8), known as the *Salone del Circo*, from the scenes of a Roman Circus shown in the mosaics. It is interesting that this circus has been recognized as the Circus Maximus in Rome. At the north end, between the Temple of Hercules and Jupiter and the 12-doored *carceres* (starting gates) of the circus, two chariots are being made ready for the races. Eight chariots are taking part, two for each of the four teams, marked red, blue, green and white. The doors of the *carceres* have been flung open and the chariots have begun the race around the arena which has a central partition ornamented with architectural niches and water-tanks, and there is a turning point at each end. At the other end of the circus the stand is packed with spectators. The various stages of the race are all vividly depicted: the dashing start with one chariot overtaking another, then a collision between two chariots, one of which is overturning; and then the awarding of the victory palm by the judge, while a man blows a long tuba to signal the end of the race. This is a particularly lively scene, full of movement and interest. Other scenes of circuses exist elsewhere, in Carthage, Spain, Britain and Gaul, etc., but this is the most complete and detailed in treatment.

The rooms to the west of this hall (9–12) are the *Bath Buildings*. (9) is the *frigidarium* with an interesting octagonal plan which is the forerunner of polygonal buildings of the Christian period, the Baptistry at Albenga, San Vitale at Ravenna, and many others. The mosaics show a marine scene with fishing cupids, nereids, tritons, centaurs and sea monsters. This again is not an uncommon scene in African mosaics. There are other mosaics in the recesses around, one of a young man with a leopard skin. (10) is a little room which may have been used for friction and massage after the bath. In fact the mosaics show a young athlete being massaged by one slave, while another holds the oil-flask, and there are two other figures whose names, Titus and Cassius, are written beside them. The *tepidarium* (11) has lost most of its pavement, but the hypocaust system for the circulation of warm air can be seen. (12) are three small rooms of the *calidarium*.

Returning to the *Salone del Circo* you go into (13) a small trapeze-shaped waiting-room with a bench round its walls. The mosaics here are interesting, for they show a mother with her son and daughters, and two slave girls carrying clothing. The woman's hairdressing is typical of the 3rd century.

(14) is a small latrine with mosaics showing figures of partridges, bustards, leopards, hares, etc. It has a marble handbasin. This room leads into the corner of the big colonnaded hall or Portico (15) with its central fountain and small shrine to the patron deity of the villa (4), as well as mosaics of animal heads encircled by garlands.

(16–22) A series of rooms, probably bedrooms, along the north side of the hall. Some of them were structurally altered in Norman times, and the first of them contains, in fact, a Norman kiln. The mosaics are mostly geometric and of little interest. Those in (21) represent the four seasons, and in (22) cupids who are fishing from gaily coloured boats. In the background a villa, with a long galleried pavilion linking its two wings, stands in its park.

(23) Known as the room of the *Piccola Caccia* (the small hunting scene). The mosaics are in five registers, and it is probable that the scenery in the background is meant to represent the surroundings of the villa. You can see the hunters setting out with their hounds in pursuit of a fox. Below this, sacrifices are being made to Diana after a good day's sport by hunters who may represent the members of the Imperial family, and men are bringing in a wild boar and a dead hare. In the middle of the room a banquet is taking place under an awning slung between two oak trees. One of the dishes contains a roast duck, and the hunters are being served by slaves (one is a negro) who are pouring out wine, tending the fire, etc. Some horses are tethered to the trees. On the left, men are hunting with falcons, and on the right others are chasing hares. Below this, other scenes show huntsmen on horseback trying to stampede deer into their nets, or attacking a boar to prevent it from savaging a fallen companion.

(26) is the next room of interest, and its mosaics are the finest in the building. It is known as *L'ambulacro della Grande Caccia* from the great hunting scene depicted. This is a long hall, about 200 feet long, with apsidal ends containing mosaics representing the personifications of two Roman provinces, one of Egypt (or more probably Arabia or Africa), and the other, very much destroyed, of Armenia. In the midst of the two seas dividing these continents is Italy, where the varied catch is being collected from different parts of the Empire for the great state feasts in Rome.

All the central part of the room is occupied by the hunting scene which is set in a varied African countryside with porticoed buildings standing among the hills, near rivers and the sea. A number of different wild animals, shown in their natural habitat, are being hunted by men armed with shields and long javelins. One man, attacked by a lioness, is being helped by one of his companions who is striking the animal. The intention seems to have been to capture rather than to kill the beasts, and in fact a leopard can be seen just about to fall into a trap baited with a slaughtered goat, while hunters wait hidden in the bushes. Another man is being pursued by a tigress while he makes off with her cubs, and he has deliberately dropped one of them to distract her attention.

The captured animals are being loaded into ships which will transport them to Rome and other cities for use in amphitheatres: some of them are in cages or are being carried in ox-drawn carts, others are being dragged along on leashes. In charge of the loading process is an imperial functionary who may even be Maximian himself. He is wearing a richly decorated white cape and a cylindrical cap, while the man beside him wears a shoulder badge with the letter H, signifying perhaps that he belonged to the *Herculia* legion, so-called in honour of Maximian.

It is strange, in this very naturalistic scene, to find one imaginary beast, a winged griffon holding a cage containing a dead man. It is thought by some scholars that this symbolizes death, the death perhaps of one of the hunters lost during the foray; but its significance is not fully understood.

(27) *The Hall of Polyphemus.* Traces of wall-paintings. The mosaic shows Polyphemus' cave on the slopes of Mount Etna. Polyphemus the cyclops is seated in the centre, about to eat a slaughtered ram which is dangling over his knee, while the rest of the flock surround him. Ulysses and his companions are about to make him drunk, and while Ulysses himself is approaching him from the left with a big cup of wine, his friends are busily filling others. This Homeric subject is quite frequently found in Roman mosaics.

(28) Some of the mosaics represent the four seasons in hexagonal frames; others show some young people playing a game like skittles.

(29) has a geometrical design with varieties of fruit.

(30) A big basilica intended for official receptions.

(31) A semicircular hall or *atrium*, consisting of a *nymphaeum* leading into a big living room. The mosaics in the *atrium* show little cupids fishing from boats or playing with ducklings. Some long porticoed buildings can be seen on the bank.

(32) A living room whose walls were once covered with marble. The pavement has a lively mythological scene of Arion among sea-creatures, naiads and cupids.

(33) *The Little Circus* room, playfully decorated with caricatures of a circus with competing *bigas* driven by children and drawn by big geese, waders, etc. whose feathers are coloured to represent the different teams.

(34) The mosaics in this room are arranged in three registers. The uppermost shows a quartet playing a cithern, a small portable organ, a double flute and tibia; the middle one, a comic chorus and big tympani on stands. It is interesting to see that above one of these tympani there are five small discs containing Greek letters indicating the various notes. In the lower register there is a tragic chorus with a poet declaiming his verses and playing a lyre.

(35) These mosaics represent the battle between Pan and Eros, while the umpire stands beside them. The onlookers again include a woman with a young boy and girl, who, for various reasons, are thought to be the Imperial family. Behind Pan and Eros stands a table decorated with vases and palm branches, and under it are bags full of money the value of which is written outside.

(36) Painted walls. Gay and humorous mosaics with children chasing hares, cocks, peacocks, etc.

(37) leads into (38) The *Sala delle dieci ragazze* where the pavement is slightly later than the others (4th century), having replaced an earlier geometric one which had suffered from damp. The design is poor in comparison with the others, and shows ten girls in bikinis doing gymnastics, competing for the victor's crown which is being presented to one of them on the lower left-hand side of the mosaic.

(39) Another living room. Fragments of a statue (a copy of the Apollo of Praxiteles) were found here, and the base for it can be seen at the end of the apse. There was a fountain in the middle of this room in which the mosaics are much damaged. They show Orpheus surrounded by real or mythical birds and animals, sensitively portrayed, which are being charmed by the music of his lyre.

(40), corridor, leads, to (41) a big elliptical court with a painted portico on three sides. Originally there was a fountain in the centre. Mosaics with figures of animals and acanthus leaves, common in Imperial Roman times.

(42–45) lead off this room. All show cupids harvesting or fishing.

(46) A big room, the *Triclinium*, with three apses, once containing statues. The mosaics show some of the Labours of Hercules, and are designed with an unusual feeling for rhythm and dramatic composition. You can see the infuriated horses of Diomede throwing their Bistonian riders, who have been shot by Hercules, the Serpent with iridescent scales guarding the Golden Apples of the Hesperides, the Cretan Bull which Hercules first caught and then liberated, the dying Nemean Lion, the Hydra of Lerna, depicted with one female head instead of many, the three-bodied monster Geryon, the Erymanthian Boar in the great jar, the Hind of Keryneia, the pitchfork and rushing water used for cleaning out the Augaean stables, and three-headed Cerberus. In the middle is Diomede thrown from his black horse. The only labours omitted are the Stymphalian Birds and the Girdle of Hippolyte.

It is strange that Hercules himself is not shown in these scenes, though he appears in some of the apses.

Other apse mosaics represent the glorification of Hercules, symbolizing the glorification of the Emperor Herculius himself. The figures are thought to allude to the successful enterprises he, or Constantius Chlorus (then Caesar), undertook in Germany (the *genius* of the Rhine shown on its knees), in Britain (the rebel Carausius at the feet of Hercules) and Africa (the apples of the Hesperides, thought to be in Morocco). In the eastern apse five giants are trying to extract the arrows, soaked in the blood of the Centaur Nessus, which Hercules has shot at them.

The south apse shows the triumph of the Dionysiac powers over Lycurgus.

From Piazza Armerina the road (117 bis) continues southwards to Gela. Alternately, if time is very short, fork off this road after 15 kms. and proceed to Syracuse via Caltagirone, Vizzini and Palazzolo Acreide. At **Caltagirone** there are two collections containing archaeological material, the Museo Civico, in Via Abate Meli, (open 9–1 on weekdays and 10–12 on Sundays); and the Museo della Ceramica, near the church of San Francesco da Paola and the public gardens.

8 · Gela and Ragusa

FIG. 23.
Coin from Gela,
showing *quadriga*
with Nike above

To leave Piazza Armerina for Gela it is necessary to rejoin the road 117 *bis* leading southwards. After 15 kms. another road (124) turns off left to Caltagirone, Vizzini, Palazzolo Acreide and Syracuse – an alternative route for visitors who have not time to go to Gela. But anyone interested in Greek antiquities should not fail to visit Gela, for apart from its splendid new museum, it also has one of the best-preserved Greek fortifications in the Western Greek world, at Capo Soprano, on the western edge of the town. There is a pleasant small hotel, the 'Autostello A.C.I.' nearby.

GELA (Fig. 24)

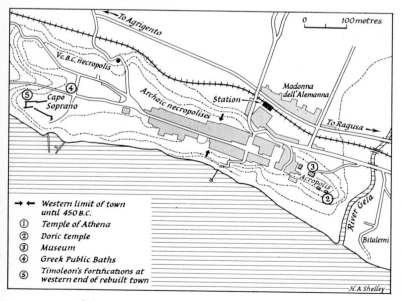

FIG. 24. Gela

Gela, built on a long low hill parallel to the coast, at the mouth of the river Gelas, was the latest of the major Dorian colonies in Sicily, founded in 688, 'in the 45th year after the foundation of Syracuse', as Thucydides wrote. He also mentioned that the colonists came from Rhodes and Crete, that they called the city after the river, and that they fortified the acropolis (the east end of the hill) and called it Lindii. The Rhodians, who mostly came from Lindos, probably formed the larger contingent of colonists, and their culture is so strongly represented that subsidiary migration from Rhodes almost surely took place from time to time. The site must have been chosen for its fertile plain, famous for wheat and for horse-breeding, and the 'fair fields of Gela', praised by Aeschylus and Virgil, seem to have soon brought wealth to the city. Relations with the Sikel population, farming on the coast and in the hinterland, must already have been tested by commercial prospectors, and there is no reason to believe that the Greeks met with any considerable resistance, for by the mid-VII century the native towns at Butera and Monte Bubbonia (perhaps the Sikel *Omphake* and *Maktorion*) and Caltagirone were already absorbing Greek customs and receiving Greek objects by trade; by the early VI century almost the whole coastal strip along the south of Sicily was in Geloan hands, and in 582 B.C. they founded Akragas.

During the VI century a temple was built on the acropolis, dedicated to Athena (Fig. 24, number 1), and decorated with the fine polychrome terra-cotta revetments which are now displayed in the museum at Syracuse. These terra-cottas are characteristic of early VI century Doric temples in Sicily and Magna Graecia, and Gela was specially renowned for their manufacture; in fact, when the Geloans built their treasury at Olympia they sent pre-fabricated painted terra-cottas to embellish it. The temple of Athena stood in a *temenos* containing a number of small shrines where offerings were made during the VII and VI centuries; these shrines, too, were decorated with terra-cotta friezes and antefixes.

In the last few years of the VI century a radical alteration was brought about in the government of Gela when a tyrant, Kleandros, seized power, and was soon afterwards (in 498) succeeded by a far abler and more ambitious man, his brother Hippocrates. This man, like Dionysius and Agathocles at a later date, loved power for its own sake; completely ruthless, and urged by his ambition to enlarge his dominions, he hired Greek and Sikel mercenaries and marched against first one place and then another, taking Naxos, Leontinoi and other towns, and capturing a prodigious quantity of booty. He was also keenly aware of the need to acquire a better harbour then could be found at Gela, where the shelving beach was suitable only for drawing up ships and quite in-adequate for docks or ship-building. So, having increased the size and strength of his army, he marched against the Syracusans, defeated them near Helorus, and approached the temple of Olympian Zeus just outside the town. At this point, however, discussions took place and, in exchange for the Syracusan colony of Camarina, Hippocrates agreed to withdraw. In the few years of his tyranny Gela grew to be the most powerful Greek city in Sicily, but Hippocrates had made one great mistake: he had tried to force Hellenization on the native peoples instead of letting its influence spread naturally through peaceful trade, and the wide-spread havoc he had wreaked led to the only concerted national move-ment the Sikels ever made – under the leadership of Ducetius. When Hippocrates was killed in one of his campaigns against the Sikels, his sons were too small to succeed him and the tyranny passed to the com-mander of his cavalry, Gelon, a direct descendant of one of the original settlers, and member of the distinguished family of the Deinomenids.

Not very much is known of the early years of Gelon's tyranny. He consolidated his position in Gela, and strengthened the bond with Akragas by marrying the daughter of the tyrant Theron with whom he later combined to win the battle of Himera over the Carthaginians in 480. At an opportune moment he supported the big landowners who had been driven out of Syracuse, and by taking that town in a moment of internal disruption, he acquired the much-coveted harbour, and then went on to destroy Megara Hyblaea, a little further north, and added its lands to the already vast area under his domination. Half the popu-lation of Gela was drafted into the new capital of Syracuse, and Gela it-self inevitably declined in importance for a few years until many of its citizens returned in 466 and it flourished once more and re-colonized Camarina. The V century was one of particular prosperity and produc-tivity, not only of terra-cottas and sculptures (witnessed by the fine and extremely sensitive horses' heads in the museum which are part of the *acroteria* of temples), but, more important still, of literature, for Gela was chosen by Asechylus as his home during the last few years of his life, and here he wrote the *Oresteia* trilogy and perhaps other works which may have been destroyed when the Carthaginians sacked the town fifty years later. He died in Gela in 456.

The whereabouts of the theatre, which must have existed in Aeschy-lus' time, is still a mystery though it was once claimed to have been identified near Capo Soprano on the western edge of the long Gela

10

ridge. If this is true a spectacular re-discovery may one day be made there: the theatre, buried by the rising sands which concealed and preserved the later Greek fortifications.

A huge number of objects, pottery (both imported and locally made), architectural fragments, including some capitals from an Ionic temple, and coins, etc., have been found in cisterns in various parts of the town, all witnessing the cultural prosperity of Gela during the V century. Another temple, now almost entirely destroyed, was built on the acropolis and dedicated to Athena; some of its elements have been incorporated in the Mother Church in Piazza Umberto I.

In 424 Gela was he seat of a famous congress, convened in an attempt to restore peace between the Siciliot cities. During the debate a notable speech was made by Hermocrates, the leading man in Syracuse, a speech reported by Thucydides, in which he urged the various Greek towns to make peace between themselves, to seek autonomy, and to resist outside interference from Greece, particularly from Athens at that time.

Before the end of the century outside interference in Sicilian matters had come in the form of the Athenian invasion, ostensibly sent to support Leontinoi and Segesta – and the story of the disastrous defeat of this invasion force at Syracuse in 413 is well known and need not be repeated. But in western Sicily the border disputes between Segesta and Selinus were still dragging on, and the Carthaginians, fearing the threat to their towns in the west of the island if Selinus were to grow too strong, landed a huge expeditionary force which proceeded to sack one Greek town after another. Among them was Gela which had received only half-hearted support from Dionysius I, the reigning tyrant of Syracuse. The walls were hurriedly rebuilt to meet the threat, but all was in vain, and the city, so distinguished and beautiful, had to be abandoned. Only after some years had passed were the inhabitants allowed to return on condition that the town was not refortified and that they paid a tribute to Carthage. Gela had, however, lost too much and it declined to such an extent that in 338 Timoleon, then tyrant of Syracuse and a man of wide vision and purpose, re-peopled it with new colonists, some of whom came from Chios.

Gela was completely laid out anew. The eastern end was terraced and houses and shops built there, while the western end of the ridge, once occupied only by the cemeteries, was redesigned as a new residential district with public buildings and streets laid out at right angles. All this new area was surrounded by walls built of masonry below and sun-dried bricks above, which enclosed the entire ridge from the old acropolis area on the east to the new fortifications at Capo Soprano on the west.

During the next years Timoleon rebuilt many of the Sikel-Greek centres in the hinterland which had been abandoned after the destructive Carthaginian campaign of 405, and offering freedom and friendship to the Sikels, he re-peopled towns such as Vassallaggi near Caltanissetta and Scornavacche near Comiso. Farms and small estates dotted the countryside, and on almost every hill around Gela traces of settlements and burial places belonging to Timoleon's time have been recovered. New money (less artistically refined than that of the VI and V centuries) was coined, and some of the sacred buildings, destroyed by the Carthaginians, were restored. Even if politically and historically Gela did not regain its former status, at least it was an ordered and peaceful town for many years, and even when Timoleon himself died the democratic and constructive example he had set continued to develop until Agathocles became the tyrant of Syracuse in 317 B.C.

At this time Gela was allied to the Carthaginians and Akragantines, and when Agathocles seized power in Syracuse the oligarchs there fled to Gela and begged for protection. Agathocles pursued them with an army of only 1,000 men, and succeeded in gaining a foothold in the town, but shortly afterwards many of his men were trapped and cut off in the streets, and the situation was only saved when Agathocles ordered his trumpeters to sound the attack from another part of the hill. Hearing the trumpets, the Geloans rushed to meet the new threat, and Agathocles managed to extricate his men, though not to take the town. Six years later he was at war with the Carthaginians, and to protect his flank he once again infiltrated soldiers into Gela and put 4,000 of the leading citizens to death and captured quantities of booty before marching on to *Ecnomus*. Here he was defeated, and once more fell back on Gela.

During his tyranny in Gela he heightened the walls of the Capo Soprano fortifications which had become partly buried in sand-dunes, added stairways and a parapet walk, and the long, buttressed spur-work, blocked some of the posterns and restored the military buildings inside.

But Gela's short renaissance was over, and an agitated and obscure period followed until the town was destroyed by the Mamertines in 282. The citizens begged assistance from Phintias the tyrant of Akragas, who transferred them to the new town which he had founded (on the site of the modern Licata), and razed the walls of Gela to the ground. Many of the buildings of that date show signs of fire and violence.

The town was still not quite wiped out, for Cicero refers to the restoration of the statues which Verres had stolen, but very shortly afterwards Strabo says that Gela was no longer inhabited. It was rebuilt in the Middle Ages.

The Capo Soprano Fortifications (Fig. 24, number 5, and Fig. 25)

Covered by sand-dunes over forty feet high until 1948, these fortifications are perhaps the most spectacular, and certainly the best preserved, Greek walls anywhere in the Western world. They have been preserved in their almost pristine state by the rising levels of the sand-dunes which necessitated the periodic raising of their height, still about seven or eight metres in places.

When, in 339, Timoleon recolonized Gela, these defences were built along the crest of a hill which dropped steeply to the sea; the level space which can now be seen outside the walls is due to recent clearing.

From the outset these massive walls were constructed in the so-called 'dual technique', in which the lower courses, designed to resist battering rams, were built in stone, and the upper courses with sun-dried bricks – a building method which was partly dictated by the necessity to economize with stone in those areas, such as Gela or Heraclea Minoa, in which it was not easily available: in fact the Capo Soprano stones were brought from several different quarries some kilometres away. It is extremely interesting to note that this same 'dual technique' was

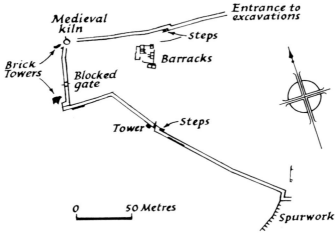

FIG. 25. Gela. The Capo Soprano fortifications

adopted by the defenders of the Heuneburg hill-fort on the Upper Danube, who rebuilt their walls in the VI century B.C. in imitation of Greek walls, interspersed with towers at short intervals; these people were in touch with the Mediterranean world through the wine trade, and were also receiving Greek black-figure ware of about 520–470 B.C.

The story of the Capo Soprano defences is as follows:

(1) After 339 B.C. the first walls were built here by Timoleon. They reached to a height of about 3 metres, and the gateway on the west was defended first by stone and later by brick towers, now hardly visible.

(2) The sand-dunes were rising steadily and by about 310 the lower 3 metres were already covered, so the wall was heightened in brick, and a battlemented parapet walk, reached by steps, was added – probably by Agathocles when he occupied Gela to resist the Carthaginians. He also built the long, buttressed spur-work whose foundations have been found to stand on 3 metres of accumulated sand.

(3) Still the sand went on rising, and the wall was again raised, but very little of this higher part still exists as it was destroyed by Phintias in 282 B.C. Just to the left of the spur-work some battlements of phase 2 can be seen, filled with brickwork of this late stage.

Some parts of the walls have been breached in antiquity and rebuilt, and some of the posterns have been bricked in. A medieval kiln stands on the site of the original stone tower in the north-west angle.

Inside the wall some military quarters were excavated, with rooms arranged around a courtyard containing wells; these barracks have now been filled in.

THE GREEK PUBLIC BATHS (Fig. 24, number 4)

Near Capo Soprano excavations have revealed the only Greek public baths so far known in Sicily; they belong to the period of Timoleon's recolonization in the late IV century B.C. There are two groups of baths (terra-cotta hip-baths with seats), one arranged in a semicircle, and the other in a ring around an area paved with terra-cotta tiles. These baths had to be filled and emptied by hand, probably by slaves, and the waste water flowed away through pipes and a stone gutter.

Originally all these baths were enclosed within a wall, but this has now disappeared, and the hot baths which formed part of the same complex (sweating baths which were later to become so popular in Roman times) were almost certainly destroyed by Phintias in 282.

THE ACROPOLIS HILL

There is little now to be seen on the Molino a Vento hill, the site of the ancient acropolis to the east of the Museum. Slight traces can be seen of two temples, both dedicated to Athena, the later of which can be identified from its one remaining Doric column belonging to the *opisthodomos*. This temple was almost surely erected to commemorate Gelon's victory at Himera in 480 B.C. The terra-cotta roof decorations from the earlier temple are in the Museum at Syracuse.

Houses and shops of Timoleon's time can be seen on the northern terraces of the hill, near the Museum.

THE MUSEUM (Fig. 24, number 3)

Opening hours. Summer, 9–1 and 3–5. Winter, 9.30–2.

This splendid new Museum is in three parts: the main display (arranged chronologically and topographically), a less important collection, similarly arranged in the basement, and a store. The basement collections are available to students on special request to the Director.

An excellent guide-book by Orlandini and Adamesteanu is available in English, and describes the collection in some detail. The following notes may, however, be of some help.

The earliest finds come from the prehistoric village which underlay the Greek buildings on the acropolis, a village of the Bronze Age Castelluccio culture which produced an extremely interesting pottery bowl containing ritual horns. These horns are not uncommon in prehistoric sites in Sicily, and they must have had some fertility significance.

Among the more interesting objects in the first cases, notice the early V century cup inscribed on the base with the name of Antiphemos, one of the founders of Gela. There are large numbers of offerings from the VII to VI century shrines near the first temple of Athena, painted and moulded antefixes from the little sacred buildings, and other offerings from the earlier phase of the town's history.

Then begins the period of Timoleon's new colony, after 339 B.C., with various finds from houses and shops which overlay the shrines destroyed in 405 by the Carthaginians. Note in the centre of the hall some fine late VI century Ionic capitals from a temple whose site is not precisely known, and behind them a stone base with part of a VI century inscription referring to one Kynaithos, evidently a famous horse-

PLATE 10. Gela. Terracotta relief of Aphrodite holding a goat. (Ashmolean Museum, Oxford)

man. In the case under the gallery there are some magnificent sculptured horses' heads from the *acroteria* of the VI to V century shrines. One of these heads is an outstanding work of art, of great sensitiveness.

The gallery contains finds from the sanctuaries in the Gela neighbourhood. Note the little terra-cotta model of an archaic shrine, and in another case a splendid painted antefix of a gorgon (early V century). In another case there is a terra-cotta *arula*, or portable altar, with relief decoration showing Herakles and a giant. Some of the finds come from the sanctuary of *Bitalemi* outside Gela, at the mouth of the river.

The North Wing. Pottery from local kilns of the VII century. The forms and designs are sometimes original and sometimes imitate imported Greek wares. Then follow finds from the Gela cemeteries, arranged chronologically from the VII century to the end of the V. The wall-cases (17, 20 and 23) contain material dating from Timoleon's recolonization until the town was destroyed in 282 B.C.

The Coin Collection. Hoards of silver coins from Gela and nearby including nearly a thousand coins of the Archaic period (all before 490 B.C.) from various Greek mints in Sicily. Another hoard of the late V century, and an important group of gold coins of late Imperial Roman times (5th century A.D.).

East Wing. Typical V century Geloan sarcophagus decorated internally with small Ionic columns. Stratigraphically arranged finds from Capo Soprano. Material from sites near Gela, including Manfria.

South Wing. Finds from the hinterland of Gela and from all over the province of Caltanissetta. Among the sites represented are *Butera* (perhaps the Sikel *Maktorion*, 20 kms. north-west of Gela) which came under Geloan rule by the VII century. Here were found four levels of superimposed tombs, some of which can still be seen on the site. One of them (just below the hill-top at Piano della Fiera) is particularly interesting for its very unusual character: it is a dolmen, complete with capstone, standing on one side of a rectangular enclosure, and one wonders whether it represents a deliberate piece of antiquarianism of the VII century, or was built perhaps by someone of non-Sicilian origin, for so far no dolmens have been definitely attested from the island. Other finds from Butera include two late VIII century carved grave slabs from the earliest tombs, the contents of tombs and of a hut of the VII century, and of IV and III century tombs.

The Early Bronze Age village of *Manfria* has produced important finds, including ritual horns and pottery, amongst which are fragments of bell-beakers.

Another site of considerable importance was at *Monte Bubbonia*, a Hellenized native hill-town surrounded by VI century walls. Finds from the VIII to V century cemetery and from a small VI century archaic shrine are preserved here.

Other indigenous centres are *Vassallaggi* near San Cataldo, *Gibil Gabib, Disueri, Monte Saraceno*, etc., and the objects recovered from many of them reflect the gradual absorption of Greek culture which spread with increasing momentum into the hinterland from Gela.

RAGUSA

Ragusa is situated on two hills, separated by ravines. The more ancient part of the town is known as Ragusa Ibla, from its early name *Hybla Heraea*, originally a Sikel settlement which later became Hellenized. Although there is now nothing of archaeological interest to see, it is worth exploring for its delightful position, surrounded by gorges whose steep sides are full of Greek-period tombs.

Ragusa is entered from the Agrigento-Gela-Syracuse road by a bridge, almost immediately after which, on the left of Via Roma, steps lead down to the *Museum*, one of the newest Sicilian museums to have been built.

Opening hours. Daily from 9.30–4. Sundays and holidays, 9.30–1. Closed on Mondays.

The main bulk of the finds come from **Camarina,** a town founded at the very beginning of the VI century by the Syracusans on the coast about 28 kms. south-west of Ragusa. Diagrams and photographs explain the various phases of its development, but since the site has so far been the object of only few excavations, we know more of its history from documentary than from archaeological evidence. Some stretches of the city wall have been found, as well as slight remains of a V century temple of Athena on the acropolis; most of the exhibits in the museum come from the cemetery of the Greek period. Note also a fine sculptured figure of a horse and rider, probably an *acroterion* from a temple, now in the Museo Nazionale in Syracuse.

The history of Camarina is one of repeated destruction and rebuilding.

Very briefly it is as follows. About 50 years after it had been founded, Camarina revolted against the Syracusans who promptly destroyed it. The site was then ceded to Hippocrates of Gela early in the V century, and he drafted in new citizens from his home town. When Gelon was the tyrant of Gela, Camarina again rebelled, and he destroyed it and transferred its people to Syracuse. In 461, however, many of its inhabitants returned from Syracuse, and Camarina was able to thrive for 60 years before it was again destroyed, this time by the Carthaginians, in 405. Soon after the mid-IV century Timoleon rebuilt it, but it was sacked in 280 by the freebooting mercenaries from Messana (the Mamertines), and again by the Romans in 258 B.C.; after this, although it apparently lingered on until the I century B.C. it was then abandoned.

Other exhibits in the museum come from the following sites:

Rito: an archaic Greek cemetery of rectangular stone-lined graves of the VI to V century, on the southern slopes of Ragusa Ibla, which has produced some fine Corinthian and Attic wares, including an Attic *kylix* (two-handled cup on a pedestal) from the school of the so-called 'griffin-bird painter', about 550 B.C.

Castiglione: a big indigenous centre, of unknown name, not far from Comiso. It seems to have first been inhabited in the VI century, and was destroyed in the early V century, probably during Hippocrates' wars against the Sikels. It was reoccupied from the IV to the mid-III century. A number of tombs of the native rock-cut type have yielded important Greek and locally made wares of the mid-VI century; these are unusual tombs in that they have a rectangular trench cut in the centre, delimiting funerary benches on three sides.

Scornavacche was founded by the Syracusans in the early VI century, at the western limits of their territory, on the long internal road which linked Syracuse with Akragas and Selinus. Destroyed by the Carthaginians in 405, it was rebuilt at the time of Timoleon on a site a few hundred yards away from its original one. It was never fortified, and was wiped out soon after 280 B.C.

It has been possible to reconstruct a IV century potter's shop and kiln. Huge jars of potter's clay stand around the big central kiln, and there are some finished pots and small objects put out on shelves.

9 · Castelluccio, Noto, Helorus, Syracuse, Palazzolo Acreide, Pantalica and Thapsos

The road from Ragusa to Syracuse passes first through Modica and then Rosolini, 7 kms. after which a secondary road forks off to the left, immediately after crossing the river Tellaro, to Castelluccio and Palazzolo Acreide.

Castelluccio, which has given its name to the most important Early Bronze Age culture in south-east Sicily, is the site of a prehistoric village and of about 200 rock-cut tombs in the steep cliffs (Cava della Signora) nearby; both the village and the tombs were excavated many years ago by Paolo Orsi. Although in the II millennium B.C. the archaeological cultures varied from one part of Sicily to another, the Castelluccio culture has been identified in the whole of the south-eastern and central part of the island.

The village, one of many of this period, stood on the top of a rocky spur flanked by deep ravines which offered a splendid natural protection. Although Orsi did not find remains of the actual huts, he not only found quantities of pottery, but he was fortunate in discovering some of the tombs still intact, their doors closed either with dry stone walling, or with stone slabs, at least two of which had been carved with spiral patterns, obviously phallic (Fig. 26). Several skeletons, accompanied with pottery and other objects, were found in each of the tombs – small rock-cut tombs with oval chambers, sometimes preceded by an antechamber, and belonging to a type which, like various other aspects of this culture, originated in the Aegean (see Plate 11).

The pottery, which is highly characteristic and little varied, is painted with criss-cross lines in dark brown on a light ground. Votive horns, also made of pottery, are not uncommon, but metal was evidently still rare, and some long bone plaques (? idols) decorated with rows of bosses and very fine incised lines, which have been found at Castelluccio and several Sicilian sites, are exactly like others from Malta, Greece and Troy, and provide an invaluable chronological link with those countries. As a result of these links, and of the similarity between the Castelluccio pottery and the Middle Helladic wares of the Greek mainland,

FIG. 26.
Castelluccio.
Carved grave slab

archaeologists have been able to date this culture to about 1800–1400 B.C., contemporary with the Capo Graziano culture in the Aeolian Islands, with the Tarxien Cemetery culture in Malta, and preceding the Thapsos culture in the Syracuse district. (See p. 195.)

Most of the finds from Castelluccio can be seen in the Syracuse Museum.

From Castelluccio the road continues northwards to Palazzolo Acreide, but Syracuse (which is the only place to stay in, and which can be used as a base for excursions to all the sites mentioned in this chapter) is more quickly reached by returning to the State road (115) and continuing through Noto.

The original site of **Noto** (Neai or Neetum) is now known as Noto Antico or Noto Vecchio, and it stands on a remote and romantic hill-top, thickly overgrown with trees and undergrowth, not many miles to the north-west of the present town, though the road is difficult to find without a detailed map. Once an important Sikel centre, it passed first into the hands of the Syracusans and then of the Romans, and is said to have been the only place which successfully resisted Verres' attempts to despoil it.

PLATE 11.
(*above*) One of the
rock-cut tombs at
Castelluccio
(*below*) One of the
sculptured figures
of Cybele at
Palazzolo Acreide
(Akrai).

The town was deserted and rebuilt on its present site after the disastrous earthquake of 1693, and no more felicitous moment in the history of local baroque architecture could have been chosen for its rebuilding: in fact it is one of the loveliest towns in Sicily. It has a newly opened museum (at the north-east end of the main street) which houses finds from the Noto district, particularly from Noto Antico, from *Helorus* (*Eloro* in Italian) on the coast a few miles away to the south-east, and from Castelluccio and Finocchito.

Helorus, a Greek town founded by Syracuse in the VII century at the mouth of the river Tellaro, is 6 kms. from Noto and is reached from the Noto–Pachino road. About 3 kms. from Noto a small road leads off to the left, and after another 3 kms. reaches a T-junction; at this point the right-hand track leads a short distance to Helorus, and the track to the left passes on its right a tall stone column standing on a rise, the so-called *Pizzuta* which for many years was thought to have been set up to mark the site of a V century battle fought in that area. This tapering column, over 30 feet high and made with carefully cut blocks of local stone, was excavated by Orsi in 1899. On the east side he found four steps leading down to an underground burial chamber sealed by a heavy stone door with an iron handle. He described his profound emotion and excitement as the door was forced open, for although he already realized that the monument could not be very early Greek work (for the stone showed signs of cementing) he at least hoped to find the burials intact. In this he was bitterly disappointed; the chamber, stuccoed in red and white, revealed only scanty traces of a wooden coffin and some funerary benches with remains of a few skeletons and some small amphorae. With one of the skeletons was a little III century bowl, and a coin of Hieron II was clutched in the hand of another, so this grandiose column was only a family tomb of the second half of the III century B.C. and it had probably already been robbed in antiquity.

Although Helorus was mentioned by various writers including Livy, Cicero and Ptolemy, very little is known of its history, and excavation has barely begun. A few stretches of walling of perhaps VI century date, some subsequent defences incorporating two rectangular and one semi-circular tower, parts of a Hellenistic Doric *stoa* and of a small theatre of the same date (now largely destroyed by river flooding) are the only extant remains, except for a few Hellenistic houses with wells or cisterns on the east side of the hill.

Possibly there was a native village on this site before it was colonized, but the pottery recovered from the tombs does not go back beyond the late VI century. Never a very large town, it evidently passed through a period of prosperity during the reign of Hieron II, but at the end of the III century it fell to the Romans under Marcellus.

A small sanctuary with quantities of votive statuettes to Demeter was found a year ago on the shore just outside the town area on the north. This sanctuary has been partly reconstructed and can be seen in Noto museum. Excavations at Helorus are shortly to be resumed.

SYRACUSE (Figs. 27 and 28)

This is one of the most beautiful and interesting towns in Sicily and the best base for visiting such sites as Thapsos, Noto, Helorus, Lentini, Megara Hyblaea, Pantalica and Palazzolo Acreide. It is well supplied with hotels, camping sites and a Youth Hostel. Information can be obtained from the *Ente Provinciale per il Turismo* in Corso

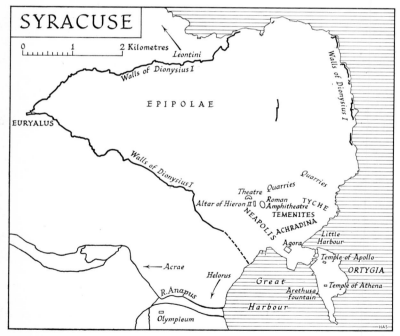

FIG. 27. Syracuse and district

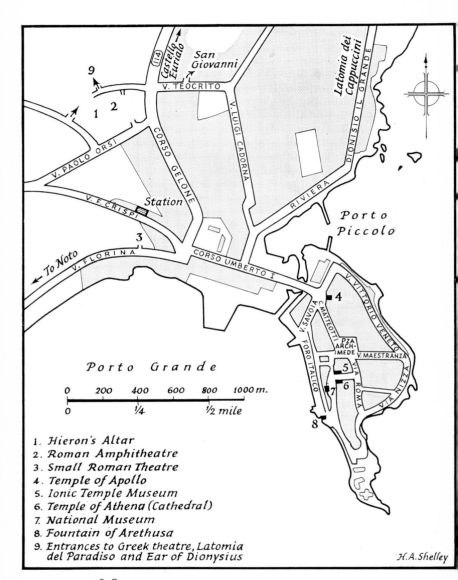

1. Hieron's Altar
2. Roman Amphitheatre
3. Small Roman Theatre
4. Temple of Apollo
5. Ionic Temple Museum
6. Temple of Athena (Cathedral)
7. National Museum
8. Fountain of Arethusa
9. Entrances to Greek theatre, Latomia
   del Paradiso and Ear of Dionysius

H.A.Shelley

FIG. 28. Syracuse

Gelone, or from the *Azienda Autonoma di Turismo* in Via della Maes-
tranza 40. Visitors without their own cars will be more conveniently
centred in the Ortygia quarter so that they can be more independent of
public transport.

The history of Syracuse is both longer and more complex than that
of any other Western Greek city; whereas other cities enjoyed periods
of prosperity, they also suffered destruction and long years of decline
or abandonment, but Syracuse, from the time of its foundation in 733
B.C., remained prosperous and potent for centuries, and one tyrant after
another, some wise and democratic, others merely ruthless and ambitious, played roles which affected not only Syracuse itself, but the
whole of Sicily.

Ortygia, a low rocky island blessed with freshwater springs and a
magnificent natural harbour to the south and another smaller one to
the north, was an ideal site for a colony – all the more so because the
fertile valley of the Anapo bordered the almost circular sweep of the
great harbour. In spite of these natural advantages it does not seem to
have been settled so early as the Thapsos peninsula a little further to
the north, for the pottery found below the foundations of the Ionic
Temple in Ortygia shows that the Sikels were not established there until
the X to the VIII century.

The colonists were Corinthians, led by Archias, and they may also
have included some Chalcidians from the toe of Italy. They must soon
have built a causeway to link the island with the mainland from which
it was separated by only a narrow stretch of water, and the urban
development spread across to Achradina. The early cemeteries of Fusco
and Giardino Spagna, whose contents are exhibited in the Museum,
were sited well outside the town, and the earliest finds from them go
back to the VIII century (see p. 172). By the mid-VI century the large
Doric temples of Apollo and Olympian Zeus were already erected, and
somewhat later the Ionic Temple was begun. Before any of these
temples were set up, the religious life of the colony had been centred
upon the early sanctuary of Athena in Ortygia.

The fact that the Ionic temple was left unfinished may have been
the result of internal changes of government: instead of the oligarchs
who had governed Syracuse until that time, a powerful tyrant, Gelon,
attracted by the potentialities for trade and ship-building offered by
the great harbour, transferred the seat of his power there from Gela,
and from that time Syracuse entered a phase of increasing strength and
wealth, destined to last many centuries. Gelon enlarged his territory by

destroying Megara Hyblaea and annexing its lands, and he also destroyed the Syracusan colony of Camarina, drafting citizens from that town and from Gela to Syracuse. His tyranny lasted from 485 to 478, only a few years, but long enough to make a considerable mark on Syracusan history. During these years Gelon turned Syracuse into a naval power, and by marrying into the family of Theron of Akragas, he strengthened his alliance with another great Greek city. Together with Theron he defeated the Carthaginians at Himera in 480 B.C. – a battle which introduced a long period of peaceful development affecting many Siciliot towns. In Syracuse itself he built ship-yards, docks, a temple to Demeter and Kore (near the later theatre), a new *agora* in Achradina, and he enriched the Temple of Apollo; more important still, he abandoned the construction of the Ionic Temple begun many years previously, and switched both man-power and wealth (much of which was derived from booty taken in the battle) to building the great Temple of Athena. He and his wife, Demarete, in whose likeness one of the most beautiful of all Syracusan coins, the so-called *Demareteion*, was struck, were buried in a sumptuous nine-towered tomb, later destroyed by the Carthaginians.

Gelon's brother *Hieron I* succeeded him in 478, the year of one of Etna's great eruptions, and reigned for twelve years, a reign noteworthy for the high cultural achievement of the poets and philosophers entertained at his court: Pindar, who described in his odes Hieron's prowess in chariot and horse-racing at Delphi, Simonides, Epicharmus, Bacchylides, and Aeschylus who is thought to have produced his *Prometheus Bound* and *Prometheus Released* on the last of his visits to Syracuse before passing his remaining years in Gela.

During these years the Etruscans were harassing the Greek towns in Italy, and Hieron defeated them in an important naval battle off the coast of Cumae. A helmet captured in the engagement and sent to Olympia as a thankoffering can now be seen in the British Museum; it bears the Greek inscription, 'Hieron, son of Deinomenes and the Syracusans, (dedicated) to Zeus Etruscan spoils won at Cumae.' This action showed that Hieron had the interests of Greeks not only in Sicily but in all Magna Graecia at heart; his other activities in the political field, however, were less distinguished, and his fame rests more on the people who surrounded him than on his own merits, for, according to Diodorus, he was 'avaricious and violent' and 'an utter stranger to sincerity and nobility of character'.

Hieron was succeeded in 466 by a far worse character, his brother

Thrasybulus, 'violent and murderous', the news of whose final over-throw was so joyfully received that two centuries later it was still an-nually celebrated at the feast of Zeus Eleutherios (the god of freedom) at the great Altar built by Hieron II. (See p. 181.)

Fortunately his short reign was no more than an episode in a long period of prosperity for the Greek towns in Sicily. After Himera the Carthaginian threat was removed for the time, and for many years the towns were ruled without tyrants and with relatively democratic princi-ples. But by 439 Syracuse began building more ships and training more cavalry, perhaps in preparation for an attack on the Chalcidians of Naxos and Leontinoi, who turned for help to their allies the Athenians. The Athenians played for time and meanwhile a congress was held in Gela in which Hermocrates of Syracuse pleaded for peace among the Greek cities in Sicily, and drew attention to the possible dangers which might result from Greek, particularly Athenian, meddling in the island's affairs; and for a time peace was restored. The Syracusans, however, soon interfered in the local politics of Leontinoi and made some clever moves which enabled them to annex both the town and its rich territory. Concerned at their growing power the Athenians decided to intervene in Sicilian affairs, taking as their pretext one of the many border disputes between their ally, Segesta, and Selinus. The wisdom of sending an expeditionary force was debated in Athens, and Thu-cydides describes how Nicias, the Athenian commander, tried to stand out against the project but was overruled by unprincipled men eager for self-glory.

In 415 B.C. a huge fleet of 134 triremes carrying both lightly and heavily armed footsoldiers, but surprisingly few horsemen, set sail from Greece and having arrived off the Sicilian coast tried to intimidate the enemy by a show of strength; sailing about (they even entered the Great Harbour) Nicias used every means to avoid the war in which he was so loath to engage. Delaying tactics proved useless and once again the Athenians sailed into the Great Harbour and pitched their camp near the temple of Olympian Zeus. Hermocrates, leader of the Syracusans, hastily built more fortifications 'all along that side of Syracuse which looks towards Epipolae,' so bringing the new quarters of Tyche and Neapolis within the defences. At that time the Athenians commanded the east end of the Epipolae ridge, and the two armies began building walls and counter-walls. The Spartans sent a force to relieve the Syra-cusans, and Nicias, still vacillating, sent to Athens to say that his ships were no longer seaworthy and that he needed reinforcements. When these arrived they were soon routed, and eventually Nicias decided to withdraw his forces, and would have done so had he not, regarding an eclipse of the moon as a bad omen, delayed departure – fatally this time, for that eclipse sealed the doom of the Athenians.

Thucydides then tells how the Syracusans blocked the mouth of the Great Harbour 'with a line of triremes broadside on, and merchant ships and other craft at anchor', and the Athenians made every attempt to escape to the open sea before they were trapped. 'They manned every ship they had, making everyone go on board who was old enough to be any use at all. Altogether they manned about 110 ships and put on board them large numbers of archers and javelin throwers', and Nicias exhorted them: 'Do not be driven back on the shore, but when ship meets ship make it your resolve not to break off the action until you have cleared the enemy's decks of their hoplites. . . .' They intended to use grappling irons, a danger which the Syracusans overcame by stretching hides over the prows and upper parts of their ships to prevent them from getting a good grip. Thucydides continues to tell the story in great detail, how the defeated Athenians tried to escape with the remains of their army but only to find all the escape routes blocked by the enemy. Forced to surrender at last, they were imprisoned in vast numbers in the stone-quarries.

Thucydides described this as 'the greatest action that we know in Hellenic history – to the victors the most brilliant of successes, to the vanquished the most calamitous of defeats. . . . Their losses were, as they say, total; army, navy, everything was destroyed, and out of many, only few returned.'

With Syracuse weakened and Athens out of the fight, the Carthaginians were soon ready to exploit the moment to grab more possessions in Sicily, and the Syracusans, now led by the tyrant Dionysius I, concluded a treaty which gained them time to prepare to meet this new danger, while the great force landed by the Carthaginians sacked one after another of the great cities in the island.

Dionysius I ruled from 405 to 367 B.C. and his ruthlessness and passion for warfare, though despicable in themselves, perhaps saved the fate of the Greeks. He built the great walls defending the Epipolae ridge and fortified its western end, building there the first of the Euryalus forts (see p. 187), and he turned Ortygia into a military base, surrounding it with a double wall interspersed with towers. Although during his reign he waged four wars against the Carthaginians, he never quite succeeded in dislodging them from the west, but he so extended his

dominions outside Sicily that under his leadership Syracuse rose to
become a strong naval power and the most formidable state in Europe.
After he had sacked the Carthaginian base at Motya, the Carthaginians
besieged Syracuse; plundered some of the outlying temples, and
destroyed the tomb of Gelon and Demarete. But the new defences
(combined with the malaria from the infested marshes near the Punic
camp, which decimated the enemy army) saved the town. As a man
Dionysius was 'cruel, vindictive, and a profane plunderer of temples',
and he showed scant respect for the distinguished writers and philosophers who visited his court – such men as Philistus (who wrote his
life), Philoxenus (who was thrown into prison for criticizing his poems),
and Plato. Such was his profound ignorance that he even tried to kill
Plato, but the latter was saved by his friends and lived to try to teach
democratic government to Dionysius' successor, his son Dionysius II.

Dionysius II who reigned from 367–343 was at first assisted by his
uncle, Dion, an idealistic and just man who invited Plato to return to
Syracuse and instruct the new tyrant in the principles of democratic
rule, but Dionysius was too autocratic and perhaps too young to profit
from his teaching and eventually showed himself so incapable of ruling
that Dion had to use force against him. Many confused years followed.
Neither Dionysius nor Dion was popular with the Syracusans who
eventually (some years after Dion had been murdered) appealed for
help from Corinth who sent Timoleon, with the result that Dionysius
was defeated and sent into exile, where, according to Plutarch, he spent
his life 'loitering about in the fish-market, or sitting in a perfumer's shop
drinking the diluted wine of the taverns, or squabbling in the streets
with common women'.

Timoleon, who ruled from 343–337, was the wisest and most beloved
of all the tyrants, and the one whose peaceful administration affected
many towns in Sicily. Only a few years ago it was thought that very
little work could be attributed to the IV century and that a period of
utter stagnation followed the destruction of many towns by the Carthaginians between 409–405, but in the last fifteen years or so the great
achievement of Timoleon has been recognized from new archaeological
excavations which have revealed the recolonization and reconstruction
carried out by him in one Greek town after another. Syracuse itself
had suffered from years of strife under Dionysius II and was described
by Plutarch who wrote, 'through solitude and want of people the
market-place was overgrown . . . with rank herbage.' Timoleon sent to
Corinth for new settlers, demolished the fortifications of the tyrants

and set up Courts of Justice in their place. He waged war not only against the Carthaginians with whom he concluded a treaty after defeating them at the battle of the Krimisos river, but also against petty tyrants in other Greek towns. He then initiated a vast plan for rebuilding and for instituting justice and democratic rule in the Greek cities, and although he died in 337 before his work was complete, the peaceful conditions he had brought about lasted for many more years, and would have lasted still longer had he not been succeeded some years later, in 317, by *Agathocles*, a brilliant and ambitious soldier, reckless, wantonly cruel and destructive, who enjoyed war for its own sake. He carried the war against the Carthaginians across the sea to Africa, and by so doing risked losing Syracuse to the enemy who, led by Hamilcar, attacked the Epipolae ridge (perhaps the Euryalus fortress which Agathocles must have modernized); but they were driven back and Hamilcar himself was captured and shamefully put to death. Agathocles was devoid of any sense of loyalty and always acted from expediency even if that entailed sacrificing his allies, and he was universally hated. Although a number of towns led by Akragas united against him and tried to war both against him and against the Carthaginians, their success was only limited, and in time Agathocles gained control of almost all of Sicily. But he made no provision for a successor, and when he died in 289 a period of confusion followed. Syracuse fell under the domination of Hiketas. The disbanded mercenaries (the so-called Mamertines) seized power in *Messana* and founded a state of plunderers who ravaged far and wide over eastern Sicily. The position of the Greeks in Sicily was precarious: when the Carthaginian fleet entered the Great Harbour in Syracuse and threatened the city, an appeal for help was sent to Pyrrhus, king of Epirus, son-in-law of Agathocles and the most powerful prince of his time, who was at that moment warring in Italy against the Romans. Pyrrhus' aim was to free all Western Greeks from all barbarians and from Carthaginians and Romans as well, and he nearly succeeded. Landing at *Tauromenion* he marched to liberate city after city, but one Carthaginian stronghold, *Lilybaeum*, proved too strong for him, and *Messana* too held out against him. For a short time he returned to Syracuse, and then withdrew from Sicily to fight the Romans on the mainland. His campaign, which promised to be so splendidly successful, had proved in the end a failure: the Carthaginians regained many towns, while the Syracusans, still free and strong, elected Hieron, one of Pyrrhus' officers, as their leader.

Hieron II reigned longer than any other tyrant (from 275–216), and under his wise leadership the town grew and flourished as never before. Hieron himself evidently combined military ability with foresight and vision in politics. Friendly at first to the Carthaginians as well as to the Romans, he defeated the Mamertines at *Longanos*, and soon afterwards the latter begged help from the Romans who, by landing in Sicily, inevitably clashed with the Carthaginians: this was the beginning of the First Punic War (264 B.C.). Hieron sided with the Carthaginians, but later wisely switched his allegiance to Rome, and remained a faithful ally for the rest of his long reign. With his problems of foreign policy so solved, he concentrated every effort to enrich and beautify his city. Great men such as Theocritus were welcomed at his court, and the greatest of these – a kinsman of his – was Archimedes who, apart from his scientific inventions, of the first importance, was commissioned by Hieron to design various types of war machines and siege engines, both for offence and defence. The Syracusan district of Neapolis was laid out anew by Hieron, who not only built the existing Greek Theatre with the porticoed building and the *Nymphaeum* above, but also the great sacrificial altar: all of these formed part of a grandiose conception for improving the amenities and cultural life of the town.

When, in 241, the First Punic War ended with the defeat of Carthage, Sicily fell under the dominion of the Romans, and although Syracuse still remained independent, Hieron provided Rome with grain and other material help for the wars against the Celtic tribes, and during the first two years or so of the Second Punic (or Hannibalian) War which broke out in 218 B.C. Then, at the age of 90, Hieron died and was succeeded by his grandson, a boy with many of the worst faults of a tyrant. At this time Hannibal was gaining victory after victory in Italy, and, impressed by this, the Syracusans sent an embassy in 215, offering their allegiance to him instead of to Rome – a serious mistake which was to have tragic consequences. The Romans, now led by Marcellus, began to assault the various towns which had opted for the Carthaginians, and amongst these was *Leontinoi*. Here Marcellus had to take a step which fired anger and hatred against his cause, for although he gave orders to stop the plundering soon after the town had fallen, Roman law required that 2,000 deserters who had been rounded up should be scourged and beheaded, and in Syracuse, where the pro-Carthage and pro-Rome factions were fairly evenly distributed, the balance was tipped in favour of Carthage.

Archimedes was still very active, preparing ingenious devices for defending the town: iron grabs which caught up the Roman soldiers as

they approached the walls and lifted them high in the air, pulleys for
hoisting huge stones or lumps of lead which were dropped on the
enemy ships, and other cunning contrivances. The Carthaginians came
to the relief of Syracuse but were unable to dislodge the Romans from
the positions they had won, and when summer drew on, malaria broke
out in their camp near the marshes: the leaders of both armies died, and
Syracusan courage was undermined. Eventually traitors opened one of
the gates into Ortygia and the town fell. This time Marcellus behaved
with commendable restraint, and it was through no fault of his that the
great Archimedes was accidentally killed by his soldiers. We are told by
Plutarch that when he realized that the lovely city, until then so prosperous and democratic, had to fall, 'he wept much'.

Soon after this Sicily became a single Roman province governed by a
praetor. Many towns dwindled in size and importance, amongst them
Syracuse. The small farms were now thrown into huge ranches (like
the *latifundia* which are only now being broken up again), worked by
disbanded soldiers and mercenaries of very mixed origin. Twice the
slaves revolted against the conditions imposed upon them, but the
Roman armies needed Sicilian meat and corn, and the harsh conditions
continued. The First Slave War, centred on Enna and Taormina, broke
out in 134 B.C. and lasted two years before the rebellion was put down
by Rupilius; the Second lasted from 102 to 99 B.C. Twenty-five years
later the miseries of the Sicilians were increased when Verres was made
praetor, and robbed one town after another of its works of art to adorn
his own villas, while at the same time imposing insupportably high taxes
and levies. These events are reported in the *Verrine Orations* of Cicero
who, leading the accusations against Verres, had personally to visit
towns all over the island.

In the civil war between Octavian and Sextus Pompeius, Sicily played
no great part, though for a time it was the centre of the struggle. By the
time that Octavian had been made Augustus, the island was in a wretched
state, and he drafted colonists to Syracuse, Tyndaris and other towns,
so that these enjoyed a new prosperity, at least for a century or two, but,
generally speaking, the Roman period in Sicily was far from glorious.
Some rich villas, including that at Piazza Armerina, some public buildings such as the amphitheatre and the small theatre (known as the
'Ginnasio Romano') at Syracuse, the so-called Basilica at Tyndaris, and
other buildings at Catania, Taormina, Termini Imerese and elsewhere,
reflect Roman activity. Archaeological research will one day lead to
much greater knowledge in this field.

In Early Christian times Syracuse, like Akrai, was an important religious centre, and the extensive catacombs bear witness to the number of the faithful. But the 3rd century A.D. had already seen the first of the barbarian raids on the south, and more were to follow. The Roman Empire was disintegrating and the Byzantine period, beginning in the 5th century, is marked by a strange phenomenon: fearful for their lives, the people fled to the interior, to sites such as Pantalica, which their Bronze Age forbears had occupied 2,000 years before when, in their turn, they had fled from the coast. In many of these upland sites the miserable rock-shelters and little rock-cut chapels are found side by side with the neatly cut tombs of earlier times – a strange and sad sight indeed when one remembers the glory of Syracuse, Akragas and Selinus a thousand years before.

THE ISLAND OF ORTYGIA

The National Museum (Fig. 28, number 7, and Figs. 29 and 30).
Opening hours. In summer, daily 9–1 and 3–6. Closed Sundays and holidays, mornings only. *In winter*, 9.30–4. Sundays and holidays, mornings only. Closed all day on Easter Day, May 1st, June 2nd, August 15th, Christmas and New Year's Day.

This is an extremely rich collection of archaeological material, much of which is derived from the excavations, made chiefly in eastern Sicily, by Paolo Orsi. The first floor contains all the prehistoric material and the smaller Greek and Roman finds; the ground floor is dedicated to heavy stone objects such as sculptures, sarcophagi, large pottery vessels, stone and terra-cotta elements from temples, etc.

FIRST FLOOR

I Palaeolithic and Mesolithic.
II Neolithic cultures of the IV millennium in the Syracuse district, with impressed and painted pottery belonging to cultures which originated in the Eastern Mediterranean. These are the coastal villages (particularly common in this area) which were surrounded by rock-cut ditches, at Stentinello, Matrensa, Megara Hyblaea and Ognina. Obsidian implements imported from the Aeolian Islands.
III Finds from Neolithic tombs and caves in south-east Sicily, and from the villages on the slopes of Etna. Flint implements from the Neolithic and Early Bronze Age flint-working sites.

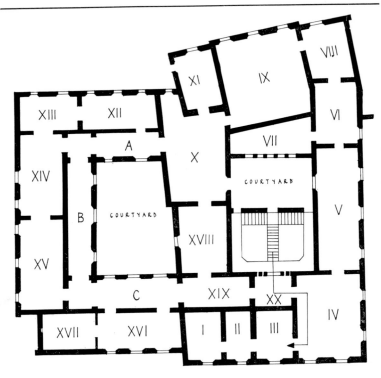

FIG. 29. Syracuse. The *Museo Nazionale*. First floor

IV Late Neolithic and Early Bronze Age (later III to early II
millennium): finds from Serraferlicchio, Sant'Ippolito,
Monte Tabuto and Castelluccio (see p. 155). Note the
models of Castelluccio rock-cut tombs, the portal stones
carved with fertility symbols, the bossed bone plaques, etc.
Cultural influences were now reaching Sicily from the
Eastern Mediterranean.

V The Bronze Age sites of the Thapsos culture (see p. 195), at
Thapsos, Plemmyrion, Matrensa, etc. The inhabitants of
these villages were trading with the Mycenaean world, and
imported pottery, beads, etc. of the XIV and XIII centuries
can be seen. Driven out by invaders from the Italian main-

land in about 1270 B.C. these people fled to the hills, and their culture continued to evolve in big centres such as Pantalica (see p. 192), Cassibile, etc. during the XIII to IX centuries.

VI Objects from the cemetery at Monte Dessueri (or Disueri) near Gela (XI–IX century) and hoards of bronze weapons, etc. from Mendolito (a Sikel town near Adrano from which an important inscription in the Sikel language has recently been found), Mulino della Badia, Giarratana, San Cataldo, etc. dating from the IX and VIII centuries.

VII The Bronze and Iron Age cultures in the Agrigento district and in central and West Sicily. XIII–VI century. Finds from Sant'Angelo Muxaro (see p. 129).

VIII The native cultures in East Sicily at the time of the foundation of the Greek colonies in the mid-VIII to mid-VI centuries B.C. Finds from the cemetery at Finocchito and from tombs at Modica. Greek influences are by now apparent and some of the native pottery imitates Geometric Greek wares. Imported Proto-Corinthian vases of the late VIII to early VII century.

(Other pre-Greek material can be seen in Room XI.)

IX Sicily at the time of the Greeks. Finds, arranged topographically, from the Hellenized Sikel sites at Monte Casale, Monte San Mauro, etc. and from the Greek towns of *Akrai* (Palazzolo Acreide, see p. 188), *Leontinoi* (Lentini, see p. 200), *Akragas* (Agrigento, see p. 107), etc. Most of this material belongs to the VII to IV century. The Greek coins of this period can be seen by applying to the custodian.

X Finds from the Sikel and Greek sites of Monte San Basilio, Serra Orlando (Morgantina, see p. 133), etc. Votive terracottas and other objects from the Etna district. Grave goods from Modica, Ragusa, etc. and native and Greek objects from tombs at Licodia Euboea.

XI The Etna district. Finds from Malpasso (X–VIII century), Calcarella (IX century, Realmese (VIII–VII century; see p. 132) and Valle Coniglio (VI–V century). All these are cemeteries in the Calascibetta district.

Corridor E. Finds from Syracuse and neighbourhood including votive objects from sanctuaries at Scala Greca and Belvedere. Mostly VIII–IV century.

XII–XIII The Fusco and Giardino Spagna cemeteries in Syracuse. The earlier cemetery is that of Fusco and the tomb groups are arranged chronologically from the VIII to the VI century. A variety of imported wares can be seen, including Proto-Corinthian, Geometric and orientalizing Corinthian, Ionian, Rhodian and Etruscan, and after about 570 B.C. Attic wares begin to appear and black-figure and red-figure vases are well represented. The Giardino Spagna cemetery is slightly later, and began in the VII century when the pottery included some of the orientalizing style, followed by black-figure and red-figure vases. (see Plate 12.)

XIV–XV Finds from Orsi's excavations in the Greek cemeteries at Gela, chronologically arranged from the VII to the V century B.C.
Corridor B. Megara Hyblaea (see p. 199). Imported and local pottery and other finds chronologically arranged from the VII century until the destruction of the town in 483 B.C.
Corridor C. Pottery made at Centuripe in the IV to the I century B.C. This rather 'baroque' pottery is peculiar to Centuripe and quite unlike anything else.

XVI More Centuripe ware and finds from the cemeteries at Camarina.

XVII Closed to the public.

XVIII Christian and Byzantine period antiquities from East Sicily.

XIX Finds from a sanctuary at Akrai, etc.

XX Pottery, etc. from the prehistoric caves of Conzo, Chiusazza and Palombara in the Syracuse district.

GROUND FLOOR

I Archaic architectural fragments from Syracuse and south-east Sicily. VI–V century.

II Epigraphic collection with Sikel, Greek and Roman inscriptions.

III Fragments of Hellenistic period architecture (III–II century B.C.) from Syracuse and south-east Sicily.

IV Architectural terra-cottas from the VI century Temple of Athena on the acropolis at Gela, and sculptured fragments from other buildings there.

V Architectural fragments of Hellenistic and Roman date, including caryatids from the scene building of the Greek

PLATE 12. Detail of a painted *krater* from the Giardino Spagna cemetery at Syracuse

Theatre at Syracuse and part of a telamon, probably from Hieron II's Altar. Inscriptions from Buscemi, etc.

VI Greek (VII–V century). Hellenistic and Roman sarcophagi, urns, etc. from various cemeteries.

VII Archaic architectural fragments from Syracuse. Reconstruction of elements of the V century Temple of Athena, including the marble cornice with lion-head spouts and parts of the terra-cotta frieze from the preceding temple (the Athenaion) of the mid-VI century and terra-cotta and stone friezes, altars, etc. from small buildings near the Athenaion and from the earliest sanctuary on the site. Parts of the frieze from the Temple of Apollo, etc. Archaic head from the sanctuary near Fonte Ciane. Three standing male figures from Megara Hyblaea (mid-VI century), Lentini and Syracuse (early V century), gorgon's head from a temple at Gela, *acroterion* in the form of a horseman from a temple at Camarina, etc.

VIII Parts of the friezes of the Athenaion and the temple of Apollo.

IX Marble statue of Venus (a Roman copy of a Hellenistic original). Small statuette of Herakles of the school of Lysippos, about 300 B.C.

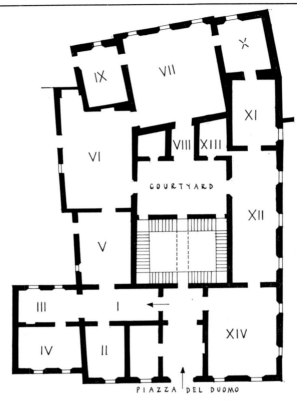

FIG. 30. Syracuse. The *Museo Nazionale*. Ground floor

   X Archaic sculpture of VII–VI century from Eastern Sicily
including a strange and interesting figure of a seated goddess
suckling twin babies from Megara Hyblaea (mid-VI century); a fine torso (early V century), and seated terra-cotta
goddess (*c.* 530–520 B.C.), both from Grammichele.

  XI Greek sculpture and Roman copies, carvings from votive
niches at Syracuse, etc., mostly V–IV century.

 XII Hellenistic and Roman sculpture from various sites. Large
head of Zeus from the amphitheatre. Statuettes of muses
from the Nymphaeum, etc. Roman mosaic pavements from
the town, etc.

XIII Hellenistic and Roman portrait busts from Sicily and North Africa.

XIV Christian and Byzantine period. Fine marble sarcophagus, probably mid-4th century A.D., decorated with biblical scenes, from the catacombs of San Giovanni. Fragments of tombs, inscriptions, etc.

At foot of staircase. Hellenistic and Roman baths, large grain jars, etc. The walls of the staircase are lined with inscriptions from catacombs.

The Coin Collection is reached from another staircase, and application must be made to one of the custodians. It is a rich collection containing coins not only from Sicily but also Magna Graecia. Among the coins from Syracuse are some going back to the time of the landed aristocracy of the VII century and commemorative issues struck after the victories at Himera in 480, and Cumae in 474 B.C. Some of the great designers such as Sosion, Euainetos and Cimon, all of whom designed Syracusan coins, are well represented.

The Ionic Temple Antiquarium (Fig. 28, number 5) is housed in two ground-floor rooms in the Palazzo del Municipio on the other side of the piazza, and the key can be obtained from the custodian at the entrance to the museum. Here are the remains of a now destroyed Ionic Temple built in about 530 B.C. – the second of the large temples of Athena, perhaps abandoned before its completion when Gelon began the present Temple of Athena (now the Cathedral) in 480, after the battle of Himera.

Much of the plan of this temple has been recovered from trenches left by stone-robbers, and from these it can be inferred that the building had 6 frontal and 14 side columns, and a 3-stepped *stereobate;* the internal divisions of the *cella* may never have been constructed. The column flutings were only roughed out, and the lower drums left smooth, perhaps with the intention of decorating them with sculptures. Nothing remains of the entablature, but the huge volutes and other elements of the capitals suggest a reconstruction closely resembling other Ionic temples, such as the Temple of Artemis at Ephesus, the Heraion of Polycrates in Samos (*c.* 525 B.C.) and others at Miletus, Sardis, Delphi, etc. This is one of the few Ionic temples in the Western Greek world to produce more than only isolated architectural elements, and it is unusually important for this reason.

The first temple to Athena, built nearby in the mid-VI century, was probably a simple megaron building with a large altar in front, and the Ionic temple, with its altar to the east, replaced it in the second half of the VI century (Corinthian, Attic and Ionian wares of 575–525 B.C. were found immediately below the foundations), but was evidently still incomplete when Gelon began to use some of its stones to build his new temple of Athena alongside in about 480 B.C.

The temples to Apollo and Olympian Zeus are thought to be some years earlier than the Ionic temple, but their exact chronological relationship is still unsure.

The Temple of Athena (Fig. 28, number 6, and Plate 13) is now incorporated in the Cathedral, and for this reason, like the Temple of Concord at Agrigento which was also adapted for use as a church, it has been spared the depredations suffered by most other temples. A great many of its columns still stand and its plan with its *cella*, *pronaos* and *opisthodomos* surrounded with 6 by 14 columns can easily be identified; the spaces between the outer colonnade have been walled in, and the *cella* wall pierced to form arcades dividing the nave from the aisles. (See Fig. 31.)

When Cicero was investigating the vandalism and robberies committed by the Roman praetor Verres in the I century B.C. he had cause to lament the many precious things (paintings of Agathocles' battles against the Carthaginians, 27 paintings including portraits of the Syracusan tyrants, ivory and gold decorations from the great doors, etc.) all stripped from the temple by Verres, 'a man whose birth, education, and mental and physical qualities suggest that he is better fitted to carry statues than to carry them off'.

The Temple of Apollo (Figs. 28 and 32). Although this has suffered from having been incorporated in a variety of subsequent buildings (in fact the door of a Norman church can be seen rather high up in the wall of the *cella*), its remains are important from an architectural point of view, for this is thought to have been the earliest of the great Doric temples in Sicily, set up, according to Dinsmoor, in about 565 B.C., a few years before the temple of Olympian Zeus, which it closely resembles in plan. Originally it had 6 frontal and 17 side columns, but today only two remain of the colonnade, and fragments of the front and side columns on the south, where remains of the *cella* wall can also be seen. On the west the *stereobate* has been rebuilt from its original dimensions, and its top step on the east bears a dedicatory inscription to Apollo by

PLATE 13. Syracuse. Inside the Cathedral. The Temple of Athena

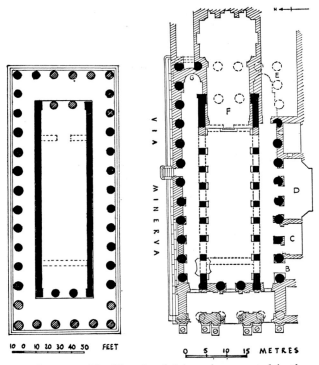

FIG. 31. Syracuse. The Temple of Athena incorporated in the present Cathedral

Cleomenes (or Cleomedes), perhaps one of the leading Syracusans of that time. Epicles was the architect. Some early writers refer to this temple as being dedicated to Artemis, and this may be explained by the fact that the cults of Artemis and Apollo are sometimes associated.

Like those of the temple of Olympian Zeus, the columns have shallow flutings and are monolithic, unlike the later temples in which the columns were built with superimposed drums. Two tall narrow triglyphs have been recovered, but none of the metopes. If the triglyphs were set only above the columns, the metopes may have been oblong like those from other early buildings at Delphi, and Dinsmoor was of the opinion that oblong metopes were a characteristic of Syracusan temple architecture; but if the triglyphs were more closely spaced, the metopes must have been tall and narrow.

The cornice was decorated with polychrome terra-cottas which can be seen in the Museum (Rooms VII and VIII on the ground floor).

The Fountain of Arethusa (Fig. 28, number 8) is one of several fresh-water springs which break out close together on the island of Ortygia, or in the sea just off its coast, and although it has been enclosed by a high wall and 'landscape-gardened' in the last centuries, it could still be described in Cicero's words as 'an incredibly large spring, teeming with fish, and so placed that it would be swamped by the sea waves but for the protection of a massive stone wall'. There are several versions of the legend attached to this spring, the earliest of them going back at least to the VI century B.C. The nymph Arethusa fled from her lover Alpheus and was changed into a spring by Artemis while her lover was changed into a river. Strabo said that the river Alpheus, which is in the Peloponnese, flowed underground until it reached Syracuse, and that a cup which had been thrown into it at Olympia was duly found at Syracuse. He also referred to the popular belief that when oxen were sacrificed at Olympia, their blood discoloured the spring in Ortygia. Pausanias, too, has his version; when Archias the Corinthian consulted the oracle at Delphi before he founded Syracuse, the words of the oracle described the site of his colony:

'An isle, Ortygia, lies on the misty ocean
Over against Trinacria, where the mouth of Alpheus
Bubbles mingling with the springs of broad Arethusa.'

(Trinacria was the early name for Sicily. The head of Arethusa appears on many of the ancient coins of Syracuse.)

THE MAINLAND

The small Roman Theatre (Fig. 28, number 3), inaccurately called the Roman Gymnasium, stands beside the road to Noto, a short distance from the Station; it has not yet been excavated but is thought to have been built in the 1st century A.D. The lower part of the *cavea* can still be seen in a rectangular enclosure originally surrounded on three sides by a portico entered from the east. Behind the stage there is a small marble shrine on a high podium, little of which now remains. A sculptured figure of the Flavian period has been found here. The need for this theatre would have been felt in the Roman period when the large Greek theatre was adapted for gladiatorial combats.

The Temple of Olympian Zeus (the Olympieion or Olympieum) stands on a rise outside the town, to the south of the river Ciane. To reach it take the Noto road (State road 115) for a short distance, and turn right immediately opposite a turning to Arenella.

Like the Temple of Apollo, this is a very early building dating from the mid-VI century. Only the stylobate and two of the columns now stand, but originally the temple shared many features with the Temple of Apollo: the long narrow *cella* with a double colonnade in front, and closely set monolithic columns (Fig. 32).

When Hippocrates of Gela threatened Syracuse in 491, he pitched his camp in this area, and according to Diodorus Siculus he arrived at this temple just when the priest and other Syracusans were in the process of removing the gold dedicatory offerings and the robe of the statue of Zeus which was also made with gold. 'And after sternly rebuking them as despoilers of the temple, he ordered them to return to the city, but he himself did not touch the dedications since he was intent on gaining a good name.'

The rest of the important monuments, with the exception of the Euryalus Fort (see p. 187), are all within a short walking distance of one another on the northern edge of the town. Visiting hours are at present as follows: mornings 9–1, and afternoons according to season. May–August inclusive, 4–7.30; September, 3.30–7; winter, about 2–5.

The Roman Amphitheatre (Fig. 28, number 2), one of the largest amphitheatres in existence, was built in the 3rd century A.D. and was not, therefore, the scene of the gladiatorial combats mentioned by Tacitus. Almost covered by soil and vegetation until the middle of the last century, the remains of the monument are still substantial even though it has been extensively robbed for building stone on the south side where, in the absence of live rock, the seats were built artificially. The elliptical arena was entered from the two ends of its long axis, with its main entrance on the south leading in from a large enclosed area, perhaps used for keeping the animals and for manoeuvring wheeled vehicles.

Some of the rounded marble blocks which topped the high parapet around the arena are still in place, inscribed with the names of the owners of the seats behind, and under these seats there runs a vaulted corridor with doors for the gladiators and wild beasts entering or leaving the arena. A curious and little-understood feature is the water-tank in the arena; whether this was merely decorative or had some functional

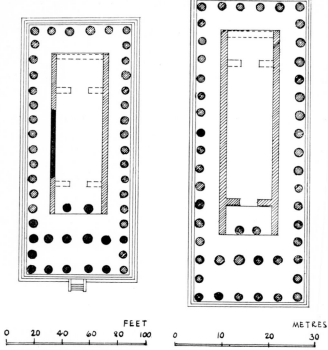

FIG. 32. Syracuse. The Temple of Apollo (*left*) and Temple of
Olympian Zeus (after Dinsmoor)

use is unknown, but certainly it was too small for any kind of aquatic
display.

Hieron II's Altar (Fig. 28, number 1). When Hieron II was reigning
in Syracuse he carried out an extensive building programme in this area,
and this huge altar, over 200 yards long, was erected between 241 and
215 B.C. at about the same time as the existing Greek theatre and the
Nymphaeum and porticoed terrace above. The whole base of this altar was
cut out of the live rock, and has not consequently suffered the despolia-
tions which have literally effaced one of the most interesting monuments
in the western Greek world, built for the sacrifice of animals at the
annual feast of Zeus Eleutherios. There is little to see now, but originally
the altar had entrances at either end, approached by ramps up which
were driven the animals destined to be slaughtered (Diodorus states that

450 oxen were sacrificed); of the statues which once flanked these entrances, only the feet of one remain on the northern end, but a figure of
Atlas, now in the Museum, may have been another. The exact appear-
ance of the altar's superstructure can only be tentatively surmised, but
it probably stood about 40 feet high and was crowned by a cornice with
lion-head spouts to carry rainwater from the roof.

The Greek Theatre (Fig. 33 and Plate 14). According to some scholars
this beautiful and impressive theatre is a palimpsest of many building
phases, but it seems more likely that the earlier theatre (of Timoleon's
time, if not earlier) must have been largely cut away when a larger
theatre was required, and the huge *cavea* of the existing structure was
made. This is the convincing theory put forward by Bulle who re-
interpreted Rizzo's basic study.

The original slope of the ground surface of the hillside can be esti-
mated from the two large rocky outcrops (C) which flank the stage, and
it can be seen at once from these that it would have been perfectly
possible for any smaller and earlier theatre, the theatre in which the
plays of Aeschylus, Epicharmus and other great dramatists were first
produced, to have been completely erased when the far more ambitious
theatre was cut out of the hillside in the III century B.C. – a work which
necessitated the quarrying of hundreds of tons of stone.

The entire *cavea* above the *diazoma* is homogeneous both in its slope
and its details, and the mouldings of the stone seats (with the exception
of those reworked in Roman times) are characteristic of the Hellenistic
period. The stage structure, too, is comparable to the other Hellenistic
theatres in Sicily, at Segesta and Tyndaris. It is sad that the upper tiers
of seats, which were not cut out of the live rock as were the lower tiers,
were pillaged for building stones during the 16th century.

A valuable clue to the more exact date of the theatre is provided by
the bold inscriptions which can be seen incised in the wall of the *diazoma*,
opposite each section of the *cavea*; these are dedicatory inscriptions to
Zeus Olympios, King Hieron, his wife Queen Philistis, and Queen
Nereis (the wife of Hieron's son Gelon, and daughter of Pyrrhus). The
missing inscription on the last section is thought to have been dedicated
to Gelon, and since he and Nereis were not married until 238 B.C. the
theatre must date from after that year.

The confusion of steps, foundations and trenches in the stage area is
not fully understood in detail, but it is clear that the orchestra was
originally approached from passages leading in from either side, and that

the front of the stage ran between the northern edges of the natural rock masses shown on the plan. The foundations of the scene structure, and the various architectural elements recovered, suggest that this may have been several storeys high and probably decorated with half-columns, caryatids, and statues of the royal family. In front was the *logeion* or platform, about 8 feet from the ground, and flanked by projecting wings with arched doorways leading to the orchestra. This scene building was evidently replaced by a pillared *proskenion* during the alterations carried out at the time of Augustus.

In front of the original stage there was possibly a small movable

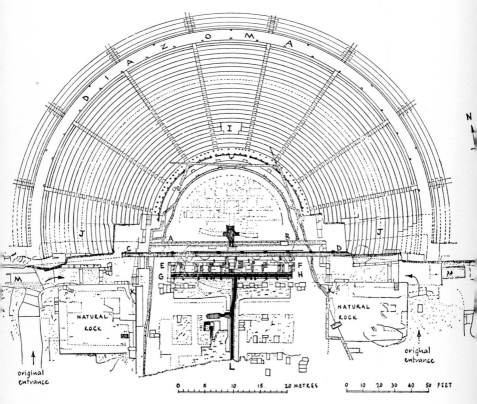

FIG. 33. Syracuse. The Greek Theatre

wooden stage (E–F) for burlesques presented by comic actors or *phlyakes*, but this interpretation is open to doubt as that type of comedy had already passed out of fashion in most parts of the Greek world by the time that this theatre was built.

During the Flavian period the Romans made basic alterations to the theatre, re-cutting the lower twelve tiers of seats, to enlarge the orchestra for use as an arena for gladiatorial combats, bringing forward the stage and cutting off the entrance passages (and so necessitating the cutting of the tunnels (J) leading in from each side), erecting a new scene building faced with coloured marble, cutting seats of honour for privileged guests (I), etc. The long trenches A–B and C–D, and the drainage channel leading southwards from the stage, belong to the Roman period.

The building was again altered in the 4th century A.D. when provision was made for flooding the arena for aquatic displays. Some rock-cut tracks in the original side passages (which were roughly enlarged) may have been made for the drawing to and fro of movable scenery.

To the west of the theatre there is a sacred enclosure which has been identified as the **Sanctuary of Apollo Temenites,** mentioned by early writers and evidently revered from the late VII century for many centuries. The earliest altar was associated with Proto-Corinthian ware; at the time of the Athenian war against Syracuse Thucydides reports a minor engagement during which some of the garrison 'fled inside the wall round the precinct of Apollo Temenites'; between the time of Timoleon and Hieron II six more altars were set up.

Nearby are the slight remains of the **Linear Theatre,** so called because its seats are arranged in a straight stairway of 17 steps cut into the live rock and divided into three sections. This may have preceded the big Hellenistic theatre, but its date is so far obscure.

The hillside above the theatre was included within the area of Hieron II's landscape gardening. A long, narrow terrace was cut into the slope, and a porticoed building set up which could provide shelter for the spectators during sudden downpours. This portico was backed by the sheer face of the cliff into which was cut an artificial grotto containing a pool fed by water from a cascade contrived from one of the town aqueducts. Framing this grotto there was once an architectural frieze with metopes and triglyphs. This delightful place was sacred to the Muses

PLATE 14
Syracuse
(*above*) The Greek
Theatre (*below*) The
Euryalus Fort,
showing some of the
towers and part of
the inner defensive
ditch with entrances
to underground
passages

(a Mouseion or Nymphaeum): several II century B.C. statues, now in
the Museum, came from here, and evidently formed part of a group of
nine muses led by Apollo.

The 'Latomie' or Quarries. The cutting of these must have started
very early in the life of the colony, and in the VI century B.C. Xenophanes of Colophon wrote of the fossil fish found in the limestone
there.

Apart from their primary function as quarries for building stone, they
also served as prisons – natural enclosures provided with water, and
perhaps some shade – where, at least during the Athenian War, the
Syracusans were able to concentrate the 7,000 or so prisoners who had
fallen into their hands. Thucydides described their sufferings in some
detail: 'There were many of them crowded together in a narrow pit
where, since there was no roof over their heads, they suffered first
from the heat of the sun and the closeness of the air, and then in con-
trast came on the cold autumnal nights, and the change of temperature
brought disease among them. . . . During eight months the daily
allowance for each man was half a pint of water and a pint of corn.'
Many must have died, and some were sold as slaves. This pitiful story
has led to much adverse criticisms of the Syracusans, but it is difficult
to know where else in this rocky land they could have imprisoned their
captives.

The 'Ear of Dionysius', entered from the Latomia del Paradiso, is a
curved artificial cavern about 200 feet long and 70 feet high, the upper
part of which follows the course of a pre-existing aqueduct tunnelled
into the rock. The cavern is carefully cut and has remarkable acoustic
properties, but as no early writers referred to its date or purpose, these
remain a mystery. A recess cut in the wall inside has been compared
in shape to the Sibyl's cave at Cumae, belonging to the VI century B.C.

Catacombs. There are several large complexes of catacombs of the
Early Christian period. Those most easily visited are on the east side of
the road to Catania (State road 114), the first turning to the left off
Viale Teocrito. They are called the catacombs of San Giovanni and are
close to the Crypt of Saint Marcian where St. Paul is reputed to have
preached.

The Euryalus Fort (Fig. 34 and Plate 14), one of the most remarkable complexes of Greek fortifications in existence, lies about 7 kms. further west and is reached from the road to Belvedere; the bus passes within 200 metres of it, and it is always open to visitors.

The fort (Castello Eurialo) was built at the western end of the long Epipolae ridge which extends westwards for several miles from Syracuse: to hold this fort was vitally important for the defence of the town. Livy says that the hill 'commands the road leading to the country and to the interior of the island, and is very conveniently placed for receiving supplies'.

Dionysius I enclosed the ridge with a strong wall provided with posterns and towers at intervals, and the earliest phase of the fort itself (built to command and protect the western gateway into the town area, which stands just below to the north) must also have originated in his time; but like all fortresses, it was continually rehandled to meet the exigencies of developing methods of warfare.

This fort is a complex mostly built between the V and late III centuries B.C. and, for lack of excavation, its various structural phases have been deduced more from a typological than a stratigraphical basis.

The complex is approached from the west, the most vulnerable side, protected by three rock-cut ditches: (A), near the custodian's house and the antiquarium; (B), and (D); the first two being unfinished. At the western limit of the fortress stands a massive wall with five huge buttressed towers built for firing heavy ballistas. Behind these towers is an inner keep (G) now separated from its eastern part (K) by a later wall – perhaps, like the small partitions on the south, of Byzantine date. The enclosure K (once provided with a tower at its eastern end where it is linked with the circuit of the town wall) contains several large water cisterns. Below, to the north, is the strongly defended 'pincer'-type gateway, which, like the fortress itself, was reconstructed and redesigned at various dates.

Space does not permit a long discussion of this complex, but F. E. Winter, in a closely reasoned article, has recently suggested the following hypothetical sequence:

(1) Dionysius I. Eastern portions of the north and south wall of the fort are all that remain: the west end has been rebuilt, and a possible natural cleft with a wall along its east side has been re-cut as Ditch D.

(2) Ditch D cut, and the pointed bastion (E) built. A gallery cut from the inner edge of the ditch to another ditch south of (G). These

modifications are unlikely to be earlier than the late IV century, and may have been the work of Agathocles.

(3) The main tower complex was probably built by Agathocles or by Pyrrhus. By their time heavy ballistas were in regular use.

(4) The two other ditches were added, to keep siege-engines and battering rams at a distance, and underground galleries and stairways made or begun. (A treatise on defensive methods written by Philo of Byzantium in the III century B.C. advocated the digging of ditches and underground passages to enable the defenders to clear out by night the material thrown into the ditches by the enemy.) The outwork (C) was never finished; carried across ditch D by a bridge (F), it was joined to the tower complex on the south, and the same design was probably intended for linking the outwork to the towers on the north. Various modifications were made to the tower complex itself. All this work was probably carried out in the III century B.C. – particularly after Hieron II had died and his successor had broken the alliance with Rome. Then Archimedes, his military adviser, must have been called upon to design defences to resist the Roman threat by Marcellus – defences which were hastily begun, but not completed by the time the town fell.

The Epipolae Gateway. The 'pincer'-type gateway (M) originally had three arches (later modified to one or two), and was protected by external cross walls. Some of these modifications are thought to have been carried out by Timoleon, and others almost certainly by Agathocles. A fragmentary inscription found here bears the Greek word for King – a title which Agathocles was the first to adopt.

Later alterations may have been made by Pyrrhus, and the long gallery (L) linking the area inside the gate with the fortress may belong to the time of Archimedes.

PALAZZOLO ACREIDE (*Akrai*)

Standing at a height of over 2,000 feet on a hill dominating a vast extent of rolling and once wooded countryside, Akrai was chosen for a military outpost of Syracuse seventy years after the parent city had been founded, i.e. in 664. To judge from the contents of its VI century tombs it seems quickly to have become a flourishing town, even if it was never a place of great importance. Of the visible remains particular mention must be made of its theatre, a little senate-house (*bouleuterion*), and some 'latomie' (or stone-quarries) the walls of which, full of recesses for

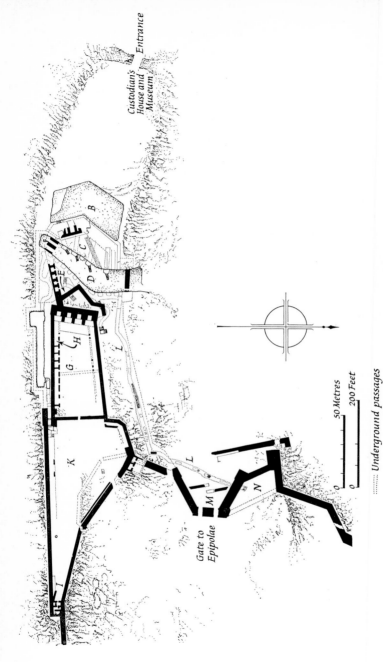

FIG. 34. The Euryalus Fort, outside Syracuse

Custodian's
House and
Museum

Entrance

B

C

E

D

G

H

L

I

K

L

M

N

Gate to
Epipolae

50 Metres

200 Feet

0

0

commemorative reliefs of the Greek period, were subsequently riddled
with Early Christian catacombs. Perhaps still more impressive is a group
of life-size figures (the so-called 'Santoni') cut in the rocky sides of a
small valley, and representing a deity, Cybele, whose cult must have
been imported into Sicily by the Greeks. Remains of a VI century
temple have been identified on the top of the hill, but so far excavation
at Akrai has barely begun.

Probably the moment of Akrai's greatest affluence was at the time
of Hieron II in the III century, but not long afterwards, when Syracuse
and its dependencies fell to the Romans, a period of decadence followed,
and the town may have dwindled to a small farming centre of little note.
For some reason it revived in the 4th–5th centuries, when it became one
of the most vital Christian centres in Sicily.

The Theatre. Though not very impressive compared with others in
Sicily, it shows some uncommon features such as frontal approaches
to the stage in place of the usual *parodoi* leading in from the sides. The
shape of the stage and some architectural details reveal a Late Hellenistic
date, and the likeliest time for its construction would seem to be towards
the end of Hieron II's long and beneficent rule in Syracuse, in the latter
part of the III century B.C. when Roman influence was already making
itself felt. The theatre was considerably rehandled in Imperial Roman
times. Remains of silos and a mill of the Roman-Byzantine period can
be seen in front of it.

Close beside the theatre there are also some very meagre remains of a
little senate-house, and the *agora* is thought to have stood nearby to the
west.

Near the theatre are two quarries thought to have been cut soon
after Akrai was founded. The first, the so-called *Intagliata*, contains rock-cut dwellings, some with several rooms, belonging to the
Byzantine period, when a large group of catacombs were cut in the
south-west corner. The second quarry, the *Intagliatella*, is reached by a
sloping path, passing a small Antiquarium. On the right, going down, is
a large sculptured relief divided into two scenes; the first is Roman in
character and shows a warrior offering a libation or sacrifice, while the
second, a typically Greek subject, depicts heroes banqueting. This unusual fusion of Greek and Roman taste is thought to belong to the I
century B.C.

The walls of the quarry have been cut to form many rectangular
recesses which once held plaques to commemorate the dead, venerated

as heroes. These plaques must have been carved in relief on marble or limestone, or were perhaps made of painted wood for people of humbler status. Some of these plaques, bearing inscriptions, were found in another quarry (*Templi Ferali*) not far away on the eastern slope of the hill. When this quarry was partially excavated, votive offerings (mostly vases with a bronze ring or a coin) were found to have been placed near the walls beneath the inscribed plaques. The earliest of these offerings dated from the time of Agathocles to the early III century B.C.

Near this quarry, about ten minutes' walk from the theatre, are the twelve fascinating sculptured figures of the goddess Cybele, some of them very worn and disfigured. To visit these you need to ask the custodian of the theatre to accompany you and unlock the doors of the huts built to protect the figures, known locally as the 'Santoni'.

All the twelve sculptures portray the goddess Cybele (see Plate 11) accompanied by various figures who are not easy to identify, though some of them can be recognized. In several of the sculptured groups little men in Phrygian caps may represent the priests of the goddess, and in one instance Cybele is shown between Hermes and the Silenus Marsyas. The Dioscuri on horseback also appear in one example, and a lion has sometimes been carved near Cybele's feet.

These lions, and the tympanum which she sometimes holds, identify the goddess as Cybele, the Magna Mater, a deity of Asiatic origin whose cult developed two different aspects in the western world. The first, the Greek cult of Cybele, was practised in Athens from the V century and spread through the Greek world; the second, orgiastic in form, was introduced direct into Rome from Phrygia in 204 B.C. and continued to be practised in the Roman world into Imperial times. The Akrai cult evidently belonged to the first group, and the importance of these figures lies in the fact that in no other place is there so rich a complex relating to Cybele.

One may ask why so many figures of the same deity should be found together in a row, and indeed this is a very rare instance. It might warrant the hypothesis that Oriental elements may have infiltrated into the Greek religion of Cybele, frequent repetitions of the figures of Buddha or other deities in one sacred precinct being a common feature in Eastern religions.

Though resembling many figures of the Cybele cult in the Greek world, those at Akrai are nevertheless richer in many respects, particularly in the number and variety of associated figures, and it is not easy to know from which part of the Mediterranean the cult was imported into Sicily. Its most probable origin was Corinth, the mother-city of Syracuse, and in fact we know that when Dionysius II was driven from Syracuse he became a priest of Cybele at Corinth. Other sculptured representations of the goddess, many of them of IV century date, have been discovered in Siciliot sites, as well as in Syracuse itself, whence the cult may have spread to Akrai. Stylistically the 'Santoni' are unlikely to be later than the III century B.C.

Returning to Palazzolo, a small collection of prehistoric, Greek and Early Christian objects can be seen on request in the Palazzo Iudica in the Corso.

PANTALICA (Fig. 35 and Plate 15)

This is a vast cemetery of rock-cut tombs of the XIII–VIII century B.C., the largest of all the tomb groups in Sicily, set in beautiful, remote

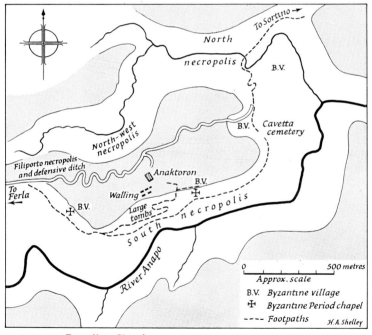

FIG. 35. Pantalica. Sketch map

and spectacular country about one hour by car from Syracuse. To reach Pantalica you leave Syracuse by the road past the station, and continue westwards through Floridia and Solarino and thence towards Palazzolo Acreide until a turning off to the right brings you to Ferla. From here a newly made but rough road leads you to the site, a high limestone plateau bounded by the river Anapo to the south and east, and by one of its tributaries to the north. (See Fig. 35.)

On this once wooded plateau stood the village. To judge from the fact that almost all the tombs which have so far been excavated were found to contain several skeletons, and as there are over 5,000 tombs, the village must have been densely populated, with many hundreds of huts, rather like one of the great Iron Age *oppida* in northern Europe. So far the village is quite unexcavated, except for the so-called *Anaktoron* (the house of the tribal chief or princeling), a few stretches of walling nearby, and a defensive ditch and wall (probably belonging to the last years of the settlement) which cuts across the approach from the west.

Those who have already visited the tombs at Thapsos (p. 195) will know that in about 1270 B.C. the small coastal villages, in contact through trade with the Mycenaean world, were abruptly abandoned and their inhabitants driven to take shelter in the high remote hills of the interior, owing to the sudden menace of warlike peoples, the Sikels, Ausonians and Morgeti, from the mainland of Italy.

The occupation of the Pantalica plateau began at the moment when villages such as Thapsos ceased to exist and their inhabitants fled to the rugged hills of the interior where, surrounded by woods and rivers, they grouped themselves into large communities whose social organization must have called for a more complex administration than that they had been used to. In fact the discovery of the prince's house implies some kind of ruling hierarchy. In many ways, however, their lives were not changed; certainly the trade which they had previously carried on with the Mycenaean world greatly diminished, but contacts were not altogether broken, and cultural links persisted with the Eastern Mediterranean rather than with the Italian mainland.

The Pantalica tombs no longer have the 'tholos' (cupola) form of the Thapsos ones, but we find that the large house, or *anaktoron* where the ruling prince must have lived, is very similar to the Mycenaean palaces, which were also 'megarons' in plan, and the same Eastern Mediterranean origin lies behind some of the bronze objects, particularly the swords from the earlier tombs at Pantalica, in the North and North-West cemeteries. Razors, brooches, mirrors and other small objects of bronze found in the tombs show that metals were no longer a rarity. The pottery forms continue to be very like those found at Thapsos, often with high tubular feet or pedestals, but they are technically more advanced and the ware is red and shiny.

Among the tombs so far excavated at Pantalica, only a few belong to the second phase of occupation (about 1000–850 B.C.) but the development of the culture can be followed in other large tomb groups such as Cassibile. A different kind of pottery, decorated with feathery designs like that of the Ausonian culture in Lipari, is found side by side with the traditional forms, and in place of the simple brooches of Pantalica I there are elbow-shaped brooches, often with a loop, a kind also found in the Ausonian culture, and probably of Eastern Mediterranean origin. Trade contacts were becoming wider, and exotic bronzes began to arrive from Spain and the Atlantic coasts of France, brought by Phoenician navigators who were busily probing the possibilities of trade with lands ever further afield.

The next phase (about 850–730) is well represented at Pantalica in the so-called South cemetery, and in the Filiporto and Cavetta ones. Probably the population had again increased. This is the time when Greek Geometric pottery first reached Sicily and the native wares were

increasingly influenced by Greek imports. According to modern research the Pantalica of this period should be identified with the legendary town of Hybla, whose king Hyblon was ruling over a vast territory
in the late VIII century when the Greeks were first founding their
colonies. In fact it was Hyblon who allowed Lamis and his followers
to settle first in Thapsos and then at Megara Hyblaea.

For hundreds of years after Pantalica had been abandoned (at about
the time of the founding of Syracuse in 733) it remained uninhabited,
to be reoccupied only in the so-called Byzantine period when people,
again driven to take shelter from barbarian raiders in the inaccessible
hideouts of the interior, chose it for their settlements; they enlarged
some of the ancient tombs to make dwellings, and built some rock-cut
chapels in which they could worship in peace.

Although no very accurate map exists of the Pantalica district, the
sketch map (Fig. 35) may help visitors to find their way to some of the
more spectacular groups of tombs, and to the *anaktoron*. In this building,
which has been re-used and partly altered in the Byzantine period,
remains were found of a metal foundry, and this has suggested the
possibility that the working of metals may have been a princely pre-
rogative. Although this *anaktoron* is not the only one known in Sicily
(there was another in the Siculo-Greek town on Monte San Mauro) it
is more complete and complex.

One of the pleasantest walks follows the southern edge of the hill,
and another starts from the point where the car can be left at the end
of the road above the Cavetta cemetery. A splendid view of the North
cemetery can be obtained by following the footpath northwards from
the end of the road, and then, after crossing the stream in the valley,
continuing a short way towards Sortino; just above the stream many of
the tombs are very close to the path.

The finds from Pantalica are displayed in the *Museo Nazionale* in
Syracuse. (Room V on the first floor.)

THAPSOS (Bronze Age rock-cut tombs)

The little peninsula of Magnisi with its extremely interesting group
of rock-cut tombs lies a few miles north of Syracuse, and about 4 kms.
from Priolo Gargallo which can easily be reached by road or rail. To
reach Magnisi you take the coast road after crossing the railway line at
Priolo.

The tombs, which are earlier in date than those in the great cemetery

at Pantalica, are of the 'tholos' or cupola type derived from the Eastern
Mediterranean. To find them you should turn up a track to the left
almost as soon as you have crossed the narrow land-strip and reached
the peninsula. Follow the track for about 200 yards and then begin looking for the tombs, the most interesting of of which are grouped along
the rocky shore to the west of the lighthouse.

On this flat and grass-grown little peninsula, Bronze Age settlers
built their villages and tombs and drew up their boats, and from here
they established trading relations not only with the local people but with
Malta and even as far afield as the Mycenaean world. The archaeological
culture to which these people belonged has been named, after this site,
the Thapsos culture, and it is thought to have developed from earlier,
related cultures in north-east Sicily, which also gave rise to the Milazzese culture in the Aeolian Islands. The Thapsos culture is particularly
well represented in coastal sites around Syracuse, such as Matrensa,
Floridia, in the Augusta neighbourhood and the Plemmyrion (the headland which closes the Great Harbour of Syracuse to the south).

So far we know much more about the tombs than the villages, but
at least one hut, rectangular and stone-walled, has been excavated at
Thapsos. The report on it has not yet been published but it produced a
quantity of pottery like that found in the tombs, and a long bronze pin
decorated with a dog and a fox.

The tombs belong to two types, and there are about 400 of them.
Most of the inland ones are reached from small vertical shafts, often
provided with a step to facilitate entry. On one side of the shaft is the
rectangular door leading into the small tomb. Near the sea the tombs
open straight on to the rocks, and from many of them a long narrow
channel leads out of the entrance to drain off the rainwater. Quite a
number of these tombs have one or more niches carefully cut in the
internal walls, and the recesses for holding the door-slab can be seen
in most of them. The number of people buried inside varied, but in
some cases there were so many that some of the skulls and bones had
been pushed back to make room for others. Buried with them were
pottery vases of local Thapsos type, bowls on very high tubular stands
(sometimes with tall, forked handles), cups with lids, etc. The decoration was generally simple and made with pairs of lines; it is very rarely
figurative. Together with these, in some of the tombs, were pots which
had been imported from the Borg-in-Nadur culture in Malta, and
pottery, bronze daggers, and paste and glass beads from the Eastern
Mediterranean (Fig. 36). These Mycenaean imports allow the Thapsos

FIG. 36. Thapsos. Native pots (top and bottom left), and imported Mycenaean pots, dagger and beads

culture to be accurately dated – the earliest of them (early Mycenaean III) belong to about 1400 B.C. – but both here, and in the other related sites nearby, these imported wares cease towards the end of Mycenaean III B, and this implies that the coastal villages were abandoned by about 1270 B.C. Peaceful trade was no longer possible; the villages were threatened by new and warlike peoples, Sikels, Ausonians and Morgeti, who came from the Italian mainland, and drove the inhabitants to take refuge in the interior, on high inaccessible hill-tops like Pantalica, where they sought safety in numbers. In fact Pantalica began to be inhabited immediately after Thapsos had been deserted.

In the late VIII century Thapsos was occupied again for a short time by Greek colonists from Megara Nisaea, under their leader Lamis. They had been driven out of Leontinoi and they sheltered provisionally in the peninsula, and here Lamis died and was buried. Shortly afterwards these people founded Megara Hyblaea, a little further up the coast. The discovery of one tomb containing late VIII century Greek pottery makes one wonder if this was not the burial place of Lamis himself.

The finds from Thapsos and from other sites of the same culture can be seen in Room V on the first floor of the *Museo Nazionale* in Syracuse.

10 · Megara Hyblaea, Lentini, Catania, Adrano, Randazzo, Naxos and Taormina

MEGARA HYBLAEA

This is the site of one of the earliest Greek colonies in Sicily and is now being excavated annually by the French archaeologists Villard and Vallet. It can be reached by the main Syracuse-Catania road (No. 114), from which, near the river Marcellino, a country lane leads off eastwards. The site of the town is on a low grassy plateau just to the south of the river Cantera, and as the approach route is subject to change it is best to ask for the '*scavi francesi*' if there is no signpost. It can also be reached by train as far as the station of Megara Giannalena, and then by following the track northwards for several kilometres.

The earliest settlement on this site was one of the many Neolithic ditch-enclosed villages which are found at intervals down the coast between here and the south-east corner of Sicily – villages such as Stentinello (just north of Syracuse), Ognina, etc., the impressed pottery and other finds from which are in the Museum at Syracuse.

Then, several millennia later, in about 750 B.C., the site was offered by the local Sikel ruler to colonists from Megara in Greece who had already settled temporarily at Trotilon and then at Thapsos (see p. 195), and these people founded their colony apparently a few years before the Corinthians chose the much more advantageous site of Syracuse. (Thucydides states that Megara Hyblaea was founded six years after Syracuse, but this is now held, by some scholars, to be incorrect). At Megara the colonists had a small anchorage but no real harbour, and some fairly fertile land around. Their prosperity was brought about partly by their maritime trade and partly by their production of fine-quality pottery.

At first the colonists settled only the northern part of the site, but by the mid-VII century the population had increased so much that a group of Megarians set off to found the new colony of Selinus, while their own town gradually expanded. The city was now fortified with a wall, traces of which can be seen on the west and north, while several semicircular towers and an oblique entrance have been identified.

Temples were built by the VII century and included one very elongated
and primitive structure with traces of a central row of wooden columns
inside. To the VI century belongs a Doric temple with terra-cotta
revetments, and votive deposits nearby which go back to about 700 B.C.,
and an Ionic sanctuary with a fine cornice block made of Parian marble.

This prosperity was brought to an unexpected end in 483 B.C. when
Gelon, tyrant first of Gela and then of Syracuse, destroyed the town
and annexed its lands; after this the site was deserted for over a century.

In the second half of the IV century Timoleon re-founded Megara
on a smaller scale, limiting the inhabited area to the northern part of
the earlier settlement, and a new cemetery was built nearby. A second
period of peaceful growth now followed, and gradually the town once
again reached the same size as before its destruction. Among the buildings belonging to this recolonization are houses, a porticoed *agora*, and
a late IV century Doric temple with Ionic decorative elements, thought
to have been dedicated to Aphrodite.

But the change of policy which led to the destruction of Syracuse by
the Romans was equally disastrous for Megara. Faced with the threatened Roman attack, the inhabitants built massive walls round the north-
east part of the town; towers were set at intervals, and the main gate,
flanked by towers, gave access to the town from the west. These defences, however, were far too old-fashioned to stand up against the
Roman attack, and in 214 B.C. Marcellus destroyed Megara, which
never grew up again. Only a few scattered houses and farms were in
time built over the ruins.

Apart from some monumental archaic tombs, stretches of walling and
a few Hellenistic houses, the visible remains are not spectacular, but
an extremely interesting *Antiquarium* has recently been opened to visitors. It contains plans and photographs showing the various phases of
the town's development, and finds which complement the very rich
collection from Megara in the Syracuse Museum, in which there are
two of the most important sculptures from the site: the archaic figure
of a goddess suckling twins, and the fine *kouros*, made of marble from
Paros or Naxos, inscribed on the right thigh, 'Sambrotidas, son of
Mandrocles', in archaic lettering.

LENTINI (Leontinoi)

The quickest way to reach Lentini from Syracuse by road is to

keep on the new main road to Catania as far as Agnone, at which point
a road forks off to Lentini. The distance is about 47 kms. At Lentini an
excellent new museum has recently been opened, and the excavations
near the south gate of the ancient town can be visited.

The ancient Greek town of Leontinoi lay to the south of the present
town and to the west of Carlentini, and was built on two hills, the Metapiccola hill to the east and the Colle San Mauro to the west, with a small
river valley between them.

Like its parent colony Naxos, this was a Chalcidian settlement,
founded in 728, and the site must have been chosen for two main
reasons: to gain control of the rich agricultural land to the north, and
to prevent the northward expansion of Syracuse. Thucydides informs
us that the colonists drove out the Sikels who had been living there, and
this may be true, for there is no lack of evidence for the presence of
native peoples on the site; there are traces of an early native village
below the Greek town on the San Mauro hill, and another on the Metapiccola hill, settled before the colonization, and of particular importance
for its unusual rectangular houses of Italic type like some in Lipari and
on the Palatine in Rome, and for the Ausonian II pottery found in them.
Perhaps this was the site of *Xouthia*, a native town said by Diodorus to
have been founded by people from Lipari. The tombs cut into the
rocky sides of the nearby valleys evidently overlapped with the period
of Greek colonization: they contained objects of the so-called Finocchito period (*c.* 750–650 B.C.), and painted pottery with geometric
designs. So the Sikels may not have been driven away immediately as
the short statement of Thucydides might suggest.

At first the new city was limited to the San Mauro hill which was
enclosed within a wall, but this circuit became too small for the growing
town by about 600 B.C. and it was enlarged to take in the valley and
the Metapiccola hill; at the same time additional fortifications were built
to defend the two gates which led out, one to the north, to the arable
lands, and one to the south, strongly defended with a gateway of the
'pincer' type, towards Syracuse.

During the VI century Leontinoi grew rich and prosperous, and
excavations have revealed the foundations of a big temple built at that
time on the Metapiccola hill, as well as some houses and a votive deposit
with locally made terra-cotta statuettes. Although Leontinoi was the
only Greek colony built so far inland, it was in touch commercially with
many parts of the Greek world, and Attic, Corinthian, Rhodian, Spartan and Chian wares have been found there.

Polybius has left a clear and useful description of Leontinoi. He says: 'The city of Leontinoi, as regards its natural position, is turned to the north. Through the middle of it runs a level valley in which stand the government offices, the lawcourts and the agora. On each side of this valley runs a ridge, precipitous from end to end, the flat ground above the brows of these ridges being covered with houses and temples. The town has two gates, one at the southern end of the valley, leading towards Syracuse, and the other at its northern end leading to the so-called Leontine plain, the arable land. . . .'

Inevitably its long period of peaceful development came to an end, and early in the V century the town was suddenly attacked and taken by Hippocrates of Gela who was striving to expand his territory. During his attack the south gate was destroyed. Later, the fortifications were abandoned, and Leontinoi passed into the dominion of Syracuse, to which town Hippocrates' successors had moved. Having regained their independence in 464, the people of Leontinoi made every possible effort to prevent their town falling into Syracusan hands again, and with this dominating fear in their minds, they rebuilt their defences and entered into an alliance with the Athenians. But all to no avail, for the Syracusans besieged Leontinoi in 427 and the war dragged on for three years before an agreement was reached. Two years later, as the result of internal political strife in the town, Leontinoi became a Syracusan dependency; the fortifications were demolished and the town used as a military strongpoint. Hopes of independence were again dashed when Syracuse defeated the Athenians in 415–413.

In 406 the Carthaginians sacked Akragas and some of the surviving inhabitants were permitted to settle in Leontinoi which declared its independence once more, and in the following year, when Dionysius of Syracuse was obliged to make a treaty with the Carthaginians, one of the stipulations made by the latter was that Leontinoi should be free – a stipulation which only expediency could have forced from such a man as Dionysius, for hopes of acquiring such rich lands must have been hard to relinquish. But he was only biding his time. He waited a few years and then besieged the town, took it and transferred its people to Syracuse, but he did not keep it for long and had to hand it over to appease his restless and discontented mercenaries – 10,000 of them, according to Diodorus.

Thenceforth the history of Leontinoi remained closely linked with that of Syracuse, in whose disasters, as Strabo points out, Leontinoi always shared, while seldom partaking of its prosperity. When Timoleon first tried to seize power in Syracuse, one of Dion's supporters, Hiketas, attempted unsuccessfully to hold out against him in Leontinoi, and it is interesting to find that when Timoleon gained possession of the town he made no attempt to refortify it, except with strongpoints which took the place of the walls. This defensive system was still in use when Pyrrhus came to Sicily to liberate the Greek towns; in 278 he was offered 'the city with its castles'. These castles, or blockhouses, must have been in the northern part of the town, and one of them is incorporated in the castle built by Frederick II.

In 263 as a result of a treaty made between the Carthaginians and Hieron II at the beginning of the First Punic War, Leontinoi's dependence on Syracuse was reaffirmed, and fifty relatively peaceful years followed. But in 214 the people of Leontinoi made a fatal mistake in changing allegiance, and declaring against the Romans, with the result that the Roman general Marcellus promptly attacked the town (whose hastily botched-up defences were of little avail) and treated the inhabitants with such severity that Syracuse, too, was induced to stand against him, and so, as we know, to lose all the wealth and beauty which it had taken generations to create.

Leontinoi fell into a state of increasing decadence during the Roman period, and when Cicero visited it he described it as a *'misera civitas atque inanis'*.

The Museum is in the Piazza del Liceo. Opening hours: daily 9.30–1; 3–5. Sundays and holidays, 9.30–1. Closed on Mondays. It houses rich finds from Leontinoi in all stages of its early history, with particularly important discoveries from the cemetery found near the Syracuse gate. This cemetery falls into two phases: the first belongs to the VI to the early V century, and the second to the IV century, when part of it was built over the fallen walls by the Gate.

A reconstructed section of the east side of the South Gate clearly shows the various stratigraphical levels. Starting from the bottom, *levels 7 and 6* are prehistoric and early Greek, ante-dating the construction of the wall. *Level 5*. The fortifications were built between the late VII and early VI century (note their foundations cutting into level 6) and were destroyed by Hippocrates between 498 and 494. The 'pincer'-type gate was destroyed, and the fortifications abandoned. *Level 4*. Signs of much movement and use. The gate rebuilt in two phases in about the mid-V century when Leontinoi temporarily regained independence and built defences against Syracuse. *Level 3*. At the end of the V century.

Destruction of the fortifications after internal strife and partial occupation by the Syracusans. Note the thick layer of collapsed wall material.
Level 2. Early IV century. The cemetery built over the remains of fallen
materials in three different stages. *Level 1* is superficial.

Other finds from Leontinoi are in the *Museo Nazionale* in Syracuse
and in the Castello Ursino Museum in Catania. It has been suggested
that the fine head of a *kouros* in the latter museum may originally have
belonged to the well-known archaic figure in Syracuse, but this cannot
be proved as the point of junction at the neck has been damaged.

The Excavated Area near the South Gate can best be reached from
Carlentini, at the southern end of which a track leads off the main road
(114), near a water trough. The various phases of the Gate's defences
can be seen, but it is difficult to understand them without first visiting
the museum at Lentini.

CATANIA (Catane)

There are not many ancient monuments to be seen in Catania, for
much of the early town, settled by Chalcidians from Naxos soon after
they had founded Leontinoi, has been destroyed by the lava flow from
Etna. The ancient acropolis has now been identified, as well as a native,
pre-Greek cemetery with imported wares going back to about 600 B.C.
The town reached a flourishing state under the Romans, and there are
some important remains of Imperial Roman date – several bath-build-
ings, a large amphitheatre, a theatre and small *odeion*.

The Theatre, entered from 47, Via Teatro Greco, is open from 9 to 1
and 2 until dusk. The various medieval and later structures which overlie the *cavea* are now being removed, and stretches of the internal
vaulted corridors are visible. The scene-structure is also partly preserved under later buildings, and some of its marble columns, their
bases richly carved with bas-reliefs, are in the Castello Ursino Museum,
together with sculptured fragments and inscriptions. It is thought that
the theatre, perhaps an entire rehandling of a previous Greek one, was
built in the 2nd century A.D.

The *Odeion,* a small theatre for music and recitations, is close by.

The Amphitheatre was of exceptionally large size, capable of holding about 16,000 spectators. It was built with lava blocks, partly encased in marble, and probably dates from the 2nd or 3rd century A.D. Its foundations can be seen near Piazza Stesicoro and Via Penninello. It is sad that many years of robbing for building stone have brought it to so poor a state.

The Castello Ursino Museum is housed in a XIII century castle built by Frederick II. Open 10–2. Sundays, 10–1. A rich collection containing a number of important objects, many of which, unfortunately, come from unknown provenances, being collectors' pieces. There is a fine Attic head of an *ephebe*, of the early V century, from Leontinoi, and a magnificent Attic *krater* of the same date, showing Perseus decapitating the Gorgon, from Camarina. There is a ground floor with three upper floors and the objects range from prehistoric times to the 18th century.

To reach Taormina from Catania, the most direct way is to follow the main road (114) but, if time allows, it is far more interesting to skirt round the edge of Etna by Paternò, Adrano, Bronte, Randazzo and Linguaglossa. This also has the advantage of allowing a visit to the new museum at Adrano, now in course of arrangement in the Norman Castle, and containing one of the richest groups of Castelluccian period pottery in Sicily, as well as some finds from the nearby site of Mendolito. *Mendolito*, famous for the great hoard of bronzes of the VIII–VII centuries, so vast that it has been thought to represent the treasure of a town or sanctuary, has recently been partially excavated, and its gateway found to bear an inscription, the longest yet known in the Sikel language. Unfortunately it is not yet readable. This site evidently preceded Adrano, or *Adranon*, founded by Dionysius I in 400 B.C. near a temple to the indigenous god of that name. (The bronzes from this site are mostly in the museum in Syracuse).

Not many kilometres to the west is the magnificently sited town of Centuripe, famed for its curious 'baroque' pottery of the Hellenistic period. It has a small museum.

At *Randazzo* there is a small collection in private hands, the Museo Vagliasindi, in the Corso, no. 205. Most of the objects come from tombs in a Greek cemetery (V to II century B.C.) at Sant'Anastasia, near Randazzo.

NAXOS AND TAORMINA

Accommodation. Information should be obtained from the *Azienda Autonoma Soggiorno e Turismo*, Taormina. Of the less expensive places outside Taormina, the small *pensione* La Lucciola, at Giardini, can be recommended, and there are camping sites at San Leo and Capo Taormina, and a Youth Hostel near Naxos in Via Sirina, Villagonia. In Taormina itself the Pensione Villa Riis is in a quiet and lovely position.

The site of Naxos, the first Greek colony in Sicily, lies not far to the south of Taormina, at Capo Schisò, near Giardini. Thucydides states that it was founded by Chalcidians from Euboea led by Thucles, and it is now thought that the colonists also included emigrants from the island of Naxos in the Cyclades. The site was no doubt chosen for its well-watered and fertile land around, and for its convenience as a landfall for ships plying between Greece and southern Italy. Until recently its date of foundation was held to be the year 734 B.C. but Villard and Vallet's work in recent years has now led some scholars to favour a date over twenty years earlier, and the date 757 is supported by the discovery of an early Proto-Corinthian cup of *c.* 750 B.C.

The earliest occupation has been archaeologically verified only in a few trial trenches on the north side of the peninsula. Thucydides tells us that the colonists 'built an altar of Apollo Archegetes which now stands outside the city', and here the competitors in the Olympic games offered their sacrifices before leaving Sicily.

A long stretch of the early walls of the town can still be seen: they are built with polygonal blocks in a technique which is widespread in areas of Ionian influence in the Eastern Mediterranean, and is also found in the colony of Lipara (founded by Cnidians in 580 B.C.). There were almost certainly earlier walls than these, but so far excavation has been too limited for this point to be verified. More defences are thought to have been built on the west and north in the late VI century when the town was attacked by Hippocrates of Gela, and again in the V century, when the whole circuit was enclosed, for Polyaenus, describing how Naxos fell to Dionysius of Syracuse in 403, refers to the towered walls.

Early sources mention a famous temple of Aphrodite, but the identification of this with the foundations of the only big temple so far found at Naxos must be regarded as very tentative. These foundations overlie an earlier sacred site with VII century walls and votive offerings including much pottery of East Greek type, but the only remains from the temple itself are painted architectural terra-cottas of the late VI century. Naxos sent colonists both to Leontinoi and Catane, but it was never a very important place. Faithful to the Athenians during the war against Syracuse, it was attacked by Dionysius some years after their defeat and almost entirely destroyed. Diodorus says that its lands then 'were given as a gift to the Sikels', and its inhabitants went into exile in various parts of Sicily until 358 when the survivors and their descendants were given a home in the new city on the hill at Taormina.

The early history of Taormina is far from clear. If Diodorus is correct the Sikels to whom Dionysius had handed over the site of Naxos did not settle there but chose instead, spurred on perhaps by the Carthaginians, to settle and fortify the hill called Monte Tauro, naming the new town *Tauromenion*. Two years later Dionysius tried unsuccessfully to storm this; leading the attack himself in wintry conditions, he nearly lost his life, and his disordered forces were driven down the snow-covered slopes. His desire was however satisfied in 392 when he concluded with the Carthaginians a treaty giving him, among other things, the right to dominate Tauromenion, and he immediately turned out the Sikels and replaced them with some of his own mercenaries.

It was not until 358 that the town was virtually refounded as a Greek city, when Andromachus (the father of the historian Timaeus) brought together the surviving Naxians from all over Sicily and established them in the new town. Plutarch writes, 'After making himself by far the most powerful of the Sicilian rulers at that time, he not only led his own citizens in the ways of law and justice but he was also known to be always averse and hostile to tyrants.' This being the case, it is not surprising to find him openly siding with Timoleon when he arrived from Greece to destroy tyranny and restore democracy in the Greek towns. In fact Timoleon made Tauromenion his operational base, and there is every reason to suppose that the town flourished at this time. A very interesting discovery was made in the last century when some inscriptions on marble turned out to be the official documents of the town's civil and fiscal administration: some of these can be seen in the small museum near the theatre. The chief administrator was the so called *Eponymos*, elected annually, and generally chosen from those who had already held lesser office. Then there were two *gymnasiarchi* responsible for the civil and religious education, in all its aspects, of the young people; two *strategi*, civil and judicial functionaries who were responsible for public buildings, etc.; and also short-term financial magistrates. At the end of each year these magistrates, together with the *Eponymos*, had to render precise accounts for their activities; in fact, they were equivalent, in standing and functions, to the Roman consuls, tribunes, and lesser magistrates. The town continued to be governed in this democratic way from Timoleon's time until 30 B.C., when instead of continuing as a *civitas foederata* (an honour given it on the death of Hieron II in 214 B.C.) it was made by Augustus into the military colony of Tauromenium.

When Agathocles succeeded Timoleon as the ruler of Syracuse, he drove Timaeus from Tauromenion, and soon afterwards a local leader, Tyndarion, took control there and was one of the men who invited Pyrrhus to Sicily. Pyrrhus landed on the coast below the town, and together they marched on Syracuse.

The III century seems to have been a period of peaceful development under Hieron II of Syracuse who used Tauromenion as a naval base against the Mamertines. It only became Roman when all Sicily became a Roman province in 201 B.C. During the Slave War of 134–132 its high position made it an admirable centre for the rebellious slaves, and for a time, until famine and treachery led to its fall, it held out against the Roman consul Publius Rupilius, who, having taken the town, massacred all the survivors.

Sextus Pompeius used Tauromenion as a naval base against Octavian, and a great sea battle was fought off the coast in 36 B.C. when Octavian's fleet was almost wiped out, but not long afterwards Octavian in his turn had his military base in Tauromenion, whose citizens he transferred elsewhere. After Pompey had been defeated, Octavian (now Augustus) recolonized the town and it flourished right through Imperial Roman times. During these centuries the Greek language apparently predominated, though Latin was the official language. The countryside around Tauromenium was famous for its choice wines, and a number of amphorae inscribed TAVR have been found in the excavations at Pompei.

Most of the surviving monuments in Taormina are Roman, and are all the more interesting for being so, for there are fewer Roman than Greek buildings of importance in Sicily. But the Roman period was long (500 years or more), and until more excavations have been carried out the exact chronological position of the various monuments must remain imprecise.

The most outstanding building is undoubtedly *the Theatre* (Plate

PLATE 16. Taormina. View of the Theatre with Etna in the background

16), standing on one of the acropoleis of the early town. This is entirely Roman in its present form, though it is quite possible that the foundations of the *cavea* may date back to the III century B.C., to the period of Hieron II. In fact some Greek inscriptions on the seats are very like some of that date in the Syracuse theatre, and the careful choice of the site itself, so placed that the full natural beauty of snow-capped Etna could delight the spectators, also suggests a Greek rather than Roman plan. Whether this proves to be so or not, the theatre was radically rebuilt in the latter part of the 1st century A.D. Around the top of the *cavea* ran a double portico with typically Roman brick arcading on the exterior, while the interior portico, decorated with niches along its façade, had a podium supporting marble columns, and from here the stairways led down to divide the *cavea* into 9 sections.

The scene-building, the only surviving one in Sicily, originally had two orders of columns supporting the architrave, but today only the lower part of the structure survives; it has three big arched apertures and some small niches, and some columns stand in front. This building was linked to the *cavea* on each side by a large vaulted room, a feature which has many parallels in Asia Minor. The theatre seems to have been entirely rehandled in late Imperial times to adapt it for the circus games which had by then become so popular. This entailed enlarging the orchestra by cutting back some of the lower seats and by removing the *pulpitum* (stage) so that the arena could extend right up to the scene-building; at the same time the arena was provided with a vaulted service corridor and with a high surrounding wall for the protection of spectators.

(The small Theatre Antiquarium stands near the entrance.)

Not far to the south-west, in Via Naumachia, leading off Corso Umberto I, is the erroneously named *Naumachia*, an impressive structure built with large bricks and thought to be of late Imperial Roman date. This now appears as a long wall terracing the hillside; its façade is ornamented with 18 large apsidal niches alternating with smaller rectangular ones. Old drawings show that behind this and for the whole of its length there once ran a water-tank or reservoir, divided by pilasters into two aisles with a vaulted roof; unfortunately this part is now covered by subsequent buildings. The exact date and character of this structure can only be ascertained by excavation, and for the time being one can only suppose that it had some function connected with public bath buildings.

There are slight remains of a small *Odeion*, or little theatre used for music or recitations, behind the church of Santa Caterina. Imperial Roman in date, and largely brick-built, its small *cavea* was originally surrounded by a gallery supported on columns or pilasters. It is interesting to find that the *stereobate* of a 2nd century Greek temple has been used as part of the scene-structure which had a brickwork façade with three niches.

Near Piazza Vittorio Emanuele a large area is now being cleared to reveal what appears to be a big public bath building of Imperial Roman date, probably 1st or 2nd century. This seems to have been an important centre of the town, for other buildings, vaulted brick structures, mosaics, etc., apparently part of the same complex, were described in the 18th century near the Porta Messina. The site of the early Roman

Forum may have been near the present barracks for from this area came some of the inscribed bases now in the Theatre Antiquarium.

There is shortly to be a *Museo della Badia*, but this is still in course of arrangement.

(Although it is not normally visible to the public, students of Roman architecture may like to know that in the Giafari district, not far away, there is a large rectangular Roman building, evidently a reservoir, brick-built and stuccoed, divided by 8 pilasters into two aisles, covered by barrel-vaulting.)

Bibliography

The following general works cover the history and archaeology of Sicily from the Palaeolithic to the Roman period, and from the bibliographies appended to many of these books scholars will be able to find references to all the more important articles.

General Works

Bérard, J. *Bibliographie topographique des principales cités grecques de l'Italie méridionale et de la Sicile dans l'antiquité.* (1941.)
Bernabò Brea, L. *Sicily before the Greeks.* (2nd edn. 1966.)
Boardman, John. *The Greeks Overseas.* (Penguin Books, 1964.)
Dinsmoor, W. B. *Architecture of Ancient Greece.* (3rd edn. 1951.)
Dunbabin, T. J. *The Western Greeks.* (1948.)
Finley, M. I. *Ancient Sicily* forthcoming from Chatto & Windus.
Freeman, E. A. *Sicily, Phoenician, Greek and Roman.* (1892.) The short version of a big *History of Sicily* in several volumes.
Harden, D. B. *The Phoenicians.* (2nd edn.)
Pace, B. *Arte e civiltà della Sicilia antica.* (4 vols., 1935–49.)
Warmington, B. H. *Carthage.* (1960.)
Woodhead, A. G. *The Greeks in the West.* (1962.)
   Among the classical writers three are of the first importance: Thucydides, *The Peloponnesian War* (Books VI and VII), Diodorus Siculus, and Cicero, *Contra Verrem.* Other main sources include Herodotus (Books V and VII), Plutarch whose *Lives* include Nicias, Dion, Timoleon, Pyrrhus and Marcellus, Polybius (Book I). See also Livy, Pindar, Silius Italicus, Strabo, Pliny, etc.
   The following short list supplements the above bibliography with some of the more important recent articles.

Chapter 1

AEOLIAN ISLANDS AND MILAZZO. Bernabò Brea, L. and M. Cavalier. *Meligunìs Lìpara* (Palermo, 1960), *Il Castello di Lipari e il Museo Archeologico Eoliano,* and *Mylai* (*Soc. Storia Patria Sicilia Orientale,* 1959).

LONGANE. *Archivio Storico Siciliano* (1950), and short reports in *Fasti Archeologici*.

TINDARI. Most recent account and bibliography is in the forthcoming volume of the *Enciclopedia dell'Arte*. See also *Archaeology*, Vol. III (1960), pp. 246–250.

Chapter 2

HALAESA. *Notizie Scavi* XIII (1959), pp. 293 ff., and short notices in *Fasti Archeoligici*.

CEFALÙ. For 'Temple of Diana' see *Notizie Scavi* (1929), pp. 273 ff., and Lucy Shoe, *Western Greek Mouldings*.

HIMERA. P. Marconi, *Himera* (1931).

SOLUNTO. *Arch. Storico Sic. Orientale*, VII (1954), pp. 27–34, and *Kokalos*, III, pp. 80 ff.

Chapter 3

ADDAURA. *Notizie Scavi*, VI (1952), p. 185, and *Bull. Pal. It.* VIII (1952–3), pp. 1–20.

SEGESTA. *Kokalos*, III, *Notizie Scavi*, LIV (1929), and *Classical Quarterly* (1961), N.S. XI, pp. 87–93.

Chapter 4

ERICE. *Enciclopedia dell'Arte* and refs.

LÉVANZO. *Notizie Scavi*, VI (1952), pp. 185 ff., and *Riv. Scienze Preist.* XVII (1962).

MOTYA. J. I. S. Whitaker, *Motya* (1921), *Archaeology*, X (1957), pp. 131–6, and XVII (1964), pp. 91–100, and *Kokalos*, VIII (1962), pp. 164–5.

Chapter 5

SELINUNTE. For foundation see *Bull. Corresp. Hellénique* (1958), pp. 16 ff. See also Santangelo, *Selinunte* (1953); *Kokalos*, III (1957), pp. 22–24, and VIII (1962), p. 156. *Atti VII Congr. Int. Arch. Class.* (1961), pp. 12–14.

HERACLEA MINOA. *Kokalos*, III and IV, *Notizie Scavi* (1958), p. 252. De Miro, *Eraclea Minoa* (1958).

Chapter 6

AGRIGENTO. See bibliography in *Enciclopedia dell'Arte*, and P. Griffo, *Agrigento, Guide to the Monuments and Excavations* (1962). For San

Biagio see *Klearchos*, 20 (1963), pp. 114–124.

SANT'ANGELO MUXARO. *Atti Acc. Palermo*, XVII (1932).

Chapter 7

SERRA ORLANDO (Morgantina). Short reports in *American Journal of Archaeology* from 1957 onwards, and recent numbers of *Fasti Archeologici*.

PIAZZA ARMERINA. G. V. Gentili and B. Pace, *La Villa Romana di Piazza Armerina* (Rome, 1951). H. P. L'Orange in *Acta ad Archaeologiam et Artium Historiam Pertinentia*, vol. II (Rome, 1965).

Chapter 8

GELA. *Notizie Scavi*, X (1956), pp. 203–401, and XIV (1960), pp. 67–246. See also *Kokalos*, II (1956), pp. 158–76, and the small Guide to Gela by P. Orlandini and Dinu Adamesteanu (available in English).

Chapter 9

CASTELLUCCIO. See Bernabò Brea, L. *Sicily before the Greeks*.

HELORUS. *Monunmenti Antichi*, XLVII (1965), and *Fasti Archeologici*, XIV.

SYRACUSE. M. Guido, *Syracuse* (4th edn. 1965) and for the Euryalus Fortress, *American Journal of Archaeology*, 67 (1963), pp. 363 ff. The Ionic Temple is to be published shortly.

PALAZZOLO ACREIDE. Bernabò Brea, L. *Akrai* (Catania, 1956).

PANTALICA. *Monumenti Antichi*, IX (1899), and XXI (1913).

THAPSOS. *Monumenti Antichi*, VI (1895).

Chapter 10

MEGARA HYBLAEA. *Mélanges d'archéologie et d'histoire* (École française de Rome) for 1952 onwards. For date of foundation see *Bulletin de Correspondance Hellénique*, LXXVI (1952), pp. 289–346.

LENTINI. See recent bibliography in *Enciclopedia dell'Arte*.

NAXOS. *Bolletino d'Arte*, April–June 1964.

TAORMINA. M. Santangelo, *Taormina e d'intorni* (Rome, 1950).

Index

Addaura (Upper Palaeolithic cave with engraved figures) 16, 23, 60, 61–64, 77, 213

Adrano 19, 29, 171, 205

Aeolian Islands, *see* Lipari Islands, and Alicudi, Filicudi, Lipari, Panarea, Salina, Stromboli and Vulcano

Aeschylus 26, 108, 144, 145, plays performed at Syracuse 162, dies at Gela 162

Agathocles, tyrant of Syracuse 27, 34, attacks Cephaloedium 48; 54, sacks Segesta 68, treaty with Carthage 89; seizes Heraclea Minoa 103; 134, 144, attacks Gela 147, strengthens Gela fortifications at Capo Soprano 149, becomes tyrant of Syracuse 166, wars against Carthaginians 166 and 176, strengthens Euryalus Castle at Syracuse 188; 208

Agrigento (*see also* Akragas) 16, 18, 19, 29, 57, 95, 99, 101, 107–130, 176, 213

Aidone (*see* Morgantina)

Akragas (Greek colony) 27, 50, 51, 52, sacked by Hannibal son of Giskon 67, 89; 90, 92, 102, history and description 107–130; 144, 145, 147, road to Syracuse and Selinus 154; 166, 169, finds in Syracuse Museum 171; 202, 213–214

Akrai (Greek colony) *see* Palazzolo Acreide

Alicudi (Aeolian island) 17, 34

Amphitheatres 52 (Termini Imerese), 180–181 (Syracuse), 205 (Catania)

Andromachus, father of the historian Timaeus, refounds Tauromenion 207

Apennine culture 38, 39

Arab domination 28, 55, 56

Archaic period, definition 29; 41, 66, 69, 150–154, 171–179, 186, 198, 200, 201, 203, 206

Archimedes of Syracuse 27, his defences of Syracuse 167 and 188, death during Roman sacking of Syracuse 168

Athenians 26, 51, send envoys to Segesta 67 and 70; 74, 113, expedition to Sicily 146 and 163, defeat at Syracuse 164 and 186, alliance with Leontinoi 202; 207

Attic pottery 32, 40, 81, 154, 172, 176, 201, 205

Augustus (*see* Octavian)

Ausonian culture 25, definition 38–39; 133, 194, 197

Bacchylides 162

Beaker pottery 24, 38

Birgi (Punic cemetery near Motya) 80–81, 83

Boccadifalco (Sant'Isodoro tombs) 60

Bossed bone plaques from Castelluccio etc. 24, 155

Bronze Age 24, 37, 38, 40, 41, 44, 60, 133, 150, 155–156, 169–171

Butera (Sikel town) 144, 152

Byzantine period 28, 44, 118, 130, 169, 172, 190, 195

Calascibetta 132

Caltagirone 17, 19, 29, 131

Camarina (Syracusan colony) 26, sacked by Hannibal son of Giskon 67, ceded to Hippocrates of Gela 145, history 153–154, destroyed

Camarina—cont.
by Gelon of Syracuse 162, finds
in Ragusa 153, in Syracuse 172
and 173, in Catania 205
Capo Graziano culture (Aeolian Is-
lands) 17, 24, 35, 38, 40, 60, 156
Capo Soprano (Greek fortifications at
Gela) 17, 18, 19, 148–149
Carthage 79, 80, 82, 89, 103, 104,
113, 138, 146
Carthaginians passim
Cassibile, Bronze Age tombs, 39,
129, finds from 171 and 194
Castelluccio, Bronze Age tombs etc.
17, 24, 38, 60, 133, 150, 155–157,
158, 170, 205, 214
Castelvetrano 18, 19, 85
Castroreale San Biagio (Roman Villa)
41
Catane (see also Catania) 26, 207
Catania (see also Catane) 17, 18, 19,
29, 50, 168, 204–205
Cefalù 17, 18, 29, 47, 48–49, 53, 213
(see also Cephaloedium)
Centuripe, finds in Palermo Museum
58, in Syracuse Museum 172, and
in Centuripe 205
Cephaloedium (Sikel town) 48, 103
(see also Cefalù)
Chalcidian colonists 26, 33, 50, 133,
161, 163, 200, 204, 206
Chthonic deities (see Demeter and
Kore)
Cicero, in Sicily investigating the
crimes of the Roman praetor Verres,
28, 34, at Tindari 44, Cefalù 48,
Lilybaeum 84, Heraclea Minoa
104–105, Agrigentum 114, 120,
121 and 122, Enna 132, Gela 148
Syracuse 168, 176 and 179, Leon-
tinoi 203
Claudius I, Emperor 75
Cnidian colonists 26, 40, 66
Coin collections 58, 152, 175
Conca d'Oro (Copper Age culture of
Western Sicily) 24, 37, 56, 60
Conzo (Copper Age culture) 24
Copper Age 23–24, 37, 60, 100
Corinthian colonists 26, 161, 165, 199

Corinthian pottery 32, 33, 40, 80,
87, 99, 116, 130, 154, 172, 176, 201
Cozzo Cannita (original site of Solus)
54, 57
Cretan colonists 26
Cretan linear script 38
Cybele, goddess, 157, 190–192

Daedalus (mythical builder of Cretan
labyrinth) 74, 100, 102, 129
Delphi 51, 162, 178, 179
Demeter and Kore (or Persephone)
goddesses 108, 115–117, 126, 128,
132, 134, 162
Demeter Malophoros, sanctuary at
Selinunte (see Gaggera)
Diana style, neolithic pottery, 37, 77
Diocletian 137
Diodorus Siculus, references in his
History of Sicily, 28, 39, 42 (Tindari), 47 (Halaesa), 51 (Himera), 54
Solunto), 66, 68 (Segesta), 75
(Erice), 80 (Motya), 83 (Lilybaeum),
87 and 89 (Selinunte), 103 (Heraclea Minoa), 113, 124, and 125
(Agrigento), 180 (Syracuse), 201 and
202 (Lentini), 207 (Naxos)
Dion, tyrant of Syracuse 26, 165,
203
Dionysius I of Syracuse 27, re-
populates Messana 34, founds
Tindari 42; 47, takes Cephaloedium (Cefalù) 48, destroys Solus
54, besieges Segesta 68, campaign
in western Sicily 74, sacks Motya
79–83, attacks Lilybaeum 84,
treaty with Carthage 89, 103, 114
and 146, tyrant of Syracuse 164–
165, builds first Euryalus fortress
187; 202, founds Adranon 205,
takes Naxos 206–207
Dionysius II of Syracuse 165, 192
Dioscuri (the gods Castor and Pollux)
42, 112, 126–127, 191
Disueri (or Monte Dessueri), Sikel
town, 153, 171
Dorian colonists 51
Drepana (see Trapani)
Ducetius (Sikel leader) founds Palica

101, at Morgantina 133, leads national movement 145

Elymians 25, 65–66, 69, 70, 87
Empedocles, philosopher, 90, 112
Enna 17, 18, 19, 131–133, Temple of Ceres 132, 168
Epicharmus 162, 182
Eraclea Minoa (see Heraclea Minoa)
Erice (Eryx) 16, 18, 19, 25, Temple of Aphrodite (Venus) 44 and 75–76, Elymian town 66–67, 69, history and description 73–76
Etna 17, 18, 19, 108, 140, 169, 171, 204, 209
Etruscans or Etruria 39, 50, 58, 88, 162, 172
Euryalus fortress at Syracuse 82, 96, 159, 166, 180, 185, 187–188, 189
Euryleon (leader of Spartan colonists at Heraclea Minoa) 103

Favignana (island), Palaeolithic caves, 61, 76, 77, 78
Filicudi (Aeolian island) 17, 34, 38, 39, 40
Finocchito, tombs 158, finds in Syracuse Museum 171, Finicchito period 201
Fusco cemetary (Syracuse) 172

Gaggera (Santuary of Demeter Malophoros, Selinunte) 60, 87, 88, 94, description 96–99, 116
Gela 17, 18, 19, Aeschylus dies at 26; 27, 29, 67, 105, 112, 114, 117, 132, history and description 143–153, Greek congress at 163, finds in Syracuse, Museum 171, 172 and 173; 200, 202, 214
Gelon, tyrant of Gela and then Syracuse, 26, wins battle of Himera 50–51, treaty with Carthaginians 81, marries daughter of Theron of Akragas 109, destroys Megara Hyblaea 145 and 200, destroys Camarina 154, reigns at Syracuse 161–162, tomb of 165, begins

Temple of Athena in Syracuse 175–176
Geometric period, defined 31 and 32; 116, 171–172, 194
Giardino Spagna cemetery (Syracuse) 172, 173
Grammichele 174
Greek colonies 25 and passim
Greek pottery styles 32
Grotta dei Genovesi (Lévanzo), Palaeolithic incised figures, 77
Grotta di Moarda (prehistoric cave near Alcofonte) 60

Halaesa (Sikel town) 17, 19, history and description 47–48, finds from in Palermo Museum 57, 213
Hamilcar Barca (Carthaginian leader) attempts to regain Panormus from the Romans 56, destroys Eryx in First Punic War 74 and 75
Hannibal, son of Giskon, (Carthaginian leader) sacks Himera 51, supports Segesta 67, sacks Gela and Camarina 67, sacks Selinus 89, 91 and 99, sacks Akragas 113
Hannibal (Carthaginian leader in Second Punic War) 167
Hanno (Carthaginian leader) base at Heraclea Minoa 104
Hellenistic period, defined 31, in Lipari 40, at Halaesa 47–48, Solunto 54, sculpture in Palermo Museum 57, theatre at Segesta 72, Motya 83, Selinunte 95 and 98, Heraclea Minoa 104–106, Agrigento 114–115, 122 and 128, Sikel settlements near Caltanissetta 131, Morgantina 134, Helorus 158, sculpture etc. at Syracuse 172–175, at Syracuse 182, theatre at Akrai 190, Megara Hyblaea 200, Taormina 208
Helorus 17, Syracusan defeat near 145, history and description 158–159; 214
Heraclea Minoa (Greek colony) 16, 18, 29, 87, captured by Pyrrhus 89, 99, history and description 101–

Heraclea Minoa—cont.
   106, traditional tomb of Minos 102
   and 129; 148
Herakles (see also Hercules) 74, 103,
   temple at Agrigento dedicated to
   120–122 and 124, sculptured figures
   at Gela 152, and Syracuse 173
Herbita (Sikel town) 47
Hercules 137–142
Hermocrates of Syracuse, at Selinunte
   89 and 96, at Gela 146 and Syracuse 163
Herodotus 102
Hieron I of Syrocuse 26, his reign
   162
Hieron II of Syracuse 26, 27, defeats
   Mamertines 34, 41 and 42, Morgantina 134, Helorus 158–159,
   Syracuse 163, his reign 166–167,
   his Altar 181–182, theatre at Syracuse 182–184, the Euryalus fortress 188, Akrai 190, treaty with
   Carthaginians in First Punic War
   203, naval base at Tauromenion
   208
Hiketas, dominates Syracuse 166, at
   Leontinoi 203
Himera (Greek colony) 16, 18, 27,
   history and description 49–52; 53,
   finds from, in Palermo 57, battle
   of Himera 50–51, 58, 67, 81, 88,
   102, 109, 112, 115, 124, 127, 145,
   150, 162 and 175, legendary visit of
   Herakles 74, temple at 52, 53,
   92 and 95, sacked by Carthaginians
   113
Himilco (Carthaginian leader), treaty
   with Cephaloedium 48, relieves
   Segesta 68, sacks Akragas 113
Hippocrates of Gela 144–145 acquires
   Camarina 154, menaces Syracuse
   180, takes Leontinoi, attacks Naxos
   206

Kamikos (Sikel stronghold) 102, 129
Knossos, Crete, 102
Kokalos (legendary Sikel king) 102,
   his stronghold at Kamikos 129

Lamis (Greek colonist) 195, dies at
   Thapsos 198
Late Bronze Age 25, in Aeolian
   Islands 38–39, finds in Palermo
   60, tombs at Sant' Angelo Muxaro
   129, and Pantalica 192–195
Lentini Greek colony of (Leontinoi)
   17, 19, 29, prehistoric site at 39,
   taken by Hippocrates 144, Athenian support for 146, annexed by
   Syracuse 163, captured by
   Romans 167, finds in Syracuse
   171 and 173; 198, history and description 200–204, finds at Catania
   205; 214
Lévanzo (island with Palaeolithic en-
   gravings) 16, 18, 23, 60, 61, 62,
   76, 77–78, 213
Licodia Eubea, tombs at 171
Lilybaeum (Carthaginian stronghold)
   83–84, 89, 114, resists Pyrrhus
   166 (see also Marsala)
Lipari (or Aeolian Islands) 17, 19,
   23, 24, 25, 33, prehistoric sequence
   in, 34–39, Greek and Roman
   periods 39–40; 42, finds from, in
   Cefalù 49, and in Syracuse 169;
   194, 196, 201, 212 (see also Capo
   Graziano and Milazzese cultures)
Livy, describes Roman capture of
   Akragas 121, Enna 132, mentions Helorus 158, describes Euryalus Fort at Syracuse 187
Longane (Sikel town) 17, 19, site
   identified 41, Mamertines defeated at 42 and 167; 213

Malophoros sanctuary (Selinunte) see
   Gaggera
Malpasso, prehistoric finds from, in
   Palermo 60, and in Syracuse 171
Malta, links with Sicily 37, 38, 155
   156, 196
Mamertines (mercenary troops from
   Messana) 34, defeated by Hieron
   II 41 and 42, destroy Gela 147,
   sack Camarina 154, ravage Sicily
   166, call for Roman intervention
   167; 208

Manfria (Early Bronze Age village) 153

Marcellus, Roman general 27, takes Helorus 159, captures Syracuse 167–168, 188, destroys Megara Hyblaea 200, captures Leontinoi 203

Marsala (see also Lilybaeum) 16, 18, 19, finds from, in Palermo 60

Matrensa (Bronze Age site) finds from, in Syracuse 170; 196

Maximian (Herculius) Emporer 136, 137

Megara Hyblaea (Greek colony) 17, 19, 26, 29, founds Selinus 87, 98 and 107, destroyed by Gelon 145 and 162, finds from, in Syracuse 169, 172 and 173, settled by colonists under Lamis 195 and 198, history 199–200; 214

Mendolito (Sikel town) finds from, in Syracuse 171, inscription in Sikel language 205

Messana (Messina) 42, seized by Mamertines 166

Messina 17, 18, 19, 29, history and museum 33–34 (see also Zancle)

Middle Bronze Age 24 and passim

Milazzese culture in Aeolian Islands, 24, 38, 39, 40

Milazzo 17, 18, 19, boat service to Lipari, 33 and 34; 38, 39 (see also Mylai)

Mineo (Sikel sacred place near) 100–101

Minos, legendary Cretan king 102, 129

Modica, finds from, in Syracuse 171

Monreale, Cathedral and mosaics 16, 18, 56, 64

Monte Bubbonia (Sikel town) 144, finds from, in Gela 153

Monte Dessueri (see Disueri)

Monte Pellegrino (see Palermo)

Monte Tabuto, prehistoric finds from, in Syracuse 170

Morgantina (Aidone), Sikel and Greek site, history and description 133–134, finds from, in Syracuse 171; 214

Morgeti (tribe from Italian mainland) 25, 39, 194, 197

Motya (Carthaginian town) 16, 18, 27, 29, 54, 56, finds from, in Palermo 57, history and description 78–83, sacked by Dionysius of Syracuse 81–83 and 165, population transferred to Lilybaeum 84, defeated by Theron of Akragas 112; 213

Mozia (see Motya)

Museums and Collections 21, list of larger museums 29, Adrano 200, Aeolian Islands 36 and 40, Agrigento 128, Calascibetta 132, Caltanissetta 131, Catania 205, Cefalú 49, Centuripe 205, Gela 150–154, Heraclea Minoa 106, Lentini 203–204, Megara Hyblaea 200, Messina 33, Motya 83, Noto 158, Palazzolo Acreide 190 and 192, Palermo 56–61, 91 and 92, 98, Ragusa 153–154, Solunto 55, Syracuse 169–175, Taormina 210 and 211, Tindari 46, Trapani 76

Mycenaean Period, links with Sicily 24, 25, 38, 102–103, 129–130, 133, 170, 193–194, 196–197

Mylai (Greek colony) 26, 33

Naxos (Greek colony) 17, 26, taken by Hippocrates 144, allied with Athenians 163, founds Leontinoi 201 and Catane 204, history and description 206–207; 214

Neolithic period 23, 36–37, finds in Palermo Museum 60; 62, 77, 78, finds in Syracuse Museum 169

Nicias (Athenian leader in war against Syracuse) 163–164

Norman period 28, in Cefalú 48, in Palermo 56, walls at Erice 76, alterations at Piazza Armerina 138 and to Temple of Apollo in Syracuse 176 (see also Monreale)

Noto (Sikel centre and baroque town) 17, 18, 19, 29, 156, 158

Octavian (Augustus) 28, sacks Mes-

Octavian—cont.
sana and drafts new colonists to Syracuse, Tyndaris etc. 168, makes Tauromenion a military colony 208

Olympia (Siciliot sanctuaries at) 51 and 144, successes in chariot races at 112, Etruscan helmet sent to 162, associations with Fountain of Arethusa at Syracuse 179

Orientalizing period, defined 31; 130

Ortygia (Syracuse) 159–179 *passim* and fig. 28

Palaeolithic period 23, finds in Palermo Museum 60, incised figures at Addaura and Lévanzo 61–64 and 77–78, finds in Syracuse Museum 169

Palazzolo Acreide (Greek town of Akrai) 17, 19, 26, 29, 156, 157, 169, finds from, in Syracuse Museum 171 and 172, history and description 188–192; 214

Palermo (*see also* Panormus) 16, 18, 19, 29, 53, 54, history and museum 56–61, 66 and 130

Palici (Sikel gods) 100–101

Panarea (Aeolian island) 17, 34, prehistoric cultures 37, 38, 39, 40 (*see also* Milazzese and Piano Quartara cultures)

Panormus (Phoenician site at Palermo) 54, 56

Pantalica (Late Bronze Age rock-cut tombs) 17, 19, 25, 39, 66, 129, bronzes of Pantalica type 129 and 132; 169, finds in Syracuse Museum 171, description of site, etc. 192–195; 198, 214

Paul, St., visits Syracuse 28

Pausanias 179

Pergusa, lake of 133

Phalaris, tyrant of Akragas, 108–109, 128

Phintias, tyrant of Agrigento 114, sacks Gela 147 and 149

Phoenicians (*see also* Carthaginians, *passim*) 25, their three main sites,

Solus 54, Panormus 56 and Motya 78–83; 130, traders before foundation of Greek colonies 194

Piano Conte (Copper Age culture) 37

Piano Quartara (Copper Age culture) 37

Piazza Armerina (Roman villa at Casale) 17, 18, 19, 28, description of villa and mosaics 135–142; 214

Pindar, in Akragas 109, 112, at Hieron I's court in Syracuse 162

Plato, in Syracuse 27, 165

Plemmyrion (Syracuse) 170, 196

Plutarch, describes Syracuse 165, its defeat by the Romans 168, describes Andromachus of Tauromenion 207

Polybius, writes of Akragas 107 and 122, and of Leontinoi 202

Pompey (Sextus Pompeius, war with Caesar 28, 34, 84, 168, at Tauromenion 208

Ptolemy, writes of Agrigentum 115, and Helorus 158

Punic Wars 34, in Aeolian Islands 40, Akragas 114, 122 and 126, Halaesa 47, Heraclea Minoa 104, Leontinoi 203, Morgantina 134, Selinus 89, Solunto 54, Syracuse 167

Pyrrhus, King of Epirus, in Sicily, joined by Segestans 68, takes Eryx 74, fails to take Lilybaeum 84, joined by Selinuntines 89 and 96, takes Akragas 114, liberates Greek cities in Sicily 166; 182, fortifications at Euryalus fort in Syracuse 188, acquires Leontinoi 203, lands near Tauromenion 208

Ragusa 17, 19, 29, history and museum 153–154, finds from, in Syracuse Museum 171

Railways in Sicily 18

Randazzo 19, small private collection at 205

Realmese (prehistoric rock-cut tombs) 132

Rhodian colonists, at Segesta 66, Akragas 107 and 109, Gela 144
Rhodian pottery 46, 83, 130, 172, 201
Rito (archaic Greek cemetery), finds from, in Ragusa 154
Rocce di Cusa (Selinunte) 85, 99
Rock-cut tombs (see especially Cassibile, Castelluccio, Malpasso, Pantalica, Realmese, Thapsos and Valle Coniglio)
Roman period 27, Aeolian Islands 40, Agrigento 114–115, 117, 122 and 127, Camarina 154, Catania 204–205, Cefalú 48–49, Erice 75-76, Gela (coins) 152, Halaesa 47, Helorus 159, Heraclea Minoa 104-105, Leontinoi 203, Lilybaeum 83 and 84, Megara Hyblaea 200, Messana 34, Morgantina 134, Palazzolo Acreide (Akrai) 190–191, Noto Antico 156, Palermo 57, 58, and 60, Piazza Armerina 135–140, Segesta 68 and 72, Solunto 54–55, Syracuse 167–168, 172–175 (museum), 179 (theatre), 180 (amphitheatre), 184 and 188, Taormina 208–211, Tindari 43–46
Roman Villas (see Piazza Armerina and Castroreale San Biagio)
Rupilius, Publius (Roman Consul) rebuilds Heraclea Minoa 104–105, quells First Slave War 168, takes Tauromenion 208

Sabucina (Hellenized Sikel settlement) 131
Salina (Aeolian island) prehistoric sites 34–40, passim
San Cono-Piano Notaro (Copper Age culture) 24
Sant' Angelo Muxaro, 'tholos' tombs 16, 60, 66, 102, description 129–130; 132, 133, 171, 214
Sant' Ippolito (Copper Age culture) 24, 37, 170
Sciacca 16, 18, 99–101, 108
Scipio Africanus 44, 68, 84

Scornavacche, founded by Syracuse, its history, and finds in Ragusa 154
Segesta 16, 18, 19, Elymian town 25, description and history 64–72; 74, frontier disputes with Selinus 87, 89, 106, 113 and 146, allied with Athenians 163; 182, 213
Selinus (Selinunte) Greek colony 16, 18, 19, 26, 27, sacked by Hannibal son of Giskon 51–52, temple metopes in Palermo Museum 57–58 and 92, votive figurines from, 60 and 96, frontier disputes with Segesta 66–67, 70 and 113, history and description 85–99; 103, 112, Demeter Malophoros sanctuary (see Gaggera), 121, 124, road from Selinus to Syracuse 154, founded by Megara Hyblaea 199; 213
Serraferlicchio (Copper Age culture) 24, 37, finds in Palermo 60, and in Syracuse 170
Sicilian Vespers, war of, 28
Sikans and Sikels 25, 39, 41, 47, 66, 87, gods of 100–101; 109, religious site at Akragas 126, shrine from Sabucina 131, at Enna 132, Morgantina 133, relations with Greeks of Gela 144, national movement under Ducetius 145, friendly treatment by Timoleon 147, settlements in the interior 153 (and others listed as Sikel towns) in Ortygia 161, finds in Syracuse Museum 171 and 172; 194, 197, 199, at Leontinoi 201, Sikel inscription 205, at Tauromenion 207
Simonides 112, 162
Slave Wars 27, 44, 104, 105, 132, 168, 208
Solus (Solunto) 16, 18, 29, street layout compared with Halaesa 47, history and description 52–55, important Carthaginian base 56, finds from, in Palermo 57, 58 and 60, houses similar to Punic houses at Motya 83; 213

Stentinello (Neolithic culture) 23, in Aeolian Islands 36, finds from in Syracuse 169 and 199
Stesichorus, lyric poet 50
Strabo 75, writes of Selinus 90, Heraclea Minoa 104, Agrigentum 115, Syracuse 179, Leontinoi 202
Stromboli (Aeolian island) 34, 40, 108
Syracuse 17, 18, 19, main tyrants 26–27; 29, Bronze Age villages near 39, First Punic War 43, defeats Carthaginians at Himera 50–51, defeats Athenians 67 and 163–164, Euryalus fort 82 and 187–188, death of Hermocrates at 89, war with Akragas 113, Fonte Ciane 133, colonizes Camarina 145, history and description of monuments and museum 159–188, Neolithic villages near 199, relations with Leontinoi 202–203; 214

Tacitus 180
Taormina (Tauromenion) 17, 19, Pyrrhus lands at 166, history and description 207–211
Temples passim, but see especially Agrigento, Gela, Himera, Megara Hyblaea, Segesta, Selinunte and Syracuse
Termini Imerese 18, 50, built by Carthaginians to replace Himera 51–52, Palaeolithic caves near 61, Roman amphitheatre 168
Thapsos (Bronze Age culture and rock-cut tombs) 17, 19, 24, 38, 39, contemporary cultures in W. Sicily 60, at Morgantina 133; 159, 161, finds in Syracuse Museum 170; 193–194, description of the site and finds 195–198; 214
Theatres, Greek or Roman, at Akrai 190, Catania 204, Gela 145–146, Helorus 158, Heraclea Minoa 105–106, Segesta 72, Syracuse 168, 179 and 182–185, Taormina 208–210, Tindari 44–46

Theocritus at Hieron II's court 167
Theron (tyrant of Akragas) 26, victory at Himera 50–51, 109, 115, 124 and 145, finds legendary tomb of Minos 102, victory over Motya 112, so-called 'Tomb of Theron' 122, temple on acropolis 128
Thucydides 48, writes of Solus, Panormus and Motya 54, the Elymians 65, date of foundation of Selinus 87, of Akragas 107, of Gela 144, reports Hermocrates' speech at Gela 146, account of Athenian defeat at Syracuse 163–164 and 184, sufferings of Athenian prisoners 186, foundation of Megara Hyblaea 199, of Naxos 206
Timaeus, historian 207, driven from Tauromenion 208
Timoleon 26, 27, liberates Messana 34, given allegiance of Tyndaris 42, battle of Krimisos 68 and 103, treaty with Carthage 89, agreement about Heraclea Minoa 103, rebuilds destroyed towns in Sicily, Akragas 114, 117, 126 and 127, Camarina and Scornavacche 154, Gela 146, 147–150, Halaesa 47, Megara Hyblaea 200, Morgantina 134, Segesta 66, Syracuse 165–166, Vassallaggi 147, modification of defences at Syracuse 188, and at Leontinoi 202–203, operational base a Tauromenion 207–208
Tindari (Greek colony) 17, 19, 29, history and description 42–46, theatre 72, 106 and 182, recolonized by Augustus 168; 213
Trapani 16, 18, 19, 29, Palaeolithic caves near 61 and 64, district occupied by Elymians 66, museum etc. 77
Tyndaris (see Tindari)

Urnfield at Milazzo 39

Valle Coniglio (rock-cut tombs near Enna) 132, finds in Syracuse Museum 171

Vallelunga (Early Bronze Age Culture) 38

Vassallaggi (Sikel centre) repeopled by Timoleon 147, finds from, in Gela museum 153

Verres (Roman praetor), crimes investigated by Cicero 28 and 168, his statue publicly demolished at Tyndaris 44, heavy levies imposed at Halaesa 47, oppressions at Cephaloedium 48, steals statue of Demeter from Segesta 68, at Heraclea Minoa 104, attempts to steal statue from Agrigentum 121, steals statues from Gela 148, unsuccessful attempts to despoil Noto Antico 156, robs works of art from Syracuse 176

Villafrati, bell-breakers from 38, finds from, in Palermo 60

Virgil, describes Eryx 73, writes of rich lands of Gela 144

Vulcano (Aeolian island) 17, 40

Wessex culture (England) 24, 38

Xenophanes of Colophon 186

Zancle (Greek colony) 33, founds Himera 50